TAKE A HIKE
WASHINGTON DC

THERESA DOWELL BLACKINTON

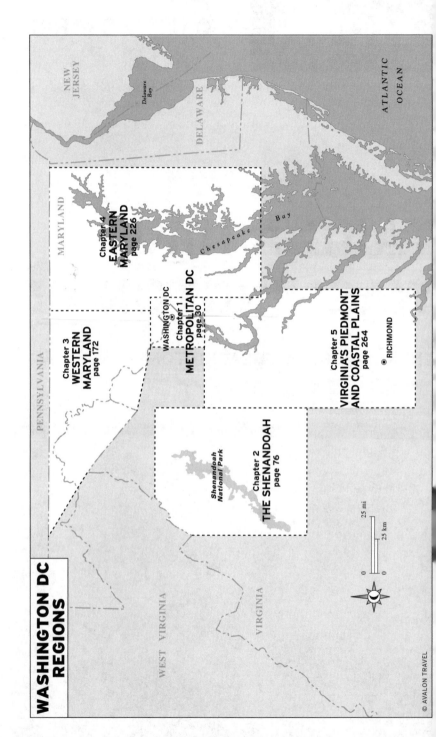

WASHINGTON DC REGIONS

NEW JERSEY

Delaware Bay

DELAWARE

ATLANTIC OCEAN

MARYLAND

MARYLAND

Chapter 4
EASTERN MARYLAND
page 226

Chesapeake Bay

WASHINGTON DC

Chapter 1
METROPOLITAN DC
page 30

Chapter 3
WESTERN MARYLAND
page 172

PENNSYLVANIA

Chapter 5
VIRGINIA'S PIEDMONT
AND COASTAL PLAINS
page 264

RICHMOND

Shenandoah
National Park

Chapter 2
THE SHENANDOAH
page 76

WEST VIRGINIA

VIRGINIA

25 mi
25 km
0

© AVALON TRAVEL

Contents

(Best Butt-Kickers   (Best Views
(Best Historical Hikes   (Best Waterfall Hikes
(Best Kid-Friendly Hikes   (Best Wildflower Displays
(Best for Solitude   (Author's Favorites
(Best for Viewing Wildlife

Chapter 4
Eastern Maryland

How to Use This Book

ABOUT THE MAPS

This book is divided into chapters based on regions that are within close reach of the city; an overview map of these regions precedes the table of contents. Each chapter begins with a region map that shows the locations and numbers of the trails listed in that chapter.

Each trail profile is also accompanied by a detailed trail map that shows the hike route.

Map Symbols

– – – – – – · Featured Trail	🛡80 Interstate Freeway	○ City/Town
– – – – – – · Other Trail	🛡101 U.S. Highway	✕✕ Airfield/Airport
Expressway	🛡21 State Highway	⚲ Golf Course
Primary Road	🛡66 County Highway	🦢 Waterfall
Secondary Road	★ Point of Interest	Swamp
═ ═ ═ ═ ═ ═ Unpaved Road	🅿 Parking Area	▲ Mountain
· · · · · · · · · · · · Ferry	🅣 Trailhead	▲ Park
— · — · — · National Border	▲ Campground	)ꞁ Pass
— · · — State Border	▪ Other Location	✚ Unique Natural Feature

ABOUT THE TRAIL PROFILES

Each profile includes a narrative description of the trail's setting and terrain. This description also typically includes mile-by-mile hiking directions, as well as information about the trail's highlights and unique attributes.

The trails marked by the **BEST** ◖ symbol are highlighted in the author's Best Hikes list.

Options

If alternative routes are available, this section is used to provide information on side trips or note how to shorten or lengthen the hike.

Directions

This section provides detailed driving directions to the trailhead from the city center or from the intersection of major highways. When public transportation is available, instructions will be noted here.

Information and Contact

This section provides information on fees, facilities, and access restrictions for the trail. It also includes the name of the land management agency or organization that oversees the trail, as well as an address, phone number, and website if available.

ABOUT THE ICONS

The icons in this book are designed to provide at-a-glance information on special features for each trail.

🔲 The trail climbs to a high overlook with wide views.

🔲 The trail offers an opportunity for wildlife-watching.

🔲 The trail offers an opportunity for bird-watching.

🔲 The trail features wildflower displays in spring.

🔲 The trail visits a beach.

🔲 The trail travels to a waterfall.

🔲 The trail visits a historic site.

🔲 Dogs are allowed.

🔲 The trail is appropriate for children.

🔲 The trail is wheelchair accessible.

🔲 The trailhead can be accessed via public transportation.

ABOUT THE DIFFICULTY RATING

Each profile includes a difficulty rating. Definitions for ratings follow. Remember that the difficulty level for any trail can change due to weather or trail conditions, so always phone ahead to check the current state of any trail.

Easy: Easy hikes are less than 5 miles long and have less than 600 feet of elevation change. They are generally level and short in distance. These hikes are suitable for all hikers, including families with small children.

Easy/Moderate: Easy/Moderate hikes are 1–8 miles round-trip and have up to 950 feet of elevation gain. They feature rougher terrain or a more difficult combination of length and elevation. These hikes are suitable for reasonably fit adults as well as active children above the age of six.

Moderate: Moderate hikes are 3–9 miles round-trip and have up to 1,800 feet of elevation gain. They feature steep sections, rugged trail, or other challenges. These hikes are suitable for fit adults and children with some prior hiking experience.

Strenuous: Strenuous hikes are 3–10 miles round-trip and have up to 1,900 feet of elevation gain. They feature significant elevation changes as well as difficult terrain. These hikes are suitable for very fit hikers who are seeking a workout.

Butt-Kicker: Butt-Kicker hikes are 7–18 miles round-trip and have up to 2,700 feet of elevation gain. They feature challenging combinations of distance and elevation gain or extremely difficult terrain. These hikes are suitable only for advanced hikers who are very physically fit.

INTRODUCTION

© THERESA DOWELL BLACKINTON

Author's Note

Let me introduce you to my Washington DC. Some parts of it will probably be familiar to you. You've visited the Smithsonian, I trust, and maybe even looked out on the Potomac while dining in Georgetown. I'm certain you've snapped a photo of the White House, toured the Capitol, maybe even listened in on a Supreme Court hearing. The monuments, yes, I agree, they're best seen at night.

But what about the National Arboretum? Have you hiked around it in the spring when the smell of magnolias perfumes the air? Have you seen the lotus in bloom at Kenilworth Aquatic Gardens or spotted a five-lined skink on the trails near Great Falls? Don't tell me that you've never hiked through the autumn splendor of Shenandoah National Park or greeted a summer morning from a trail alongside the Chesapeake Bay. These, too, are essential DC experiences.

The neat grid pattern of DC belies the fact that wilderness abounds both within city limits and just outside. Within a two-hour radius of the nation's capital—the area covered in *Moon Take a Hike Washington DC*—you can climb a 4,000-foot mountain, hike beachside trails, soak in the spray of waterfalls, and travel on foot across historic ground. Great diversity exists within the mid-Atlantic region. In the western reaches, the Blue Ridge Mountains soar, while the beaches of the Chesapeake Bay constitute the eastern boundaries. In between, rolling piedmont hills and the riparian forests of the coastal plains spread out.

If you want to see wildlife, the DC region has it: black bears, deer, bald eagles, peregrine falcons, red foxes, and hundreds of other species. If you prefer wildflowers, you will not be disappointed by the trilliums, spring beauties, lady slippers, wild geraniums, mayapples, jack-in-the-pulpits, bluebells, and other delightful flowers that grow alongside the region's trails. For those with a rugged pair of boots and a sense of adventure, hundreds of miles of hiking trails wait to be explored.

In this second edition of *Moon Take a Hike Washington DC,* I feature 85 magnificent hikes. Though this certainly isn't a comprehensive listing of every trail in the DC area, the hikes profiled here are among the best. In choosing them, I not only drew upon my years of experience hiking in the mid-Atlantic, but I also scoured maps, chatted on hiker forums, and picked the brains of park rangers, trail volunteers, outdoors-store employees, and fellow hikers. I then hiked every mile of every trail detailed in this guide, plus other trails that didn't make the cut.

In the hike profiles, you will find easy-to-follow directions; descriptions of the trail environment, flora, and fauna; and information on natural and social history relevant to the area. On any weekend, holiday, evening, or all-too-rare day off, all you need to do is pick up this guidebook and select the trail that sounds most appealing to you. Right at hand, you'll have driving directions, information on fees, a basic map, and all the details you need to successfully navigate the trail.

If you're a longtime hiker, *Moon Take a Hike Washington DC* will remind you of some of your favorite haunts as well as introduce you to fresh trails. If you're new to hiking, you'll be able to find easy trails perfect for getting your feet wet (maybe even literally), then progress through levels of difficulty until you're adding butt-kickers to your repertoire. Families with small children, those with disabilities, and those limited to public transportation will also find trails to suit their tastes and needs.

So what are you waiting for? It's time to lace up the old boots, hit the trails, and discover the wild side of Washington DC.

Best Hikes

❰ Best Butt-Kickers
Buzzard Rock, The Shenandoah, page 91.
Signal Knob, The Shenandoah, page 94.
Old Rag, The Shenandoah, page 136.
Log Roll Trail, Western Maryland, page 183.
Bull Run-Occoquan Trail, Virginia's Piedmont and Coastal Plains, page 281.

❰ Best Historical Hikes
Underground Railroad Experience Trail, Metropolitan DC, page 53.
Dickey Ridge, The Shenandoah, page 97.
Maryland Heights Trail, Western Maryland, page 192.
Chancellorsville History Trail, Virginia's Piedmont and Coastal Plains, page 269.
Lee's Woods Trail, Virginia's Piedmont and Coastal Plains, page 293.

❰ Best Kid-Friendly Hikes
Huntley Meadows Circuit, Metropolitan DC, page 64.
River Trail and Boardwalk Loop, Metropolitan DC, page 69.
Lower Trail-Cliff Trail Circuit, Western Maryland, page 210.
Calvert Cliffs Beach Trail, Eastern Maryland, page 240.
Farms to Forest Trail, Virginia's Piedmont and Coastal Plains, page 284.

❰ Best for Solitude
Fraser Preserve Circuit, Metropolitan DC, page 32.
Laurel Run, The Shenandoah, page 79.
Buck Ridge-Buck Hollow Circuit, The Shenandoah, page 112.
Catlett Mountain, The Shenandoah, page 139.
Long Pond Trail, Western Maryland, page 180.

❰ Best for Viewing Wildlife
Huntley Meadows Circuit, Metropolitan DC, page 64.

◖ Best Views

◖ Best Waterfall Hikes

◖ Best Wildflower Displays

◖ AUTHOR'S FAVORITES

Hiking Tips

HIKING ESSENTIALS
Clothing

Dressing for a hike requires that you do more than take a quick glance at the weather; you need to prepare for multiple contingencies. Temperatures at higher elevation will be colder. It can feel cooler in the shade than it does in the sun. A storm can move in suddenly, leaving you cold and wet. To keep comfortable regardless of changing conditions, wear or pack layers. Pants that convert to shorts are ideal for a range of conditions, and a waterproof jacket is always a wise choice. In winter, a hat and gloves are essential.

Cotton is generally not the best fabric for outdoor activity because it retains moisture. Keeping dry is key to avoiding hypothermia. High-tech fabrics designed to wick moisture away and dry quickly (and sometimes even protect against bugs and the sun) perform well on active outings and can be purchased at any outdoors store and at many other retailers.

The most important element of any hiking outfit is what's on your feet. Footwear options range from lightweight trail runners to midheight hiking shoes to full-coverage boots. No style is inherently better than the others; the best shoe is the one that fits you properly and comfortably and provides support where you need it. Consider how sturdy the sole is, how much ankle support the shoes provide, whether you want the shoes to be waterproof, and whether the shoes rub or slip. When you're covering multiple miles, the last thing you want is aching or blistered feet, so invest time and money in finding the right pair for you.

Food

Hiking is hard work, and since you can burn a lot of calories on the trail, it's important to regularly replenish your energy supply. Hunger can hit hard and fast and can make a hike very unpleasant, so always pack more than you think you'll need. In fact, you should bring enough food to get you through your trip plus one extra day. Food that is lightweight, packs a lot of energy, requires no preparation, and won't get smashed in your backpack is best. A few tried and true hiking favorites are trail mix (store bought or homemade), dried fruit, pretzels, energy bars, and jerky.

Water

If you bring only one thing from this list with you, make it water. The amount of water you should carry varies depending on weather conditions, the difficulty

HIKING GEAR CHECKLIST

Cell phone	Map
Compass	Multiuse tool
Emergency blanket	Sunglasses
Extra clothing layers	Sunscreen
Fire starter	Water
First-aid kit	Waterproof jacket
Food	Waterproof matches
Hat	Whistle
Headlamp	
Insect repellent (with DEET)	Optional items: camera, binoculars, field
Lip balm	guide to flora and fauna

of the hike, and your own personal needs. For decades, the primary method for carrying water was in bottles, but in recent years water bladders have gained in popularity. These bladders can carry multiple liters, slip into or are already incorporated into backpacks, and make staying hydrated easy since you don't have to stop and grab your water bottle but can instead drink from the bladder's hose as you walk. In the end, however, it doesn't matter how you carry your water, so long as you don't set out on any hike without it. You may also want to put an extra bottle or two in your car so you can hydrate both before and after the hike. If you don't bring your own water or enough water, you need to carry a water filter. Never drink untreated water from natural sources because you could end up seriously ill. Also, be aware that some water sources in the area dry up during all but the wettest periods, so it's unwise to rely solely on finding water along the trail.

Navigation Tools

Always carry an up-to-date map of the area where you are hiking. Maps are frequently available for free at ranger stations, visitors centers, and trailheads. They can also often be ordered in advance from the trail's managing agency. A compass is another useful item to carry, as it will get you headed back in the right direction should you get off course. If you prefer high-tech tools, consider investing in a handheld GPS device, which can provide maps, directions, distance tracking, and elevation data.

TRAIL MARKING SYSTEMS

The majority of trails in the Washington DC area are marked by blazes, which are generally rectangular-shaped, colored marks that are about two inches by six inches in size and are painted on trees along the trail to mark the way. Different

Methods for marking trails include blazes and posts.

color paints are often used to identify different trails. Sometimes the color is different for every trail within the park; other times specific colors are used to mark specific types of trails. For example, in Shenandoah National Park, white blazes are used to mark the Appalachian Trail, blue blazes are used to mark all other hiking trails, and yellow blazes are used to mark horse trails. Often, but not always, double blazes are used to indicate intersections or significant bends in the trail.

Other trail marking systems include wood or concrete posts inscribed with trail information or informational signs that appear at intersections or at regular intervals along the route. Sometimes these systems are used in addition to blazes; other times they stand alone.

Light Source

Even if you've carefully planned your trip to be off the trail or to have set up camp before dark, you should still carry a light. Bad weather can hasten the fall of darkness, hikes can take longer than predicted, or you may have to spend the night outdoors unexpectedly. Headlamps are an excellent option since they are lightweight but provide a strong stream of light. Additionally, they free up your hands, so you can easily look at your map, maneuver over rocks, or dig through your backpack. A spare set of batteries provides a safety net.

Sun Protection

The sun's dangers are real and extend far beyond the discomfort of a sunburn.

Thirty minutes before you go outside, apply sunscreen. Take a small bottle with you to reapply after a few hours or as soon as you get wet or sweaty. Protect your eyes with sunglasses and your lips with a balm with SPF. You may also want to wear a hat and clothes that keep your skin well covered.

First Aid

Because trails present multiple injury hazards—sharp rocks, uneven ground, stinging plants and insects—you should carry a first-aid kit with you. Essential items include bandages in a variety of sizes, moleskin for blisters, tweezers for splinters, alcohol wipes for cleaning cuts and scrapes, antibiotic ointment, hydrocortisone cream, ibuprofen, and an Ace bandage. If anyone in your group requires prescription medicine or has outdoor allergies, be sure to carry the appropriate supplies with you.

Emergency Gear

No one expects to get lost or stranded, but it can happen, and smart hikers prepare for the possibility. Adding a few small items to your pack can make a big difference should you find yourself in a bad situation. A whistle can help rescuers locate you and is both louder and longer lasting than your voice. A multiuse tool such as a Swiss Army Knife or a Leatherman, waterproof matches and a fire starter, and an emergency space blanket (lightweight, small as a deck of cards, and designed to trap and reflect your body heat) can literally be lifesavers. Carrying a cell phone is not a bad idea, but you should not be reliant on it since your phone is unlikely to get reception in many wilderness areas. You may want to keep it turned off until you need it since searching for a signal can wear down the battery.

ON THE TRAIL
Trail Etiquette
HIKING WITH CHILDREN

You can instill a lifelong love of hiking in your children by taking them out on the trails with you. You must, however, consider their particular needs when planning the hike. Short trails with minimal elevation gain are often best for young ones, as they'll be able to make the hike without much assistance. This instills confidence in them and keeps you from having to carry a child back to the car. Budget more time for the trail than you normally would, and try to choose a trail where there are many things for children to discover—bugs, birds, wildflowers, and wildlife. Remember that children might not always let you know they are thirsty, hungry, or tired until they're about to reach their limits, so take frequent breaks and encourage kids to eat and drink as you go. Don't let children get ahead of or fall behind you. They should be in sight at all times. However, it's important that children know what to do if they should get separated from you. Teach them to stay exactly where they are as soon as they realize they are lost and have them carry a whistle that they know to blow so that they can be more easily located.

HIKING WITH DOGS

Restrictions for hiking with dogs vary from site to site, but on nearly all trails that allow dogs, your canine companion is required to be on a leash. Always obey trail restrictions, not only because you can be fined if you disregard them but also for the safety of your dog and the protection of the environment. Even the best-trained dog can become excited in a new environment and run off. Unfortunately, many dogs are lost each year while out hiking with their owners. Additionally, a dog's natural inclination to bark and give chase can disturb wildlife in their natural habitats, and a curious dog can easily uncover or destroy a nest. In bear country, it's wise to leave your dog at home, as a dog can incite a confrontation. Finally, remember that although you love dogs, not everyone else does, so don't allow your dog to approach other hikers unless they first indicate an interest in your pet.

LEAVE NO TRACE

Leave No Trace is a simple policy that helps protect our natural spaces and ensure that they are around for future generations. What it means is that you leave the area you hike exactly as you found it or, even better, improved. Return with everything you brought in with you, including trash. Do not disturb plant or animal life. Don't pick flowers, carve your name on a tree trunk, or trample off trail. If the weather has been poor in the days preceding your hike, consider postponing, since wet trails can easily be torn up by foot traffic. The wilderness can appear tough, but it's actually quite fragile and requires your protection. If you really want to help, carry out not only your own trash but any other litter you come across as you hike, and consider taking part in a clean-up day at your favorite park. For more information on Leave No Trace, visit www.lnt.org.

Wildlife

BEARS

Black bears are native to Maryland and Virginia, with the largest populations found in the mountainous regions in the western sections of the two states. Though bears generally avoid human contact, you may spot one while out on a trail. Knowing what to do if you encounter a bear is important. First, seek to avoid encounters by alerting bears to your presence by making noise as you hike. You can do this through conversation with hiking partners or by something as simple as tying a small bell to your backpack. When camping, keep all of your food sealed in a bear-resistant container and hang it at least 10 feet off the ground in an area away from your tent. Don't take food (or any other scented items) into your tent and dispose of all garbage in designated facilities.

If you do spot a bear, try to maintain a distance of at least 300 feet. In most cases, the bear will immediately scamper off. If the bear doesn't and appears to be upset by your presence, slowly back away while talking to the bear and waving your arms. Do not turn and run as black bears take this as a signal to pursue. Should the bear follow you as you back up, stop, stand your ground, and make yourself as big as possible. You can do this by raising your pack up over your head and huddling together with others. You will also want to make noise, although you should not squeal or imitate bear sounds. Avoid eye contact because bears may see this as a challenge. If a black bear does attack (a very rare occurrence), fight back, focusing on the bear's eyes and nose. Pepper spray is sometimes effective, but only if you know how to properly use it and you won't also incapacitate yourself. Finally, report any aggressive encounters with bears to park staff.

SNAKES

While hiking the areas covered in this guide, you can encounter more than 20 species of snakes, nearly all of which are harmless. Only two species of venomous

© THERESA DOWELL BLACKINTON

A copperhead hides among dead leaves.

WILDLIFE WATCHING

One of the joys of hiking is spotting animals in their natural habitat. While hiking the trails featured in this guide, keep your eyes out for the following:

MAMMALS
Beaver
Black bear
Coyote
Groundhog
Opossum
Raccoon
Red fox
River otter
Striped skunk
White-tailed deer

REPTILES
Black rat snake
Common snapping turtle
Eastern box turtle
Eastern fence lizard
Eastern garter snake
Eastern painted turtle
Five-lined skink
Northern copperhead
Red-eared slider
Timber rattlesnake

AMPHIBIANS
American toad
Bullfrog
Green tree frog
Red-backed salamander
Red-spotted newt
Spotted salamander

BIRDS
Bald eagle
Baltimore oriole
Cardinal
Eastern bluebird
Great blue heron
Great horned owl
Green heron
Peregrine falcon
Purple martin
Red-tailed hawk
Ring-necked pheasant
Ruby-throated hummingbird
Scarlet tanager
Wild turkey
Yellow-throated vireo

INSECTS
Eastern tiger swallowtail
Monarch butterfly
Praying mantis
Spicebush swallowtail
Stick insect
Zebra swallowtail

snakes—the timber rattlesnake and the northern copperhead—live within the region, and these snakes are rarely aggressive, only attacking when they feel threatened. Snakes are protected by law and are an important part of the ecosystem, so do not harm them. The best thing to do when you see a snake is maintain your distance. The snake, upon sensing you, will usually slither away. While hiking, watch where you put your hands and feet, since snakes often like to curl up in crevices, under logs, or in brush or rock piles. Wearing pants and boots can help prevent a bite from a surprise encounter.

Being able to identify the timber rattlesnake and the northern copperhead is a skill worth having. The rattlesnake, which is rarely longer than six feet, has brown or black markings down its back against a background ranging from dull gray to bright yellow. Its most identifying feature is the segmented rattle at the end of its tail. The copperhead is reddish-brown with dark hourglass markings on its back. Usually under three feet long, the copperhead has a bright copper head (hence the name) and a pinkish belly.

If a venomous snake should bite you, immediately proceed to the nearest medical facility. You should also wash the bite with soap and water and immobilize the bitten area below your heart. Do not apply ice or tourniquets or attempt to cut the wound open or suck out the venom. Only a handful of people are bitten by venomous snakes each year in this region, and it is extremely rare that someone should die from a bite, so be aware but not alarmed.

Insects

TICKS

Ticks are a significant concern for hikers in this region, especially because these insects can carry serious diseases, such as Lyme disease and Rocky Mountain spotted fever. Nearly 90 percent of all Lyme disease cases in the United States occur in the northeastern region of the country because it is the primary habitat of the tiny deer tick that transmits the disease. Ticks cannot fly or jump; rather they require direct contact in order to pass from the high grass and brush where they live to humans or other hosts. Thus areas in which you rub up against plants or must forge your way through overgrowth are most dangerous.

Take steps to protect yourself against tick bites. Cover as much of your skin as possible with clothing—long pants, long sleeves, and a hat. For maximum protection, tuck your pants into your socks, but don't think that this is a no-fail defense. Ticks are crafty and manage to get places you'd never expect. Protect exposed skin with a bug repellent that contains at least 30 percent DEET. After hiking, inspect your body for ticks, and enlist the help of a friend to check your scalp, back, and other areas you may be unable to see yourself. Be aware that some ticks, including the deer tick, are a mere 2–3 millimeters in size, so make sure that anything that looks like a freckle is actually a freckle. If you find a tick, use tweezers to grab the tick by the head and remove it with a slow, steady pull. Wash the area with antiseptic, and kill the tick using rubbing alcohol. If you should fall ill within a few weeks of exposure to ticks, be sure to alert your doctor to your exposure. Rashes are an early symptom of both Lyme disease and Rocky Mountain spotted fever. Other symptoms include flulike indicators, such as fever and musculoskeletal pain. See a doctor immediately if you suspect you have either disease.

MOSQUITOES

Mosquito bites are not only annoying but can also lead to illness. Though your chances of getting West Nile virus are slim, mosquitoes that act as carriers have been found in this region. The long pants, long sleeves, hat, and DEET protection that you should use to prevent tick bites play a double role in preventing mosquito bites. You should also try to avoid stagnant water because this is breeding ground for mosquitoes.

Poisonous Plants

Poison ivy and poison sumac are indigenous to the broad area this guide covers. Poison ivy is a vine found primarily in wooded areas, while poison sumac is a shrub located in wet or flooded areas

Poison ivy grows up a tree.

such as swamps and marshes. Poison oak, also a shrub, is less common in this area, but it can be found in some forests. All three of these plants produce urushiol, a skin irritant that results in itchy rashes in the majority of those who come into contact with it.

Learn to identify these plants so that you can avoid contact with them. Poison ivy has three leaves and is usually deep green, though leaves can have a reddish tint. It creeps along the ground and climbs trees. The poison sumac bush has branches containing 7–13 leaves. It is also usually green but can appear red at various times during its lifespan, and it produces white berries. Poison oak grows as a shrub with clusters of three leaves that resemble oak leaves, hence the name. The leaves usually turn orange or yellow in the fall.

The best way to avoid contact with these plants is to wear protective clothing and stay on the trail. If you do rub up against one of these plants, immediately wash the area with soap and cold water. Over-the-counter antihistamines provide relief for many people, but if your symptoms are severe, see a doctor for further treatment.

Health and Safety

Fitness

Hiking is a wonderful way to get in shape and stay in shape. While enjoying the beauty of your surroundings, you can improve your fitness level. As with any form of vigorous physical activity, you should begin at an easy level and gradually work your way up to longer distances and more challenging elevation gains. Adding exercises to your workout regime that aim to strengthen your knees, ankles, legs, and core muscles can prove beneficial when you hit the trails. Stretching before and after a hike is also a good idea.

Hiking Solo
The safest way to hike is with a partner. Sometimes, however, the joy of a hike is in being alone with nature. If you do decide to hike alone—regardless of whether the hike is short or long, in an urban area or in the wilderness—alert someone to your plans. Provide a trusted friend or family member with written information about where you are going and when you expect to return home. If a trail has a log book, sign in and note your time, and if there's a visitors center or ranger station, stop in and say hello. The more people who know where you are the better. Once on the trail, be aware of your surroundings and use the same common sense you would elsewhere.

Hunting Season
Some of the trails featured in this guide run through regions open for hunting during designated seasons. Inform yourself of the hunting regulations at the location you plan to hike by calling the trail headquarters or visiting its website. During hunting season, wear blaze orange to make your presence known to hunters.

CAMPING

Many of the hikes in this guide are located in close proximity to one another but may be up to two hours away from Washington DC. A great way to enjoy these more distant hikes is to plan for a full weekend of camping and hiking. The following parks allow camping (either in a campground or in the backcountry) and/or rent cabins. For specific information on camping fees and seasons, contact the park.

Bull Run Regional Park (7700 Bull Run Drive, Centreville, VA 20121, 703/631-0550, www.nvrpa.org/park/bull_run)

Cacapon Resort State Park (818 Cacapon Lodge Drive, Berkeley Springs, WV 25411, 304/258-1022, www.cacaponresort.com)

Catoctin Mountain Park (6602 Foxville Road, Thurmont, MD 21788, 301/663-9388, www.nps.gov/cato)

Cedarville State Forest (10201 Bee Oak Road, Brandywine, MD 20613, 301/888-1410, www.dnr.maryland.gov/publiclands/southern/cedarville.asp)

Cunningham Falls State Park (14039 Catoctin Hollow Road, Thurmont, MD 21788, 301/271-7574, www.dnr.maryland.gov/publiclands/western/cunningham.asp)

Elk Neck State Park (4395 Turkey Point Road, North East, MD 21901, 410/287-5333, www.dnr.maryland.gov/publiclands/central/elkneck.asp)

Gambrill State Park (8602 Gambrill Park Road, Frederick, MD 21702, 301/271-7574, www.dnr.maryland.gov/publiclands/western/gambrill.asp)

George Washington National Forest (Lee Ranger District, 95 Railroad Avenue, Edinburg, VA 22824, 540/984-4101, www.fs.fed.us/r8/gwj)

Greenbrier State Park (c/o South Mountain Recreation Area, 21843 National Pike, Boonsboro, MD 21713, 301/791-4767, www.dnr.maryland.gov/publiclands/western/greenbrier.asp)

Green Ridge State Forest (28700 Headquarters Drive NE, Flintstone, MD 21530, 301/478-3124, www.dnr.maryland.gov/publiclands/western/greenridgeforest.asp)

Lake Anna State Park (6800 Lawyers Road, Spotsylvania, VA 22551, 540/854-5503, www.dcr.virginia.gov/state_parks/lak.shtml)

Little Bennett Regional Park (23701 Frederick Road, Clarksburg, MD 20871, 301/972-6581, www.montgomeryparks.org/facilities/regional_parks/little_bennett)

Patapsco Valley State Park (8020 Baltimore National Pike, Ellicott City, MD 21043, 410/461-5005, www.dnr.maryland.gov/publiclands/central/patapsco.asp)

Pocahontas State Park (10301 State Park Road, Chesterfield, VA 23832,

© SABRINA YOUNG

Tents vary in complexity, size, and price.

804/796-4255, www.dcr.virginia.gov/state_parks/poc.shtml)

Prince William Forest Park (18100 Park Headquarters Road, Triangle, VA 22172, 703/221-7181, www.nps.gov/prwi)

Rocky Gap State Park (12500 Pleasant Valley Road, Flintstone, MD 21530, 301/722-1480, www.dnr.maryland.gov/publiclands/western/rockygap.asp)

Shenandoah National Park (3655 Highway 211 East, Luray, VA 22835, 540/999-3500, www.nps.gov/shen)

Susquehanna State Park (4122 Wilkinson Road, Havre de Grace, MD 21078, 410/557-7994, www.dnr.maryland.gov/publiclands/central/susquehanna.asp)

Tuckahoe State Park (13070 Crouse Mill Road, Queen Anne, MD 21657, 410/820-1668, www.dnr.maryland.gov/publiclands/eastern/tuckahoe.asp)

Westmoreland State Park (1650 State Park Road, Montross, VA 22520, 804/493-8821, www.dcr.virginia.gov/state_parks/wes.shtml)

METROPOLITAN DC

© THERESA DOWELL BLACKINTON

BEST HIKES

Ask someone to describe DC, and they'll probably reference the White House and the Capitol, the legions of lobbyists and politicians, the profusion of think tanks and nonprofits. Perhaps they'll also mention the city's many museums and monuments, hallmarks of the American capital. As for green space, the only place they're likely to note is the National Mall. That's where their description falters.

Inside the Beltway – the phrase locals use to describe the area that falls within the I-495 loop – and just outside of it, green space abounds. You can find it on the islands of the Potomac River or tucked inside the 1,754 acres that make up Rock Creek Park. In an arboretum and an aquatic garden, you can commune with nature without traveling far from the city center. In fact, many of the trails are surrounded by heavily traveled thoroughfares and lively neighborhoods, although once you begin your hike, you'll quickly forget that you're in one of the busiest metropolitan areas in the country. Additionally, public transportation provides access to some of these trails, so even without a car, you can take advantage of the city's hiking opportunities.

For those in search of an afternoon away from the hustle and bustle, easy escapes are plentiful. Located along the Anacostia River in northeast DC, the tidal marsh habitat of Kenilworth Aquatic Gardens is reminiscent of the District's constitution before human engineering did its best to drain the swampland and control the rivers. Wander the garden trails in late July to witness the blooming of the lotus plants, whose bright pink flowers and impressive height dazzle all who see them. At the nearby National Arboretum, you can hike the rolling hills and enjoy delicate dogwoods, fiery azaleas, magnificent-smelling magnolias, and the city's famed cherry trees. These are the plants that you'll find throughout the wild spaces of DC, but only at the arboretum will you find them in such abundance.

It's not all a stroll through the park, however; in the rocky region along the Potomac River at Great Falls, you'll encounter more challenging hikes. Dropping 76 feet in less than a mile, the Potomac crashes over huge boulders, creating churning rapids as it narrows drastically to rush through Mather Gorge. You'll be hard-pressed to find a more awe-inspiring natural site in the metropolitan area, so it's fortunate that multiple trails run alongside the river on both the Maryland and Virginia sides, allowing you to observe the falls from a variety of vantage points and to note the state of the river a few miles before the falls and a few miles past. While on any of the trails near the Potomac, you'll want to take at least a few opportunities to look up in hopes of catching sight of our national bird. Bald eagles have returned to the DC area and begun to reproduce along the river's shores. You're far more likely, however, to spot deer, turtles, woodpeckers, and maybe even a snake or two.

Although part of the appeal of hiking is escaping the city, it's not really necessary to journey far. Step off a Metrobus and into the woods of Rock Creek Park and immediately swap honking horns for crackling underbrush. Leave behind the potted plants of your office for the bird- and butterfly-attracting blooms of Huntley Meadows Park. Swap out the gym's treadmill for a hike around Lake Frank or along the Rachel Carson Greenway. Or pack a picnic and enjoy an urban island adventure on Teddy Roosevelt Island. If you're going to take a hike, DC, you might as well start in your own backyard.

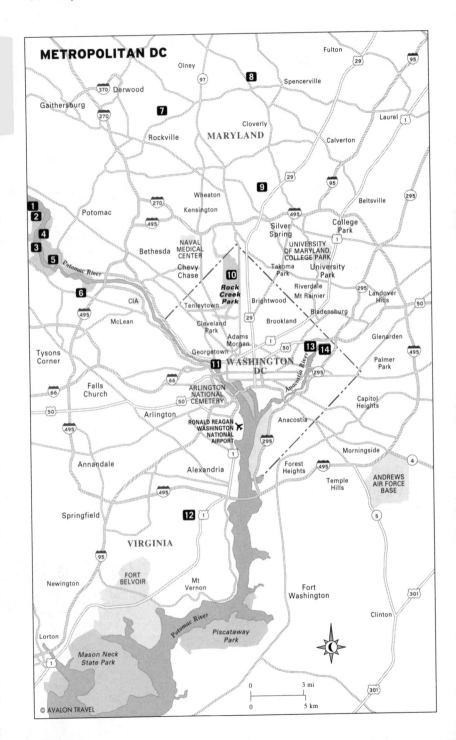

TRAIL NAME	LEVEL	DISTANCE	TIME	ELEVATION	FEATURES	PAGE
1 Fraser Preserve Circuit	Easy	4.4 mi rt	2 hr	320 ft	(icons)	32
2 Potomac Heritage Circuit	Easy	3.0 mi rt	1.25 hr	300 ft	(icons)	35
3 Difficult Run	Moderate	5.8 mi rt	2.5 hr	300 ft	(icons)	38
4 Gold Mine Loop	Easy	3.2 mi rt	1.5 hr	250 ft	(icons)	41
5 Billy Goat Trail, Section A	Moderate	3.8 mi rt	2 hr	250 ft	(icons)	44
6 Stubblefield Falls	Easy/Moderate	3.5 mi rt	1.75 hr	500 ft	(icons)	47
7 Lake Frank	Easy	3.5 mi rt	1.5 hr	250 ft	(icons)	50
8 Underground Railroad Experience Trail	Easy	3.7 mi rt	1.75 hr	100 ft	(icons)	53
9 Rachel Carson–Northwest Branch Circuit	Easy/Moderate	6.1 mi rt	2.75 hr	400 ft	(icons)	55
10 Western Ridge and Valley Trail Northern Circuit	Easy/Moderate	6.0 mi rt	2.75 hr	600 ft	(icons)	58
11 Theodore Roosevelt Island Circuit	Easy	1.75 mi rt	0.75 hr	60 ft	(icons)	61
12 Huntley Meadows Circuit	Easy	1.8 mi rt	1 hr	20 ft	(icons)	64
13 Arboretum Circuit	Easy	4.5 mi rt	2.25 hr	450 ft	(icons)	66
14 River Trail and Boardwalk Loop	Easy	2.4 mi rt	1.25 hr	35 ft	(icons)	69

1 FRASER PRESERVE CIRCUIT   BEST ☾

Fraser Preserve

Level: Easy

Hiking Time: 2 hours

Total Distance: 4.4 miles round-trip

Elevation Gain: 320 feet

Summary: Bird-watching and wildflower-spotting opportunities abound on this hike through quiet forest along the Potomac.

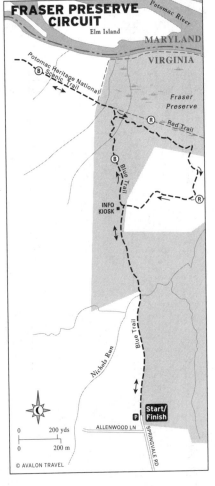

The Nature Conservancy acquired the 220 acres that is now Fraser Preserve in 1975 and has overseen the land since then with the goal of maintaining the preserve in its natural state and protecting its plants and animals. Prior to becoming the peaceful refuge that it currently is, the land was used for farming, with wheat grown here as early as 1790. Even earlier, the land was inhabited by Anacostan, Piscataway, and Tauxenent tribes, and evidence of their lives has been found along the river.

Now this rugged stretch of riverfront property is home to more than 100 species of birds and 300 species of wildflowers as well as mammals such as white-tailed deer and red fox. Tucked away in a well-to-do neighborhood, Fraser Preserve offers solitude to those wishing a quiet walk through the woods.

Even if the preserve gate is open, please follow the preserve's wishes and park on the street outside the gate. Then begin your hike by walking down the gravel road. The road rolls up and down, with mature deciduous trees as well as some pines and hollies on both sides. Part of the preserve is used seasonally as a summer camp and church retreat, and the first evidence of that is the camp waterfront on your left and the canoes tucked among the trees. Enjoy the sound of hammering woodpeckers and the music of songbirds as you walk the 0.5 mile to where the road crosses Nichols Run. Look for congregating yellow swallowtails and even hummingbirds here.

The gravel road ends about 0.1 mile later at an info kiosk. Turn left onto the blue-blazed Blue Trail, a dirt path leading downhill. After about 0.3 mile, the trail itself will turn right, but you'll want to go left to take the connector trail along the sewer-line right-of-way to the Potomac Heritage National Scenic

The forest is bright and open and filled with birdsong at Fraser Preserve.

Trail for an out-and-back to the river. From the connector, you can turn right onto the navy blue–posted Potomac Heritage Trail or stay straight; you'll want to stay straight for about 1.0 mile, avoiding any side trails to the left, until you see the Potomac River on your right. A side trail leads to the Potomac, and you can follow a small footpath along the river for about 100 yards if you wish. The partial sections of stone wall you'll find in this stretch are remnants of 18th-century canals. The rare purple fringeless orchid likes swampy areas, so look for it here and at other wet, marshy spots along the trail.

After enjoying the river, retrace your steps back to the Blue Trail, then turn left to continue along the loop it creates through the forest. At the intersection with the Red Trail, stay right. The loop will end back at the info kiosk, where you will turn left to follow the gravel road back to the preserve entrance.

Options

The Potomac Heritage National Scenic Trail is a network of trails spanning more than 800 miles on both sides of the Potomac River through Pennsylvania, West Virginia, Maryland, and Virginia. You can add distance to your hike by further exploring the trail in either direction.

Directions

From southbound I-495, take exit 44 and merge onto Georgetown Pike in the direction of Great Falls. Drive 6.4 miles, then turn right on Walker Road. After

2.3 miles, Walker Road turns to the left and becomes Beach Mill Road; continue on it for another 0.6 mile, turning right to stay on Beach Mill Road. Make an almost immediate right onto Springvale Road. In 0.4 mile, Springvale Road will end at the preserve. Park on the road.

Information and Contact

There is no fee. Dogs are not allowed. The preserve is open from dawn to dusk daily. Trail maps can be downloaded from the website. For more information, contact The Nature Conservancy, 490 Westfield Road, Charlottesville, VA 22901, 434/295-6106, www.nature.org.

2 POTOMAC HERITAGE CIRCUIT   BEST €
Riverbend Park

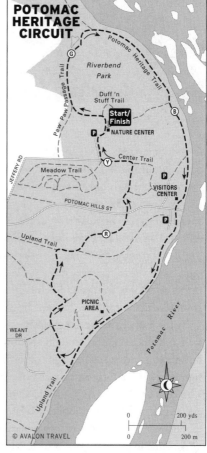

Level: Easy   **Total Distance:** 3.0 miles round-trip

Hiking Time: 1.25 hours   **Elevation Gain:** 300 feet

Summary: A gentle hike ripe with opportunities for bird watching and wildflower spotting.

More than 10 miles of trails snake through Riverbend Park, which stretches along the Potomac River and encompasses a swath of upland forest. The trails, which are primarily short but can be pieced together to form longer paths, attract trail runners, hikers, and horseback riders. The 3.0-mile circuit outlined here shows off some of the best assets of the park, including the spring wildflowers that carpet the floodplain forest along the Potomac. The delicate white petals of bloodroots and trilliums and the periwinkle clusters of Virginia bluebells provide the first signs that the forest is wakening from its winter slumber.

Begin your hike on the paved path to the right of the Riverbend Nature Center, where a sign directs you to the green-posted Paw Paw Passage Trail. You'll shortly turn left onto a dirt trail that leads downhill and over a bridge, and then turn right into a lightly canopied forest that allows plenty of sunlight to reach the namesake pawpaw trees that grow in the midstory. At about 0.4 mile, you'll approach a pond, where you might spot frogs, turtles, fish, ducks, or even a foraging star-nosed mole.

After another 0.1 mile, you'll arrive at the river and a junction with the portion of the navy blue–posted Potomac Heritage Trail that runs through Riverbend Park.

The Potomac is placid where it passes through Riverbend Park.

A work in progress, the Potomac Heritage Trail will one day run along both banks of the Potomac River, from the Chesapeake Bay to the Allegheny Highlands, but for now the trail is only piecemeal. Turn right onto it and follow the path along the river, which flows shallow and peaceful here. When the weather's nice, this stretch of river is popular with canoeists. In the fall, keep an eye out for migrating tundra swans. After about 0.5 mile on the Potomac Heritage Trail, you'll pass the visitors center. Continue past the boat launch and through the parking area, picking up the trail at the end of the lot. The trail is rather wide and open for the next stretch of 0.7 mile, and you might encounter horseback riders in this area. If so, give the horses room to pass by, stepping to the side of the trail.

At the end of this broad segment, there's a picnic area and a junction with a trail on your right. Stay straight and forge through a 0.2-mile section of boulder-heavy trail before turning right onto the Upland Trail, which is marked with a sign. The trail is aptly named, as you'll begin by going uphill over ground rough with rocks and roots. As you wind your way back toward the nature center, you'll encounter multiple trail junctions. Fortunately, the Upland Trail is mostly well marked with trail posts with red lettering, so you must only follow the signs. The only confusing spot is after you cross the road leading to the visitors center after 0.8 mile on Upland Trail. A sign directs horses to the right but doesn't indicate the way for hikers. You want to go straight.

About 0.1 mile after crossing the road, you'll reach a signed wildlife clearing. Look for wild turkey and the American woodcock, which performs a spectacular aerial dance as part of its mating ritual. Nearly 0.1 mile past the clearing, you'll arrive at the paved and yellow-posted Center Trail, which you will turn left onto. The nature center parking area will then be on your right.

Options

Instead of turning right off of the Center Trail into the parking area, turn left to access Meadow Trail, a 1.25-mile natural surface path that loops through old fields that are a bird-watcher's delight. You may also spot weasels and foxes. Interpretive brochures at the trailhead highlight the wildlife you can find here.

Directions

From I-495, take exit 44 to go west on Georgetown Pike. Drive 4.5 miles, then turn right on River Bend Road. After 2.2 miles, turn right on Jeffery Road, and drive 1.5 miles to the nature center parking area.

Information and Contact

There is no fee. Dogs on leash are allowed. The park is open 7 A.M.–dusk daily. Trail maps are available at the visitors center (9 A.M.–5 P.M. weekdays, noon–5 P.M. weekends Mar.–Nov., and 11 A.M.–4 P.M. daily Dec.–Feb.) or online. The nature center is open for scheduled events only. For more information, contact Riverbend Visitor Center, 8700 Potomac Hills Street, Great Falls, VA 22066, 703/759-9018, www.fairfaxcounty.gov/parks/riverbend.

3 DIFFICULT RUN

BEST 🄲

Great Falls Park

Level: Moderate

Total Distance: 5.8 miles round-trip

Hiking Time: 2.5 hours

Elevation Gain: 300 feet

Summary: Follow the Potomac as it crashes through a gorge, then walk alongside a creek that replicates the falls on a smaller scale.

Great Falls, which drops 76 feet in less than a mile through a series of cascading rapids and waterfalls, might be DC's most magnificent natural site. Fortunately the site is easily accessible thanks to two parks run by the National Park Service,

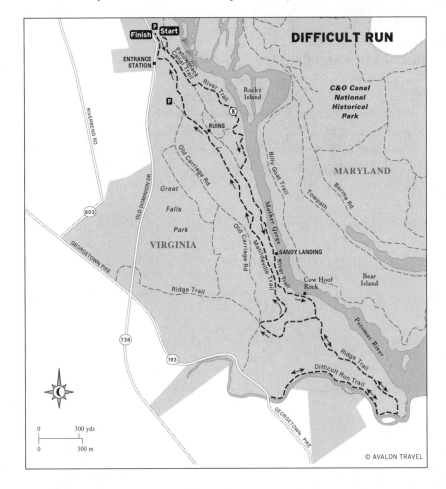

A stop at one of the overlooks reveals the power of the Potomac as it passes over the fall line.

each occupying an opposite bank of the Potomac at the point where this wonder occurs: C&O Canal National Historical Park on the Maryland side and the appropriately named Great Falls Park on the Virginia side. At Great Falls Park, three overlooks allow for stunning views of the falls, which are at their most powerful in the spring but are spectacular year-round. Much of the crowd that flows into the park doesn't venture far beyond these overlooks, but if you really want to observe the falls as well as explore the surrounding landscape, then you need to take a hike.

The circuit outlined here begins south of the Great Falls Visitors Center on the Patowmack Canal Trail. You'll pass all three overlooks, and then reach a sign indicating that the blue-blazed River Trail begins to the left. Make the turn and enjoy the nearly 1.5-mile section of this hike that runs along the terrace situated atop 30- to 70-foot cliffs that line the river. Peek down to see rock climbers ascending the steep walls and look across to see a parade of people traversing the Billy Goat Trail on the Maryland side.

After you pass Sandy Landing, the trail, which has until this point been nearly flat, begins a steep ascent. You'll first pass through a boulder-strewn gulch. Stay high on the inland side to cross it, then clamber up the last stretch of the River Trail to Cow Hoof Rock. This is the most challenging part of the hike, but it rewards with a sweeping view of the river. If you're lucky, you might spot herons, cormorants, or eagles.

The River Trail ends at a junction with the Ridge Trail. Stay left to follow the wide path through upland forest. After 0.6 mile, you'll turn right and head downhill to the Difficult Run Trail. When you reach the creek, turn right. After a few yards, you'll notice a small path to the left leading down to the water. Though it is a steep, slippery scramble, it's worth the side trip. Difficult Run imitates the Potomac River here, tumbling and churning on a reduced scale as it also flows across the fall line, and you'll get a nice waterfall view from the bank. Farther down Difficult Run, the creek broadens and the embankment levels out so that you're walking next to the creek, rather than above it.

Upon reaching Georgetown Pike after 0.7 mile, turn around and retrace your steps along the Difficult Run and Ridge Trails. When you reach the intersection with the River Trail, turn left to stay on the Ridge Trail for another 0.3 mile. At that point, you'll meet the Old Carriage Road. Do not cross it, but instead, make a sharp right turn back into the woods on the Matildaville Trail. This trail leads downhill before leveling out and running nearly parallel to the River Trail. At some points, just a few yards will separate the trails. You'll want to stay on the Matildaville Trail, however, in order to see the ruins of a town that flourished in the brief period between 1790 and 1820. Built to house those working for the Potomac Canal Company, the town was abandoned after the C&O Canal across the river proved to be the better of the two canals. After 1.1 miles on this trail, you'll turn right onto Old Carriage Road for the final 0.2-mile walk back to the overlooks and visitors center.

Options

If you don't want to backtrack, you can turn right on Georgetown Pike and walk 0.15 mile before turning right onto Old Carriage Road. At the meeting point of the road with the Ridge and Matildaville Trails, switch to the Matildaville Trail and follow the preceding directions. This will shave about 1.2 miles off the hike, but Georgetown Pike is a busy, winding road with no shoulder. Do not attempt this with children.

Directions

From I-495, take exit 44 to go west on Georgetown Pike. Drive for 4.1 miles, then turn right on Old Dominion Drive, which leads to the entrance station. A small parking lot will be to your right, but it's often full, so proceed to the larger lots straight ahead. The visitors center is at the south end of the parking lot.

Information and Contact

There is a fee of $5 per vehicle, which covers admission for three consecutive days. A $20 annual pass is available. America the Beautiful passes accepted. Dogs on leash are allowed. The park is open 7 A.M.–dark daily except Christmas. Maps available at the entrance station and visitors center (10 A.M.–5 P.M. daily spring–fall). For more information, contact Great Falls Park, c/o Turkey Run Park, George Washington Memorial Parkway, McLean, VA 22101, 703/285-2965, www.nps.gov/grfa.

4 GOLD MINE LOOP
C&O Canal National Historical Park

Level: Easy

Hiking Time: 1.5 hours

Total Distance: 3.2 miles round-trip

Elevation Gain: 250 feet

Summary: Escape the park's waterfront crowds by looping through the forest, scoring a glimpse of the river from an overlook.

Named in homage to the Maryland Mine, which ran intermittently from 1890 to the 1940s after a tiny amount of gold was found here during the Civil War, the Gold Mine Loop traverses a forested section of C&O Canal National Historical Park, offering a quieter alternative to the popular waterfront trails. The hike outlined here covers the entirety of Gold Mine Loop, then uses Overlook

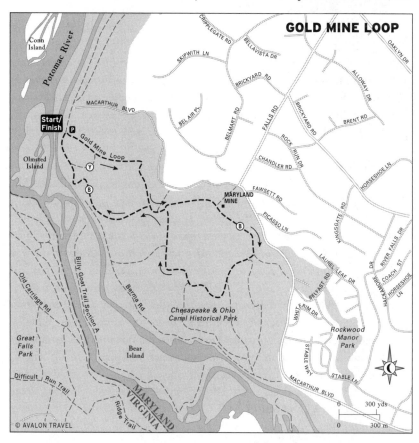

GOLD MINE LOOP

© AVALON TRAVEL

© THERESA DOWELL BLACKINTON

Along the Gold Mine Loop, deer are abundant and not particularly fearful of humans.

Trail for the return trip to add variety to your hike.

You'll find the trailhead just past the visitors center on the left, marked by a set of rough stairs. Go up the stairs to begin your hike on the light blue–blazed trail. The trail proceeds uphill through pawpaw trees, passing an intersection with Lock 19 Loop on your right. Upon reaching a small ridge, the trail levels out and passes through deciduous forest with little understory. At a double-blazed branch, turn right; when the trail reaches a concrete post marking the Overlook Trail, continue straight.

After about 0.75 mile, the trail will go slightly uphill, then meet with the loop part of this hike at a T intersection. Turn right, and then turn right again at the split. Multiple spur trails will branch off this loop to your left; stay right at all of them. For the first half of the loop, MacArthur Boulevard will be to your left, and you'll be able to hear and see it at times. This doesn't seem to bother the park's deer, which are abundant here and which don't seem to mind people either, rarely giving up their grazing to retreat.

On the back side of the 1.7-mile loop, you'll pass the ruins of the Maryland Mine. There's not much to see, but a signboard provides historical details. The loop is mainly flat, but once you pass Anglers Spur, you'll go downhill until you reach a small brook at the Woodland Trail intersection. From there, you'll proceed uphill a bit before the trail levels back out and you complete the loop.

Upon reaching the end of the loop, turn left and start back down the way you came, but instead of retracing your entire route, turn left at the post directing you to Overlook Trail. This nonblazed trail weaves up and down much more than Gold Mine Trail does, running alongside a stream, diving down into gulches, and then rising back up. The hills are steep in sections, but not for long. An overlook along the trail provides views out to the Potomac and its rapids.

Overlook Trail ends at an intersection with Lock 19 Loop. Turn left onto it, and make your way down over the heavily bouldered, yellow-blazed trail to a narrow footpath, which delivers you to Lock 19 on the canal. You'll see the visitors center and parking lot to your right.

Options

Overlook Trail is a bit more difficult than Gold Mine Loop, so if you want to keep things easy, just return the way you came.

Directions

From I-495, take exit 41 at Carderock and proceed 1.7 miles on westbound Clara Barton Parkway. Turn left onto MacArthur Boulevard, which leads to the entrance station. The parking lot is on the right, and the visitors center is south of the parking lot, along the canal.

Information and Contact

There is a fee of $5 per vehicle, which covers admission for three consecutive days. A $20 annual pass is available. America the Beautiful passes accepted. Dogs on leash are allowed. The park is open from sunrise to sunset daily except New Year's, Thanksgiving, and Christmas. Maps are available at the entrance station and the visitors center (9 A.M.–4:30 P.M. daily). For more information, contact C&O Canal National Historical Park, 1850 Dual Highway, Suite 100, Hagerstown, MD 21740, 301/767-3714, www.nps.gov/choh.

⑤ BILLY GOAT TRAIL, SECTION A   BEST ◖

C&O Canal National Historical Park

🏛 🦌 🐾 ❄ 🏞

Level: Moderate   **Total Distance:** 3.8 miles round-trip

Hiking Time: 2 hours   **Elevation Gain:** 250 feet

Summary: Grand views of Mather Gorge and the rushing rapids of the Potomac River are the rewards offered by this challenging scramble.

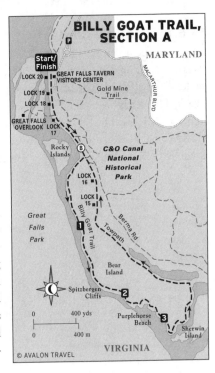

You'll want to wear sturdy shoes for this hike because you'll be jumping from boulder to boulder and even climbing along a cliff face as you cover rough and rocky terrain. The Billy Goat Trail is one of the most popular hiking destinations for DC residents and visitors, and there are plenty of reasons why. It's just outside the Beltway, so no long drive is required. The scramble is a lot of fun—it's like being a kid on the best playground you've ever seen. And the scenery is outstanding. Huge, jagged, darkly colored rocks rise from the river, causing the water to churn, swirl, and crash its way through. Virginia pine and riverbank goldenrod root themselves in crevices, and wildflowers and tall grasses create riverside prairies as a result of periodic flooding.

Start your hike by walking south from Great Falls Tavern Visitors Center for about 0.5 mile along the wide, gravel towpath. After you pass Locks 19, 18, and 17, look for Stop Gate Detour Bridge, which crosses over the canal. Just before the bridge, you'll find the trailhead on your right. Tracing the perimeter of Bear Island, the blue-blazed trail leads you along cliffs 50 feet above the Potomac.

For the short stretch that it travels east, the trail is flat and relatively easy, but as soon as it makes a turn to the south, the trail becomes a clamber over boulders of all sizes, though increasingly large. Some you'll be able to walk around; others you'll need to climb over and leap between. Though you'll spend

The Billy Goat Trail parallels the Potomac, offering fantastic views.

serious time looking at where your feet are going, take time to enjoy the scenery. Look across to Virginia to see rock climbers scaling the walls, and glance down at the Potomac to watch intrepid white-water kayakers brave the rapids. When you come across a vernal pool, search for tadpoles, newts, and frogs. You may also spot a five-lined skink, a reptile with bright markings that range from red and yellow at its head to turquoise and blue at its tail. To protect the fragile plant life, stay on the path.

Before you arrive at the second of three trail markers spread along the 1.7-mile nontowpath section of the hike, you'll hit the Spitzbergen Cliffs, which you'll ascend via a 60-foot stretch of near-vertical trail. Though it's not for those with a fear of heights, plentiful hand- and footholds mean the climb is not particularly difficult. If someone is already descending when you arrive at the cliffs, you'll want to give them the right of way, because there's not really room for two-way traffic.

The trail later descends to Purplehorse Beach, an ideal spot for a rest. Don't even think of entering the river, however, as dangerous currents have swept away unsuspecting swimmers. Upon reaching the south end of Bear Island, the trail turns back toward the canal. When you reach the towpath, turn left and proceed back 1.6 miles to the starting point while counting the many turtles you're certain to pass. If you see a ranger giving a demonstration of the locks, stop and learn about the history of the canal and the vital role it played in providing for cities and towns along the Potomac River in the 19th century.

Options

To extend your hike, turn right when you exit onto the towpath and continue about 0.6 mile until you reach Section B of the Billy Goat Trail, a more moderate 1.4-mile hike. Section C, which is 1.6 miles long, is another 0.4 mile down the towpath from the end of Section B.

Directions

From I-495, take exit 41 at Carderock and proceed 1.7 miles on westbound Clara

Barton Parkway. Turn left onto MacArthur Boulevard, which leads to the entrance station. The parking lot is on the right, and the visitors center is south of the parking lot, along the canal.

Information and Contact

There is a fee of $5 per vehicle, which covers admission for three consecutive days. A $20 annual pass is available. America the Beautiful passes accepted. Dogs are not allowed on Section A. The park is open from sunrise to sunset daily, except New Year's, Thanksgiving, and Christmas. Maps are available at the entrance station and the visitors center (9 A.M.–4:30 P.M. daily). For more information, contact C&O Canal National Historical Park, 1850 Dual Highway, Suite 100, Hagerstown, MD 21740, 301/767-3714, www.nps.gov/choh.

6 STUBBLEFIELD FALLS
Scott's Run Nature Preserve

Level: Easy/Moderate

Total Distance: 3.5 miles round-trip

Hiking Time: 1.75 hours

Elevation Gain: 500 feet

Summary: Visit a waterfall and enjoy picturesque river views as you make your way through a maze of trails.

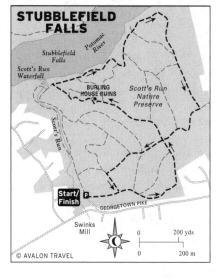

It's hardly possible to have a nature preserve closer to an interstate than Scott's Run, but don't let its seemingly dubious location prevent you from enjoying a lovely waterfall and a scenic stretch of the Potomac. You can hear traffic in only a few spots thanks to the heavy cover provided by hemlock, oak, beech, and wild cherry trees. Under these forest giants, mountain laurel thrives along with wildflowers such as trailing arbutus, Virginia bluebells, and trillium.

If there is one thing to complain about, it's the poor marking of trails. The crisscrossing paths are not named or blazed, and the maps indicating your location are wholly inadequate and often not around when you most need one. Fortunately, you can't get lost—only temporarily confused—because the 384-acre preserve is bordered on the west by Scott's Run, the north by the Potomac, the east by a neighborhood, and the south by Georgetown Pike. If ever there were a hike where you might want a compass, however, this is it. Then, should you make a wrong turn, you'll at least have an idea of where you are and in what direction to proceed.

Begin by climbing the stairs from the parking lot and taking a right. Three trails will branch off to your left, but you'll want to stay straight for 0.45 mile until you near the east parking lot. At that point, you'll turn left to head north. About 0.2 mile after making the turn, you'll reach a junction with a trail on your left. Continue straight through the junction, then proceed for another 0.1 mile to a trail intersection, where you will again stay straight. When the trail forks shortly after the intersection, go left. In another 0.25 mile you will approach a stone chimney,

© THERESA DOWELL BLACKINTON

Scott's Run forms a waterfall before flowing into the Potomac.

which is all that remains of the house of Edward Burling, who once owned the land upon which you are hiking.

From the ruins, go west (left if facing the chimney) along a trail that will end with a set of stairs leading to a wide gravel path. Turn right at the bottom of the stairs to hike downhill until you reach the Potomac about 0.25 mile after you passed the ruins. The waterfall created by Scott's Run will be to your left. Enjoy the falls, but don't venture into the water because it is, unfortunately, polluted.

Once you're ready to move on, backtrack to the gravel path and then continue east along the river, the water flowing to your left. After about 0.4 mile, you'll encounter a rocky outcrop at Stubblefield Falls, where the Potomac repeatedly plateaus and then drops. It's a beautiful spot for a break. After the outcrop, follow the trail as it makes a steep but short uphill climb. Where the trail branches, turn left and hike along a narrow ridge covered in moss and ferns while enjoying the striking views. After following the river for a total of about 0.9 mile, the trail turns south.

Follow the trail uphill, through an intersection and past a trail on your right. When the path ends at a junction about 0.6 mile after you left the Potomac, turn right and begin the westbound trek to the end. In the next 0.5-mile stretch, you will encounter multiple junctions: Stay to the left at the first fork, proceed straight though two trail intersections, and stay left at the second fork. This path will then dead-end at a junction, where you will turn left. A final right at the next trail intersection will have you back in the parking lot 0.25 mile later.

Options

For a 1.5-mile, child-friendly hike to the falls and back, take the gravel path that leads north out of the parking lot. Cross the creek at 0.2 mile and again at 0.4 mile. Then stay straight to reach the falls. For a challenging rock scramble, don't make the second creek crossing, but instead follow the path to the left.

Directions

From I-495, take exit 44 to go west on Georgetown Pike. Drive 0.5 mile to the west (second) parking lot.

Information and Contact

There is no fee. Dogs on leash are allowed. The preserve is open from dawn to dusk daily. Map D from the Potomac Appalachian Trail Club covers this region and can be purchased at www.patc.net. For more information, contact the Fairfax County Park Authority, 12055 Government Center Parkway, Suite 927, Fairfax, VA 22035, 703/324-8702, www.fairfaxcounty.gov/parks.

7 LAKE FRANK
Rock Creek Regional Park

Level: Easy

Total Distance: 3.5 miles round-trip

Hiking Time: 1.5 hours

Elevation Gain: 250 feet

Summary: Make an easy loop around a lake in this suburban oasis.

Rock Creek Regional Park preserves nearly 1,800 acres of green space in Montgomery County, Maryland. Though surrounded on all sides by neighborhoods and the trappings of suburbia, the park is a retreat of quiet trails that wander along tumbling streams, circle lakes where painted turtles sunbathe, and cut

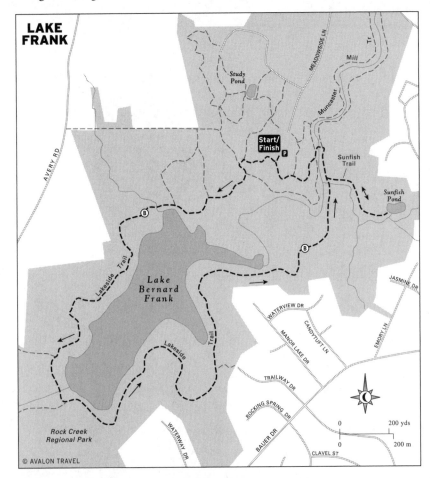

through meadows and forests that are home to ring-necked peasants, great horned owls, and plenty of songbirds. The loop outlined here runs around the serene 54-acre Lake Bernard Frank, detours to a small pond, and finishes with a creek crossing.

You'll find the trailhead just past the raptor aviary behind Meadowside Nature Center. Stay right at the split to wind downhill along Meadow Trail to a bridge over the creek, which you'll cross. Make an immediate left onto Muncaster Mill Trail, followed shortly by a right onto Lakeside Trail, which you'll travel along for the majority of this hike. All intersections are marked with posts you can reference should you get confused. At all other times, look for the blue blazes.

In the first stretch, a forest heavy with tangled undergrowth will be on your right, and a marsh will be on your left. Just over 0.1 mile after turning onto Lakeside Trail, you'll reach a pine-lined intersection. Turn left toward the lake, which glistens through the trees. As you travel along the west side of Lake Frank, which was created in 1966 to aid in flood control, you'll pass through gently rolling terrain and cross a few footbridges over creeks. The white-barked birch trees stand out beautifully in this area, and the beech trees make their presence known in the winter when their leaves remain clinging to the branches long after all others have fallen.

Near the southern end of the lake, the trail turns into a paved path, which leads left over the dam and then up along the east side of the lake. The red maples in this section provide a touch of color, especially in the spring, when they're budding. Multiple connector paths come in from the right, but stay on the main path, passing through two abandoned parking lots slowly returning to their natural state. At the end of the second lot, the trail becomes dirt again. Soon after, you'll leave behind the lake for the creek that feeds it.

About 2.75 miles into the hike, you'll cross a branch of the creek. Turn right to make a 0.5-mile round-trip along the Sunfish Trail to a pond. Upon returning to the main trail, turn right and continue for less than 0.1 mile, at which point you'll reach a signpost on the bank of Rock Creek, indicating a crossing to the Muncaster Mill Trail on the opposite bank. Bound across the creek via stepping stones, turn left once back on dry land, and then take the Backbone Trail branching off to your right. The Backbone Trail quickly connects you to the Rocky Ridge Trail, which will lead you back to your starting point about 0.2 mile after hopping across Rock Creek.

Options

Add another mile to the end of your hike by following the Meadow Trail from the nature center as you did at the beginning of the hike. Rather than cross the bridge, however, turn right and go uphill. Cut through the meadow and pass the picnic area before veering left to the fence-lined Pioneer Trail. Go clockwise around the Study Pond to approximately nine o'clock, and then take the stairs on the left to the Wildflower Loop. You'll take a footbridge across the creek, then another that leads back over, before reaching Valient Covered Bridge. Turn left after crossing the bridge, and proceed until you reach another bridge on the left. Cross it, turn right onto the Meadow Trail, and return to the nature center.

Directions

Take northbound I-270 to exit 4A and proceed east on Montrose Road. At the intersection with Rockville Pike, turn left. Drive 2.1 miles before turning right on 1st Street. After 4.1 miles, turn left on Muncaster Mill Road and travel 1.4 miles to Meadowside Lane. Turn left to arrive at the nature center parking lot.

Information and Contact

There is no fee. Dogs on leash are allowed. The park is open from sunrise to sunset daily. Maps are available at the nature center (9 A.M.–5 P.M. Tues.–Sat.). For more information, contact Rock Creek Regional Park, 6700 Needwood Road, Derwood, MD 20855, 301/948-5053, www.montgomeryparks.org/facilities/regional_parks/rockcreek.

8 UNDERGROUND RAILROAD EXPERIENCE TRAIL   BEST 【

Rachel Carson Greenway Trail Corridor

Level: Easy

Total Distance: 3.7 miles round-trip

Hiking Time: 1.75 hours

Elevation Gain: 100 feet

Summary: Gain a better understanding of what escaped slaves endured on their trip north on this history-heavy trail.

Though merely a tiny fragment of the route that freedom-seeking slaves traveled on the Underground Railroad, this trail brings to life textbook history and provides a hint of the hardships slaves suffered. To make the most of the experience, print out the trail guide before you go, since it contains interpretive text that corresponds to eight marked points on the path. Great for families, the hike is not just educational but also an agreeable walk through fields and forests.

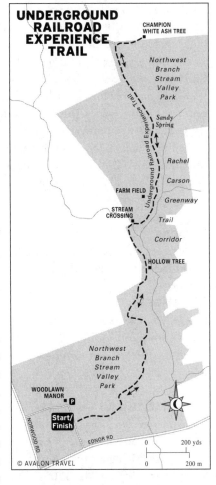

The trail starts on the grounds of Woodlawn Manor, which was owned by a Quaker family said to have sheltered escaped slaves in their stone barn as the slaves made their way north. Plans exist to turn the barn into a visitors center, but as of this writing information is limited to a bulletin board at the trailhead. Head straight from the bulletin board and first marker down the greenway that extends between a pond on the right and a fenced-in field on the left where park police graze their horses. After 0.2 mile, you'll reach the second marker at the edge of the woods. Take a minute to reflect on what it must have been like to forge your own path through this heavy forest with slave catchers in pursuit and your life at risk. Then set out down the trail that is now clearly defined and well marked.

As you walk you'll notice that brambles grow thick in this stretch, and the text that goes with marker three, which is 0.2 mile past the previous marker, explains that though thorny and uncomfortable, bramble patches made excellent hiding spots for fugitive slaves in need of rest. Continue on, paying attention to the markers at trail intersections so as to stay on the correct path rather than veering onto one of the many neighborhood connectors. At 0.75 mile, explore the hollow tree, in which those who provided assistance along the Underground Railroad could have hidden food. You'll walk along a stream for the next 0.25 mile before crossing over it by way of a replica period bridge. At this point, you'll emerge into an open field, which you'll traverse by staying close to the tree line.

The spring from which the town of Sandy Spring takes its name is located at the edge of the trees. Well maintained with benches and flowering plants and trees, it's a nice spot for a break before the final 0.5-mile walk down a gravel road bisecting a grassy field. Upon reaching the wood fence separating the park from the residential area, turn right and follow the dirt single-track until you arrive at the final point on the trail—a champion white ash tree, which has witnessed three centuries of U.S. history, including the dark years of slavery when the Underground Railroad provided a sliver of hope to slaves. When you're ready, return the way you came.

Options

Join a free guided tour on Saturday mornings at 10 A.M. from April through October to learn more about the Underground Railroad.

Directions

From I-495, take exit 28A to northbound New Hampshire Avenue/Route 650. Stay on Route 650 for 6.4 miles, then turn left on Norwood Road. After 2 miles, cross Ednor Road, then turn right to park at Woodlawn Manor at 16501 Norwood Road.

Information and Contact

There is no fee. Dogs on leash are allowed. The trail is open from sunrise to sunset daily. Download a map with a key from the park's website. For more information, contact Montgomery County Department of Parks, 9500 Brunett Avenue, Silver Spring, MD 20901, 301/774-6255, www.montgomeryparks.org/PPSD/ParkTrails/trails_MAPS/Rural_legacy.shtm.

9 RACHEL CARSON-NORTHWEST BRANCH CIRCUIT
Rachel Carson Greenway Trail Corridor

Level: Easy/Moderate

Total Distance: 6.1 miles round-trip

Hiking Time: 2.75 hours

Elevation Gain: 400 feet

Summary: This riverbank hike allows you to splash through streams and introduces you to a plant you probably won't want to grow at home.

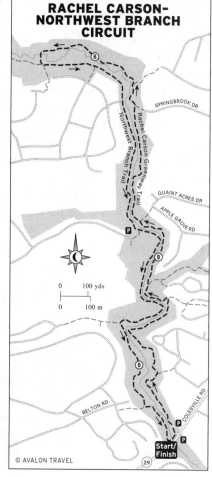

RACHEL CARSON-
NORTHWEST BRANCH
CIRCUIT

In the city of Silver Spring in the early 1960s, Rachel Carson penned her revolutionary book *Silent Spring*. With this book, the environmental movement gained momentum and the effect of pesticides on the natural world and its inhabitants became a focus for scientists, activists, and politicians. Fortunately, decades after the book's publication, we have avoided that terrifying "silent spring," but the environmental problems we face remain daunting.

Thankfully some steps are being taken to protect green spaces, even in heavily developed areas. To honor Carson, Maryland's Montgomery County has established the Rachel Carson Greenway, a corridor that will stretch 25 miles; as of this writing it is only partially complete. One of the sections open to hikers is the southern section alongside Northwest Branch, a tributary of the Anacostia River. The hike outlined here runs north from Colesville Road on the Rachel Carson Greenway Trail and then connects with the Northwest Branch Trail for the return.

Embark on your hike by going up the stairs to the right of the dam and then immediately going down another set of stairs to reach the riverbank. Reserved for hikers, the Rachel Carson Greenway Trail is a narrow path that winds up and down and repeatedly edges near the water before backing off. Though covering much the same ground as the Northwest Branch Trail that runs along the opposite bank, the Greenway Trail meanders more, following each curve of the river much more closely than the trail across the river. The key to staying on course is to always follow the water and to look for the blue blazes, particularly at the intersections with connector trails.

Northwest Branch separates the two trails you'll take on this hike.

With multiple streams interrupting the trail, this hike isn't for those averse to getting their feet wet. Depending on the season and the water level, you may have to cross water up to 10 times. Sometimes a good leap will get you across; other times a network of stepping stones leads the way. Once or twice, you simply have to walk right through.

After just over 3.0 miles of hiking through mature forest and areas where mountain laurel clusters, you'll reach the bridge marking the end of the Greenway Trail. Cross the bridge, and then turn left onto Northwest Branch Trail, which is wider, straighter, and flatter than the Greenway Trail and is also open to horses. Only the last mile is blazed, but signposts provide adequate directions at all intersections.

As you walk, you may find yourself wrinkling your nose at what seems to be the foul odor of a skunk. Don't assume, however, that the striped woodland creature has sprayed nearby. Instead take a look around for a collection of green plants that have scrolled-up leaves when they first emerge in late winter and then produce egg-shaped fruits with a brainlike surface in the summer. This is skunk cabbage, which is common in marshy areas in this region. When cut or injured, it is just as odiferous as the animal from which it takes its name. Though abundant on this bank of Northwest Branch, on the opposite bank of the trout-stocked river it is much less prominent; instead, the much more attractive crocus and daffodil bloom there.

With a final stream crossing, the hike ends at Colesville Road, where a dirt single-track leads you back to the parking lot and the rush of suburban life.

Options

After crossing the bridge at the end of the Greenway Trail, turn right and travel less than 0.5 mile to reach **Brookside Gardens and Nature Center** (1800 Glenallen Avenue, Wheaton, MD 20902, 301/962-1400, www.montgomeryparks. org/brookside, sunrise to sunset daily, free), where you can explore 50 attractive acres before returning along Northwest Branch Trail and completing the hike.

Directions

Take 16th Street NW to the DC–Maryland border. Turn right onto Colesville Road and travel 3.2 miles to the Burnt Mills Dam parking lot, which will be on your left at 10700 Colesville Road.

Information and Contact

There is no fee. Dogs on leash are allowed. The trail is open from dawn to dusk daily. Download a map from the park's website. For more information, contact Montgomery County Department of Parks, 9500 Brunett Avenue, Silver Spring, MD 20901, 301/625-7207, www.montgomeryparks.org/PPSD/ParkTrails/trails_ MAPS/NorthwestBranch.shtm.

10 WESTERN RIDGE AND VALLEY TRAIL NORTHERN CIRCUIT

Rock Creek Park

🦌 ✈ 🌿 🐕 🚌

Level: Easy/Moderate

Total Distance: 6.0 miles round-trip

Hiking Time: 2.75 hours

Elevation Gain: 600 feet

Summary: Explore DC's best-known urban park on a hike that leads you along the ridge and through a creek valley.

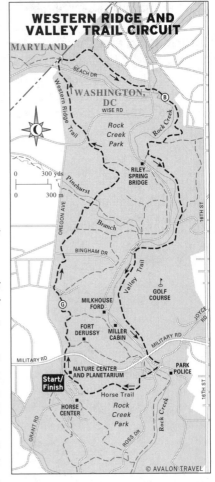

WESTERN RIDGE AND VALLEY TRAIL CIRCUIT

New York City's Central Park may be America's best-known urban oasis, but DC's Rock Creek Park is nothing to scoff at. In fact, this 1,754-acre refuge in the heart of the city is twice the size of Central Park. Within its boundaries are an amphitheater where free Shakespeare performances take place in the summer, a tennis stadium that hosts U.S. Open Series matches, Civil War forts, horse stables, and a planetarium. Of course, Rock Creek Park is also home to miles and miles of trails. Unfortunately, information on many of these trails can be difficult to locate. The Potomac Appalachian Trail Club has, however, done an admirable job of blazing and maintaining a number of prominent hiking trails, including the two featured in this listing.

Depart from the Rock Creek Nature Center, following the signs toward Fort DeRussy. Cross Military Road, turn right, and then turn left off the paved path onto the green-blazed dirt trail. You're now officially on the Western Ridge Trail, and you'll stay on it for 2.2 miles to the Maryland-DC line. Because the trail wanders along a ridge, you'll enjoy views east across the park,

© THERESA DOWELL BLACKINTON

The Valley Trail runs along Rock Creek, for which the park is named.

through a forest that is home to great horned, barred, and screech owls; red and gray fox; and since 2004, coyotes. At dawn and dusk, it's nearly impossible not to spot white-tailed deer, and you may also see a raccoon; in fact, no other area in the United States has as high a population density of raccoons as Rock Creek Park.

In the first 0.75 mile on the Western Ridge Trail, you'll pass through a community garden and cross Bingham Drive. In both instances, you'll end up on a paved bike path after the crossing, but you'll quickly return to the dirt track of the Western Ridge Trail. About 0.4 mile after crossing Bingham Drive, you'll reach Pinehurst Branch Creek. A yellow-blazed trail runs parallel to the creek, but follow the green blazes to skip across a shallow, narrow section of the water, and then continue uphill. You'll then cross Wise Road and Beach Drive before hitting Boundary Bridge, which marks the end of the Western Ridge Trail.

Pass over the bridge, and you'll find yourself on the blue-blazed Valley Trail, which runs south along Rock Creek and bursts with wildflowers in spring. At any point where the trail approaches a road, stay low and use the underpasses rather than climb up to street level. Erosion along the sandy banks of the creek causes some sections of the trail to be closed at times, so watch for detour signs and obey them should you see any.

After 3.1 miles, you'll reach Military Road. Cross under it and turn right onto Joyce Road, passing over Rock Creek. Stay right toward picnic area 22, and then pick up the horse trail, which runs uphill behind it. This 0.6-mile path will return you to the nature center.

Options

Turn this into a 10.2-mile loop by continuing straight on the Valley Trail past Military Road for another 2.6 miles. At this point, you'll reach Bluff Bridge. Turn north back onto the Western Ridge Trail and continue 2.2 miles until you return to the nature center.

Directions

From downtown, take northbound Connecticut Avenue. Turn right on Military Road. After 1.1 miles, turn right on Glover Road and follow signs to the nature center, located at 5200 Glover Road.

Public Transportation: Take Metrorail's Red Line to the Friendship Heights station. Then board bus E2 or E3. Exit at the intersection of Glover and Military. The nature center is up the trail to your left.

Information and Contact

There is no fee. Dogs on leash are allowed. The park is open from sunrise to sunset daily. A general park map is available for free at the nature center (9 A.M.–5 P.M. Wed.–Sun.). Map N from the Potomac Appalachian Trail Club covers this region and can be purchased at www.patc.net. For more information, contact Rock Creek Park, 3545 Williamsburg Lane NW, Washington, DC 20008, 202/895-6070, www.nps.gov/rocr.

11 THEODORE ROOSEVELT ISLAND CIRCUIT

George Washington Memorial Parkway

Level: Easy

Total Distance: 1.75 miles round-trip

Hiking Time: 0.75 hour

Elevation Gain: 60 feet

Summary: Loop around an island that pays tribute to our nation's most conservation-minded president.

Only a footbridge separates Theodore Roosevelt Island from the heavily trafficked George Washington Memorial Parkway, so you can't expect wilderness. Yet the city life scenes that you glimpse as you circle the island still manage to catch you by surprise thanks to the marsh, swamp, and forest environments that the trails traverse.

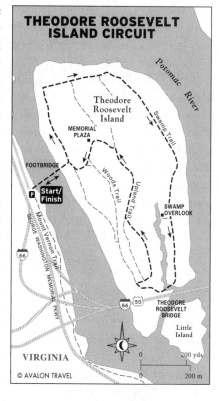

An outdoorsman and renowned naturalist, Teddy Roosevelt established the U.S. Forest Service and set aside more land for national parks and nature preserves than any of the presidents preceding him. Dedicated in 1967—after having previously existed as a Civil War plantation, a recreation site, and a Civilian Conservation Corps (CCC) project—the 91-acre island honors our 26th president through its preservation of nature and pays tribute to him with a memorial.

Begin your hike by crossing the footbridge and then turning left at the bulletin board. The dirt trail is often muddy along this stretch, and blowdowns may block the path, but you can always go under, over, or around without much difficulty. Follow the trail as it turns west. You'll pass two trails that lead off to the right, but you'll want to stay straight until you reach the third turnoff on your right. Shortly after you make the turn to head south along the island, the trail will turn into a boardwalk. This section is officially named the Swamp Trail, and even during the summer droughts, you'll find pools of water off to your right.

Multiple rest areas with benches are situated along the boardwalk. Stop at the benches located near the boardwalk extension and look through the trees to your left for a peek at the Kennedy Center and Watergate Hotel across the Potomac. Then take the extension on your right to the swamp overlook. Try to spot a redwing blackbird, which nests just a foot or two above the high-water mark.

After about 1.0 mile, you'll reach the southern end of the island, which is aligned with the Theodore Roosevelt Bridge. The overhead traffic doesn't

A boardwalk leads over the more marshy parts of the island.

provide the best ambience, but before you hurry along this section, look through the bridge supports for a view of the Lincoln Memorial. You may also see local crew teams plying the waters. After turning east, you'll cross a small bridge and then come to the end of the boardwalk. The trail then turns back to the north. As the trail turns, you'll see a rest area straight ahead and a branch in the trail to the right. Take the branch uphill, past another branching trail on your left, before turning left at the top of the small hill. Named the Upland Trail, this stretch will take you past the remains of a mansion built by John Mason in the early 19th century.

At about 1.4 miles, you'll catch sight of the memorial to Teddy Roosevelt to your left. Take the path that leads to it and explore the water features and 17-foot bronze statue of the president, designed by famous sculptor Paul Manship. Before exiting the memorial via the trail opposite the statue, read the four tablets engraved with Roosevelt's thoughts on nature, manhood, youth, and the state. The quote "The nation behaves well if it treats the natural resources as assets which it must turn over to the next generation increased and not impaired in value" seems particularly apt. After departing the memorial, turn right. The footbridge to the parking lot will be on your left.

Options

From the island, you can head south and cover as many of the 18.5 miles of the Mount Vernon Trail as you choose. The Navy and Marine Memorial is less than

1.5 miles to the south, and Gravelly Point, a popular spot for watching the planes take off and land at National Airport, is just another 1.5 miles farther south.

Directions

Take 14th Street across the Potomac to exit 10C toward Arlington Cemetery. Merge north onto George Washington Memorial Parkway. The parking lot is on the right after 2 miles.

Information and Contact

There is no fee. Dogs on leash are allowed. The island is open 6 A.M.–10 P.M. daily. Download a map from the park's website. For more information, contact Theodore Roosevelt Island, c/o Turkey Run Park, George Washington Memorial Parkway, McLean, VA 22101, 703/289-2500, www.nps.gov/this.

12 HUNTLEY MEADOWS CIRCUIT   BEST ☾
Huntley Meadows Park

Level: Easy

Hiking Time: 1 hour

Total Distance: 1.8 miles round-trip

Elevation Gain: 20 feet

Summary: See how many frogs, turtles, and birds you can spot along the marsh on this wildlife-rich walk.

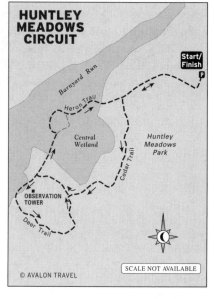

A tiny gem tucked away in the Northern Virginia suburbs, Huntley Meadows Park, a 1,424-acre park containing forest, meadow, and wetlands, is easy to overlook, which is a shame. The hiking at the park is not challenging, but it's what you'll see along the trails, rather than the trails themselves, that make this a destination worth visiting. The plentiful and easy-to-spot wildlife means you'll want to budget far more time than you normally would for such a short hike; it also makes Huntley Meadows Park a great place to introduce children to the joys of outdoor exploration.

Begin your adventure by following the paved path 100 yards from the parking lot to the visitors center. With great displays about the park's flora and fauna, the visitors center should be a stop either prior to or after your hike. To start hiking, head straight out from the center on the 0.6-mile Cedar Trail, a broad gravel and dirt path. As you hike through the forest of tall trees with a grassy understory mixed with a few fern groves, listen and look for woodpeckers and songbirds. Small numbered signs line the trail, and at sign five, the trail splits. Stay left to stay on Cedar Trail.

You'll notice the next sign is 15, but don't worry about it; by going this way instead of sequentially, you'll save the best part of the park for last. If you're a dessert-first kind of person, feel free to do the hike in reverse of how it's written here. The Cedar Trail continues through the woods until it meets the 0.4-mile Deer Trail at sign 12. Turn right onto Deer Trail and head toward the marsh. Upon reaching the boardwalk at the marsh's edge, turn left toward the observation tower. Climb the tower and scan the marsh, which was created by hardworking beavers, for belted kingfishers, red-shouldered hawks, king rails, mallards, and green and great blue herons.

Once you're done on the tower, continue left, passing through cattails, button flowers, and crimson-eyed rose mallows that attract butterflies and dragonflies. The boardwalk will give way to gravel as you continue on the loop. Once back to where the Cedar Trail and Deer Trail met, stay on the Deer Trail to return to the boardwalk, but this time turn right onto the 0.6-mile Heron Trail. This trail meanders along the marsh. Walk quietly and take the time to search the cattail stems for green tree frogs, scan the

You have to look closely to see a green tree frog perched on a cattail stem.

water for painted turtles, and listen for the call of a bullfrog. When the trail splits, turn left to follow the loop that goes farther out into the marsh. Where the trails come back together, turn left, following the Heron Trail until it connects with the Cedar Trail at sign five. Turn left here and proceed back to the visitors center.

Options

After you've completed the circuit, make another one. Maybe this time you'll see a northern water snake, a barred owl, or a great egret.

Directions

From southbound I-395, take exit 8C to merge onto southbound U.S. 1. Drive 8.5 miles to Lockheed Boulevard. Turn right and drive 0.6 mile to the park entrance on the left.

Information and Contact

There is no fee, although donations are welcome. Dogs are not allowed on the boardwalk trail, but dogs on leash are allowed on the park's other trails. The park is open from dawn to dusk daily. Maps are available at the visitors center (9 A.M.–5 P.M. weekdays except Tues. Mar.–Nov.; noon–5 P.M. weekends Mar.–Apr. 15 and Nov.; 9 A.M.–5 P.M. weekends Apr. 16–June and Sept.–Oct.; 9 A.M.–1 P.M. weekends July–Aug.; 11 A.M.–4 P.M. daily except Tues. Dec.–Feb.). For more information, contact Huntley Meadows Park, 3701 Lockheed Boulevard, Alexandria, VA 22306, 703/768-2525, www.fairfaxcounty.gov/parks/huntley-meadows-park.

13 ARBORETUM CIRCUIT
U.S. National Arboretum

Level: Easy

Hiking Time: 2.25 hours

Total Distance: 4.5 miles round-trip

Elevation Gain: 450 feet

Summary: Follow the blossoms on a loop around the ever-bountiful arboretum.

While hordes of people are cramming the sidewalks of the Tidal Basin, angling for the perfect photograph of the cherry blossoms, you can marvel at the elegant pink and white flowers in practical solitude. Just head to the U.S. National Arboretum, where botanists maintain multiple species of the famed trees, with blooming times extending from mid-March to late April.

But cherry trees aren't the only reason to visit the arboretum. There are also the azaleas that catch fire in spring, the magnolias that perfume the park, and the daylilies that burst open in the hot stretch of summer, not to mention hollies, herbs, ferns, conifers, and acres of hardwood forests. The hike outlined here covers ground that is at its best in mid- to late spring, but you shouldn't limit your visits to the arboretum to spring; throughout the year, you'll find flora to enjoy.

The first stop on this loop is the National Capitol Columns, a striking architectural display of columns from the former east-central portico of the U.S. Capitol, dismantled in 1956 and reconstructed here in 1990. Reach the columns

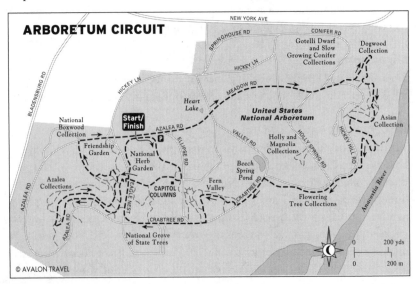

© THERESA DOWELL BLACKINTON

The National Capitol Columns are framed by a cherry tree.

by exiting the visitors center, turning left, passing the herb garden, and taking the paved walkway on your right. Wander among the columns, and then walk past the reflecting pool, following the faint mown path through the field scattered with daffodils to the overlook on Eagle Nest Road opposite the columns.

Next, cross Eagle Nest Road and pick up the mulch path that winds through 40 hillside acres of azaleas. Stay left through the riotous blooms of fiery pink to reach the Morrison Garden, where some of the 15,000 azalea plants in the collection are formally arranged. Pass through it and then turn right to follow the trail up Mount Hamilton. Though only 240 feet high, this is one of the most elevated points in DC, and you can see the Capitol from the peak. Remain on the trail as it loops around and heads back down the mountain. At the end of the loop's return section, stay left to visit the Lee Garden and its serene pool. Finish your 1.0-mile stroll through the azaleas by turning right on the paved foot trail.

The footpath will end at Azalea Road. Turn right onto it and walk roadside for 1.0 mile until you reach the Dogwood Collection. Make a left turn, and then proceed down the grassy run to the fountain set amid the dogwoods. On your return trip, stop at the shelter on your left to take in a panoramic vista of the Anacostia River. Then connect to the Asian Collection trails, where the *Camellia japonica,* a tree with large roselike flowers, stands out. Follow the trails south, visiting the pagoda before ending up back on the road.

Proceed left on the road, turning left again when the road reaches a junction. Shortly after you make the turn, you'll reach Fern Valley on your right. Use the

0.5-mile series of paths to explore the ferns growing alongside a brook. Finish your hike by turning right onto Crabtree Road, and then making another right at Eagle Nest Road. Move onto the sidewalk on your right, and follow it as it curves back to the visitors center.

Options
Endless hiking loops, including many that are wheelchair accessible, can be created with the help of a map and the arboretum's handout on average blooming dates, which is also available online. Visit the arboretum's website to view a calendar of events, as there are many programs offered, many at no cost. With plenty of advance planning, you can sign up for a coveted spot on the monthly full-moon guided hikes. It's an entirely different experience from daytime hiking.

Directions
Follow New York Avenue east to the intersection of Bladensburg Road. Turn right onto Bladensburg Road and go four blocks to R Street. Make a left on R Street and continue two blocks to the arboretum gates. Park in the visitors center lot.

Public Transportation: On weekdays, take Metrorail's Orange or Blue Line to the Stadium Armory station. Transfer to Metrobus line B2 and ride it to R Street. Walk two blocks down R Street to the entrance. On weekends, take the X6 bus from Union Station directly to the arboretum.

Information and Contact
There is no fee. Dogs on leash are allowed. Arboretum is open 8 A.M.–5 P.M. daily. Maps are available at the visitors center. For more information, contact U.S. National Arboretum, 3501 New York Avenue NE, Washington, DC 20002, 202/245-2726, www.usna.usda.gov.

14 RIVER TRAIL AND BOARDWALK LOOP

Kenilworth Aquatic Gardens

BEST **⟨**

Level: Easy

Hiking Time: 1.25 hours

Total Distance: 2.4 miles round-trip

Elevation Gain: 35 feet

Summary: Wander among lotus and water lilies in the wetlands of the Anacostia River on this colorful hike.

Hidden away in southeast DC is a park unlike any other run by the National Park Service. In more than 35 ponds nestled together on 12 acres of land, the Park Service cultivates water-loving plants, including water lilies and lotus. In the prime blooming season of late May to early August, the gardens are a wonderland of color. The saucer-shaped water lily flowers range from bright red to magenta to pink, and from lavender to light blue to dark purple. Less prevalent are yellow, bronze, copper, and peach flowers, but they can all be found in the Kenilworth lily ponds. Lotus plants tower high over the ponds, shooting up stalks as tall as five or six feet from which pink and white flowers bloom. Some of the flowers are night blooming, and nearly all of them close when temperatures rise above 80°F, so you'll want to visit early in the morning.

Although the park's star attractions only come out in summer, Kenilworth is a year-round destination. Wildlife spotting peaks in the early spring when the

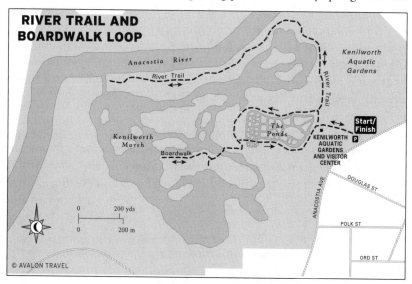

RIVER TRAIL AND BOARDWALK LOOP

Anacostia River

River Trail

Kenilworth Aquatic Gardens

River Trail

Kenilworth Marsh

The Ponds

Boardwalk

Start/Finish

KENILWORTH AQUATIC GARDENS AND VISITOR CENTER

ANACOSTIA AVE

DOUGLAS ST

POLK ST

ORD ST

0   200 yds

0   200 m

© AVALON TRAVEL

Lilies bloom in the pond in front of the bridge, while lotuses fill the pond behind it.

weather is fair but the trees are still bare, providing you with an opportunity to catch a glimpse of whatever it is you hear rustling in the underbrush. It might be a red fox or a raccoon looking to make a meal out of Canada geese eggs. Expect loud honking and hissing and wild wing flapping should any animal (including humans) come too close to these nests. Great blue heron, standing regally on the dikes separating the ponds or flying low over the water, are also frequently seen.

The trails at Kenilworth are short and flat, but be prepared to spend more time here than you'd think because you'll be stopping to admire the natural beauty every few feet. These qualities also make Kenilworth ideal for children; the walking is easy, and there is plenty to inspire awe and wonder. When the lilies and lotus peak—truly an astonishingly beautiful sight—expect a full parking lot and more photographers than you can count. The rest of the year, however, you'll likely be left in solitude.

Begin your hike on the River Trail, which is to the far right after you pass through the entrance gate. A 0.7-mile dirt track will lead you along some of the 70 acres of freshwater tidal marsh within the park. Some sections of the marshes have been re-created after the dredging and filling of the 1900s destroyed them, but other sections are remnants of the original swampland that once covered DC. What you see here is very similar to that which pre-Columbian people, including the Nacotchtank Indians native to this area, encountered. The trail dead-ends at a tributary of the Anacostia River that flows in from the river on your right to fill the marsh on your left.

After returning to the starting point of the River Trail, take the first right turn to follow the wide trail that loops 0.5 mile around the ponds. While enjoying the lilies and lotus, keep an eye out for frogs and turtles. After making the turn around the top of the ponds, you'll find a boardwalk on your right. The 0.25-mile-long structure leads you out over the marsh, where you might see beaver and other aquatic animals. Upon returning to the ponds, turn right and complete the loop around Kenilworth.

Options

Extend your hike by wandering the inner pathways that separate the various ponds. You'll get a better look at some of the plants that are hard to see from the outer loop. Be aware, however, that this is prime nesting ground for Canada geese, and you may be chased away by protective parents in the spring.

Directions

Take Route 295 south to the Addison Road/Aquatic Gardens exit and merge onto Kenilworth Avenue. Turn right on Quarles Street after 0.2 mile, and then turn left onto Anacostia Avenue when Quarles Street ends. The parking lot at 1550 Anacostia Avenue will be on your right.

Public Transportation: Take Metrorail's Orange Line to the Deanwood stop. Use the pedestrian overpass to cross Kenilworth Avenue, then go left on Douglas Street. Turn right on Anacostia Avenue and enter through the gate on your left.

Information and Contact

There is no fee. Dogs on leash are allowed. Aquatic gardens are open 7 A.M.– 5 P.M. daily in summer, 7 A.M.–4:30 P.M. daily fall–spring, except New Year's Day, Thanksgiving, and Christmas. Very basic maps available at the visitors center. For more information, contact Kenilworth Park, 1900 Anacostia Drive SE, Washington, DC 20020, 202/426-6905, www.nps.gov/keaq.

THE SHENANDOAH

© THERESA DOWELL BLACKINTON

BEST HIKES

Hidden within the haze of the Blue Ridge Mountains

southwest of DC are some of the best hiking trails in the region. A defining characteristic, the haze gives the mountain range a blue appearance, hence its name. Although the oxidation of natural emissions from trees and plants is the root cause of this feature, human activity has contributed to it, especially in recent decades. Yet even on days when the haze is particularly thick, the hiking is still good.

Around 300 square miles of the Blue Ridge Mountains fall within the boundaries of Shenandoah National Park, which stretches 70 miles through Virginia. East of the park, the gentle hills of the Virginia piedmont roll toward the coast, while the Shenandoah Valley spreads out to the west. With more than 500 miles of trails, including 101 miles of the illustrious Appalachian Trail, located within the boundaries of Shenandoah National Park, hikers could spend a lifetime exploring the park's hardwood forests, sylvan streams, and prominent peaks. In order to keep driving time to trailheads at around two hours, this guide only includes hikes in the northern and central sections of Shenandoah, but even with that restriction, the options are numerous.

In spring, when the waters are flowing freely, choose one of the waterfall trails. Later in the summer, many falls will slow to a trickle, but in spring, they gush and provide a refreshing spray of mist. Near the park's streams and along old fire roads you'll find myriad wildflowers. See how many of the 862 species that call Shenandoah home you can identify. When the heat and humidity hit the city, follow in the footsteps of President Herbert Hoover, who built himself a summer retreat in the area. With temperatures averaging 10°F cooler than DC, Shenandoah is the ideal getaway. Fall brings brilliant color to the park as the oaks, hickories, chestnuts, tulip poplars, birches, and other deciduous trees put on a show. Skyline Drive will be packed with leaf-peepers, but you can find solitude on a number of trails. And though heavy snows can close park roads in winter, the views from the peaks this time of year are unbeatable, with no leaves to impede them and less haze to obscure them.

Lying to the west of Shenandoah National Park is George Washington National Forest, which encompasses more than one million acres in Virginia and West Virginia. Lee Ranger District, the area of the forest most accessible to DC, includes a number of long, and sometimes strenuous, summit climbs that will be a welcome challenge to hiking enthusiasts. The fact that these trails are much less popular than those in Shenandoah is a bonus for those who prefer quiet communes with nature.

In both wilderness areas, as well as on the three trails located outside these two parks, wildlife flourishes. Peregrine falcons, which were successfully reintroduced to the area in the mid-1990s, nest on the tallest peaks in the area, and some lucky hikers witness chicks trying out their wings for the first time. If you're fortunate, you'll spot some of the region's more elusive animal residents, which include the spotted skunk, bobcat, and black bear, on a hike through the Blue Ridge. A few sightings of cougars have even been reported in Shenandoah, although park staff has not yet been able to verify the presence of this impressive cat.

With so much ground to cover and so many different types of hikes at hand – tough climbs up peaks, restorative treks to waterfalls, and family-friendly walks through the woods – this region demands that you return again and again. You may even want to reserve a space at a campground or pack your backcountry gear and turn a trip to the Blue Ridge Mountains into a multiday adventure.

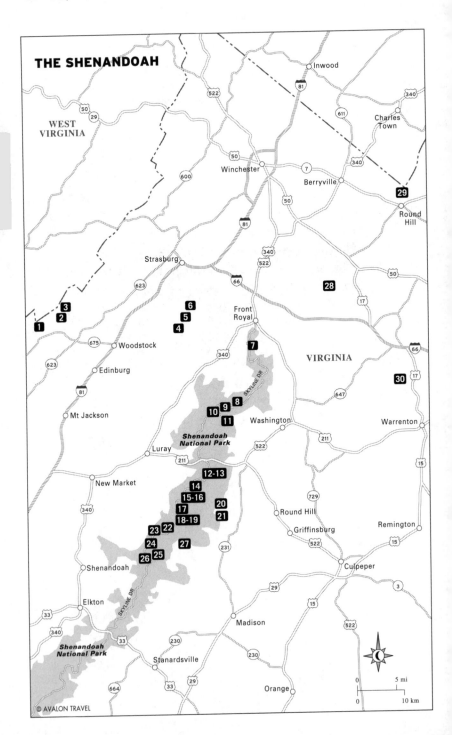

TRAIL NAME	LEVEL	DISTANCE	TIME	ELEVATION	FEATURES	PAGE
1 Laurel Run	Strenuous	6.6 mi rt	3.5 hr	1,600 ft		79
2 Big Schloss	Moderate	4.4 mi rt	2 hr	1,035 ft		82
3 Tibbet Knob	Moderate	3.1 mi rt	1.75 hr	830 ft		85
4 Veach Gap	Moderate	7.0 mi rt	3.5 hr	1,050 ft		88
5 Buzzard Rock	Butt-Kicker	8.6 mi rt	5 hr	2,510 ft		91
6 Signal Knob	Butt-Kicker	10.7 mi rt	6 hr	2,680 ft		94
7 Dickey Ridge	Easy/Moderate	5.2 mi rt	2.5 hr	850 ft		97
8 Big Devils Stairs	Easy/Moderate	4.7 mi rt	2 hr	600 ft		100
9 Overall Run Falls	Moderate	6.4 mi rt	3 hr	1,100 ft		103
10 Piney River Falls	Moderate	6.8 mi rt	3.25 hr	1,300 ft		106
11 Little Devils Stairs	Strenuous	5.5 mi rt	2.75 hr	1,500 ft		109
12 Buck Ridge–Buck Hollow Circuit	Strenuous	5.6 mi rt	2.5 hr	1,800 ft		112
13 Hazel River Falls	Easy/Moderate	5.4 mi rt	2.5 hr	800 ft		115
14 Mary's Rock	Moderate	6.8 mi rt	3 hr	950 ft		118
15 Corbin Cabin Circuit	Moderate	4.0 mi rt	2 hr	1,190 ft		121

TRAIL NAME	LEVEL	DISTANCE	TIME	ELEVATION	FEATURES	PAGE
16 Stony Man Mountain	Easy/Moderate	3.3 mi rt	1.5 hr	860 ft		124
17 Whiteoak Canyon Falls	Butt-Kicker	7.3 mi rt	4 hr	2,300 ft		127
18 Limberlost Trail	Easy	1.3 mi rt	0.75 hr	130 ft		130
19 Robertson Mountain	Moderate	6.2 mi rt	3 hr	1,300 ft		133
20 Old Rag	Butt-Kicker	7.2–8.8 mi rt	5 hr	2,510 ft		136
21 Catlett Mountain	Butt-Kicker	10.5 mi rt	6 hr	2,010 ft		139
22 Cedar Run Falls	Strenuous	3.4 mi rt	2 hr	1,600 ft		142
23 Hawksbill Mountain	Easy	2.1 mi rt	1 hr	400 ft		145
24 Rose River Falls	Easy/Moderate	4.0 mi rt	2 hr	875 ft		148
25 Dark Hollow Falls	Easy/Moderate	1.4 mi rt	1 hr	440 ft		151
26 Lewis Spring Falls	Moderate	3.3 mi rt	1.5 hr	800 ft		153
27 Stony Mountain	Strenuous	10.1 mi rt	5 hr	1,840 ft		156
28 Thompson Wildlife Circuit	Moderate	7.5 mi rt	3.5 hr	1,670 ft		159
29 Raven Rocks	Strenuous	4.8 mi rt	2.5 hr	1,530 ft		162
30 Wildcat Mountain Circuit	Moderate	5.2 mi rt	2.5 hr	1,510 ft		165

1 LAUREL RUN

BEST **☾**

George Washington National Forest

Level: Strenuous

Total Distance: 6.6 miles round-trip

Hiking Time: 3.5 hours

Elevation Gain: 1,600 feet

Summary: A hike up to and along the ridge of Great North Mountain.

The one million acres of land that make up the George Washington National Forest are ripe with vistas. From peak after peak of the Appalachian ranges that run through the forest, you can count distant summits and gaze down into valleys—some populated, others seemingly undisturbed by humans. Trying to determine which vista is best is impossible and any judgment is entirely subjective, but it would be hard to argue that the panoramic views from Great North Mountain, which you'll encounter on this hike, are anything but brilliant.

If you want the views, you're going to have to earn them, because this hike starts with a long climb. You'll begin by walking around the closed gate at the head of yellow-blazed Laurel Run Trail and hiking a short distance before the trail splits; veer to the left, crossing over a small stream. The trail, which starts out grassy but quickly becomes studded with rocks, begins to climb at this point, and though it's never particularly steep, it also never relents. Additionally, there is little canopy, so in summer the sun beats brutally down. Without much tree coverage, you have good views to your right of Devils Hole Mountain. You may also be treated to displays of wild flag irises as well as pink lady slippers in May. In June, mountain laurel and rhododendron bloom, while July welcomes ripe blueberries.

On the 2.1-mile climb to the ridge, you'll pass through two wildlife clearings where you might spot wild turkeys or white-tailed deer. Toward the top, as the trail begins to level out, you may hear a cacophony of frog croaks. Look for an

Great mullein fills a meadow through which the trail passes.

opening on your left where you'll find a small pond. Not far beyond the pond, Laurel Run Trail ends. A forest road lies to the right, and orange-blazed Great North Mountain Trail runs to your left. Turn onto Great North Mountain Trail, which traverses the ridge of the mountain, crossing a series of knolls.

After about 0.7 mile, as you ascend a knoll, a white-blazed spur trail will branch off to the left. Follow it to a small pine-enclosed overlook. Back on the orange-blazed trail, descend into a saddle as the trail narrows. Scramble onto one of the many rocks on your left for expansive views that take in Devils Hole Mountain, Tibbet Knob, Long Mountain, and a bit of Big Schloss. Continue up and over a knoll, then cross a meadow filled with yellow goatsbeard—which looks like a huge dandelion once it's gone to seed—and great mullein before making one more ascent. About 1.6 miles past the spur trail, you'll reach a junction with purple-blazed Stack Rock Trail. Turn left onto this trail, which winds steeply downhill over rocky terrain, passing first through ferns and large boulders, then through dense mountain laurel and blueberry bushes. A series of switchbacks tempers the upper part of this trail, but as the grade decreases, the switchbacks end.

Stack Rock Trail will end at blue-blazed Laurel Run Spur Trail (Forest Road 252) after 1.3 miles. Turn left onto this gravel road and hike 0.9 mile back to your starting point.

Options

Continue past the junction with Stack Rock Trail, instead turning left just a short distance later on yellow-blazed Falls Ridge Trail. Follow this trail as it gently descends 2.0 miles to blue-blazed Laurel Run Spur Trail. Turn left and hike 2.4 miles back to your car for a total distance of 8.8 miles.

Directions

Take I-495 to westbound I-66 to southbound I-81. After 17.4 miles, take exit 283 and turn right onto Route 42. Drive 5.2 miles, then make a right on Union Church Road followed by a quick left onto Route 623. After 0.2 mile, turn right onto Wolf Gap Road. Drive for 2.9 miles; stay to the left to continue on Liberty Furnace Road. After 2.5 miles, turn right onto Cool Spring Road and drive for 0.5 mile. Then turn left onto Forest Road 252, following it for 1.1 miles past the first gate, parking on the right just before the gate at the trailhead. On occasion, the first gate is locked, and you have to park outside of it and walk the 1.1 miles to and from the trailhead, turning the hike into an 8.8-mile round-trip.

Information and Contact

There is no fee. Dogs on leash are allowed. Map F from the Potomac Appalachian Trail Club covers this region and can be purchased at www.patc.net. For more information, contact the Lee Ranger District, 95 Railroad Avenue, Edinburg, VA 22824, 540/984-4101, www.fs.fed.us/r8/gwj.

2 BIG SCHLOSS   BEST [

George Washington National Forest

🎒 🦌 🐾

Level: Moderate   **Total Distance:** 4.4 miles round-trip

Hiking Time: 2 hours   **Elevation Gain:** 1,035 feet

Summary: Relish one of the best views in the region from an outcrop on Great North Mountain.

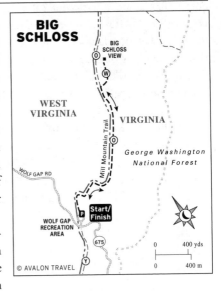

The German word *schloss* translates to castle, and though there's no formal royal structure awaiting you on this hike, once you make it to the end of the trail, you'll understand why German immigrants gave this spot such a name. Many a king would envy this location high atop the ridge of Great North Mountain in the Appalachians, with views that encompass a broad swath of the valleys below as well as the other ridges that rise to the east and west.

Start your hike on rocky orange-blazed Mill Mountain Trail, which cuts between campsites 8 and 9 in the Wolf Gap Recreation Area and then heads up the mountain. The majority of the George Washington National Forest is young because the area was extensively logged for nearly two centuries, from the early pioneering days of the nation until the 20th century. Mountain laurel grows hardily, not having to compete with a heavy canopy for light, and berry bushes also thrive. In late July, the blueberries are particularly bountiful and make for a tasty treat as you hike. You might notice some charred vegetation as well as tender new growth; this is the result of an April 2012 fire, which was started by campers carelessly dumping their ashes. Fortunately, the fire primarily consumed dead and downed vegetation, sparing the trees and the living understory.

After about a mile of uphill hiking, you'll reach the ridge. Grass invades the trail here, often hiding large rocks that can trip you if you're not careful. The trail turns to the left, and partial views begin to open to your right, allowing you to look east toward Shenandoah National Park. Continue along Mill Mountain Trail as it traverses the ridge for 0.9 mile before meeting Big Schloss Trail at a marked

The summit of Big Schloss offers king-sized views.

intersection. Leave the orange-blazed trail to turn right onto the white-blazed trail. This trail again leads uphill, and soon views open to both sides. You'll pass a couple of prime campsites and then reach a wooden bridge that extends over a deep crevice. Once across, you'll maneuver over and through some large sandstone boulders before arriving at what just might be the best viewpoint in the George Washington National Forest.

Take a seat on the sandstone outcrop and take in the view. As you look straight out toward the northeast you'll be staring down the spine of the ridge you have just climbed. To the immediate east lies a valley and then another parallel ridge, and in the distance you can see the peaks contained within Shenandoah National Park. To the west, you'll see another Appalachian valley and ridge, these lying within West Virginia. Sunrise and sunset are particularly stunning from this perch, with the surrounding mountains and valleys bathed in beautiful light. You will, however, need a headlamp if you plan to arrive for sunrise or stay for sunset because the trail is difficult to hike in the dark.

The return trip is along the same set of trails and is primarily downhill. Watch your footing on the loose gravel in the last section.

Options

Visit Big Schloss on a strenuous 12.2-mile circuit by beginning at the Little Stony Creek Trail parking area on Forest Road 92 (turn right off Wolf Gap Road 1.3 miles before the campground, and then drive 3.7 miles to the lot). Hike uphill for

3.7 miles on Little Stony Creek Trail. Turn left onto Tuscarora/Pond Run Trail and hike about 0.5 mile to Mill Mountain Trail. Turn left again, passing Big Schloss Cutoff Trail after 3.3 miles and continuing about 0.9 mile to Big Schloss Trail on your left. Proceed 0.3 mile to the overlook, and then backtrack to Big Schloss Cutoff Trail, which leads a steep 1.7 miles downhill to Forest Road 92. Turn left here and return to your car, arriving at the lot in 0.6 mile.

Directions

Take I-495 to westbound I-66 to southbound I-81. After 17.4 miles, take exit 283 and turn right onto Route 42. Drive 5.2 miles, then make a right on Union Church Road followed by a quick left onto Route 623. After 0.2 mile, turn right onto Wolf Gap Road. Follow Wolf Gap Road for about 6 miles, turning right into the Wolf Gap Recreation Area. The trailhead is to the right of campsite 9, which is at the end of the loop.

Information and Contact

There is no fee. Dogs on leash are allowed. Map F from the Potomac Appalachian Trail Club covers this region and can be purchased at www.patc.net. For more information, contact the Lee Ranger District, 95 Railroad Avenue, Edinburg, VA 22824, 540/984-4101, www.fs.fed.us/r8/gwj.

❸ TIBBET KNOB
George Washington National Forest

Level: Moderate

Hiking Time: 1.75 hours

Total Distance: 3.1 miles round-trip

Elevation Gain: 830 feet

Summary: Peer out at the valleys and ridges of West Virginia from this peak that sits atop the Virginia–West Virginia border.

Running along the same ridge but in the opposite direction as the Big Schloss hike, the Tibbet Knob hike is not quite as popular or as long as its sister hike, but it is a bit more difficult. You can combine the two hikes for a full day or a leisurely weekend of exploration. The Wolf Gap Campground makes a good base, as do the more primitive sites located along the trails. In fact, the primitive sites within the Lee Ranger District of the George Washington National Forest are undoubtedly among the best in the DC region. Each site is large, well maintained, and features a stone fire ring, and the locations of these sites—set upon ridges with excellent views or cozily tucked in among the trees—are unbeatable.

As you begin this hike on yellow-blazed Tibbet Knob Trail, you'll first meander past a few campsites before beginning what will be a nearly constant climb to the ridge through young forest dominated by blackberry and blueberry bushes as well as the occasional mulberry. After about 0.5 mile, you'll reach a lower summit; from there you can peer northeast toward Big Schloss and Mill Mountain. Beyond this small summit, the trail descends through mountain laurels and conifers. Pine needles pad the path, and their crisp scent perfumes the air. The descent doesn't last long, and you'll soon begin another uphill slog. In summer, this can be a very hot hike because the canopy is nearly nonexistent in some places and the sun beats down with fierce intensity.

About 0.4 mile after you began ascending, you'll reach a very steep and rocky section of trail that requires you to scramble upward using both hands and feet. Be sure to look where you're grabbing since rattlesnakes are known to like rocky

© THERESA DOWELL BLACKINTON

Mountain range after mountain range can be seen from Tibbet Knob.

areas and aren't entirely uncommon in this area. Though the climb is tough, it's short, and the trail levels out beyond it before reaching another rocky scramble. When you've reached this point, you're almost at the top, so there's no need to rush. In fact, once you make it up over the last boulder, it's only about 200 yards to the overlook. A panorama of the north and west spreads out before you, and large sandstone rocks make for first-class seats. In autumn, Tibbet Knob is an excellent location for marveling at the changing colors without the leaf-peeping crowds of nearby Shenandoah.

After you've relaxed and enjoyed the view (consider packing a picnic lunch), complete the hike by retracing your steps to the trailhead.

Options

If you just can't get enough of the view, consider spending a night atop this peak. About 20 yards farther along the trail, you'll find an excellent campsite. Just remember that this is bear country, and if you'd like to sleep here under the stars, you should be prepared with proper food storage. Additionally, there are no water sources nearby, so pack in everything you will need.

Directions

Take I-495 to westbound I-66 to southbound I-81. After 17.4 miles, take exit 283 and turn right onto Route 42. Drive 5.2 miles, then make a right on Union Church Road followed by a quick left onto Route 623. After 0.2 mile, turn right onto Wolf Gap Road. Follow Wolf Gap Road for about 6 miles, turning right into the Wolf Gap Recreation Area. Cross back over Wolf Gap Road to reach the trailhead, directly opposite the parking lot.

Information and Contact

There is no fee. Dogs on leash are allowed. Map F from the Potomac Appalachian Trail Club covers this region and can be purchased at www.patc.net. For more information, contact the Lee Ranger District, 95 Railroad Avenue, Edinburg, VA 22824, 540/984-4101, www.fs.fed.us/r8/gwj.

4 VEACH GAP
George Washington National Forest

Level: Moderate

Hiking Time: 3.5 hours

Total Distance: 7.0 miles round-trip

Elevation Gain: 1,050 feet

Summary: Make a gentle ascent to a vista from which you can see The Point, a sharp bend in the Shenandoah River.

The Veach Gap hike provides a sample of some of the best features of the George Washington National Forest. You get a bit of the elevation gain common to almost every hike in the region thanks to the ups and downs of the Appalachian ridges and valleys, but the distance moderates the ascent, keeping it a few notches less strenuous than other nearby hikes. You'll be introduced to the excellent primitive campsites scattered throughout the forest as you pass two, including one with a sunrise view that would cost big bucks if you were in a hotel. And you'll enjoy varied scenery as you hike alongside a creek and across a ridge to the perfect view of a bend of the Shenandoah River.

Yellow-blazed Veach Gap Trail branches off to the left of the parking area. Mill Run flows down below you to your left, and a meadow riotous with summer wildflowers lies to your right. This part of the trail is flat and easy, unencumbered by the rocks typical to the area. For 1.0 mile, you'll continue along the creek, through second-growth forest. As the trail approaches the creek crossing, large rocks begin to pave the path. Once on the bank, look across and to your right, and you'll see that the blazes continue on the opposite side. Negotiate the usually shallow water, and then continue through a rocky bed running alongside the creek before returning to the dirt trail. About 0.1 mile beyond the creek

© THERESA DOWELL BLACKINTON

The Veach Gap hike starts on a broad, easy-to-traverse trail.

crossing, you'll reach an intersection with Massanutten/Tuscarora Trail, blazed in both orange and blue.

Turn left here to begin the ascent of Little Crease Mountain. At points, you may see blazes in only one color, but don't let that worry you; so long as you stay straight on the main path, you're fine. The ascent is very gradual, and though the trail becomes rockier here, it's not so uneven that you have to watch your every step. After about 0.5 mile, look for a white tent symbol on a tree, and notice the trail leading off to your right. Situated here is a great campsite.

Continue up the Massanutten/Tuscarora Trail. The forest isn't particularly old, with many tree trunks that an average adult could nearly circle with their hands. Additionally, pines, one of the first species to move into an area as forests regenerate, have a heavy presence here. About 1.4 miles past the campsite, the trail makes a 90-degree turn to the right. It later turns back to the left and passes a rockslide, reaching the ridge about 0.3 mile past the right turn. You'll have multiple views to your right, though many are partially obscured by foliage during all but winter months.

For the best panorama, hike just over 0.2 mile along the ridge to a campsite on your left. Across from this site is a rock outcrop that offers a stunning view of a U-shaped bend of the Shenandoah River. If you pitch a tent at the campsite, you'll be greeted by the sun rising gloriously over Shenandoah National Park. If you'd rather just stay for the day, retrace your route to complete the hike.

Options

For the serious backpacker, Massanutten Trail makes a 71-mile loop around Fort Valley and Crisman Hollow. Follow the orange blazes for a multiday hike that will allow you to enjoy the forest's first-rate campsites, scenic vistas, and mountain, valley, and creekside terrain.

Directions

Take I-495 to westbound I-66. Drive 58 miles, and then take exit 6, turning left onto southbound U.S. 340. After 1.2 miles, turn right onto Route 55 and drive 5.1 miles. Turn left onto Fort Valley Road, drive 10.2 miles, and then turn left on Veach Gap Road. Follow the road to where it ends at the trailhead parking lot.

Information and Contact

There is no fee. Dogs on leash are allowed. Map G from the Potomac Appalachian Trail Club covers this region and can be purchased at www.patc.net. For more information, contact the Lee Ranger District, 95 Railroad Avenue, Edinburg, VA 22824, 540/984-4101, www.fs.fed.us/r8/gwj.

⑤ BUZZARD ROCK　　　　　　BEST ◖

George Washington National Forest

🏕 🦌 ✈ 🐕

Level: Butt-Kicker　　　　　　**Total Distance:** 8.6 miles round-trip

Hiking Time: 5 hours　　　　　　**Elevation Gain:** 2,510 feet

Summary: Navigate difficult ascents and descents to reach an overlook named for the raptors that soar above it.

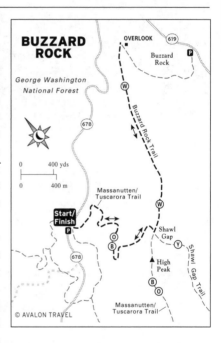

The Elizabeth Furnace picnic area is a place of leisure. Large groups gather at pavilions and picnic tables and share in enormous spreads of food. In summer, the laughter of those trying to escape the heat with a dip in Passage Creek rings loudly. Amid all this frivolity, it's hard to believe that one of the region's toughest hikes lurks. Don't let yourself be fooled, because the Buzzard Rock hike is breathtaking (literally) in its difficulty.

Finding the trailhead is the first difficulty. Three openings line the back of the parking lot. Take the one closest to the parking lot entrance, proceeding past a picnic area on your left and keeping an eye out for the orange and blue blazes of Massanutten/Tuscarora Trail. You'll stay straight to Elizabeth Furnace, then circle around it, remaining straight along Passage Creek as you pass a trail going uphill to your right. You'll soon cross a small wooden bridge and then begin the uphill hike. About halfway up the 2.3-mile ascent, the trail will turn right and then cross over another trail. Continue climbing, turning back to the left and intersecting the trail you already passed over once again, this time shortly before the ridge line.

Beyond the second intersection, the trail becomes much rockier and the ascent much steeper. At points, boulders create a natural staircase. With a final turn to the right, you'll reach the ridge. Don't celebrate yet, however, as this isn't your typical hike. Whereas walking along the ridge is usually easy—the culminating reward after the hard work of an ascent—on this hike, the most strenuous section of trail

A pretty panorama is your reward for managing the trail's ups and downs.

still awaits. When you're ready to tackle it, turn left at the four-way intersection onto white-blazed Buzzard Rock Trail and proceed along the increasingly narrow ridge. You'll continue climbing for about 0.5 mile, at which point you'll encounter large rock formations on your right. Take a break here to enjoy views to the east.

Beyond this peak, the trail begins to descend. Very steep, rocky descents are broken by short level stretches and even a few small ascents, but for the most part you're going downhill at a difficult grade over terrain that requires careful footing. About 1.5 miles past the peak, you'll reach a series of rock outcrops on your left. Decide for yourself which one has the best view, and then take a seat. You'll need to reenergize for your way back, and you'll want to take in the scene. You can gaze down on the road as it snakes between mountains, stare out toward near and distant peaks, and watch raptors lazily coast in the thermals above.

When you're ready, begin the hike back via the same route. Do not underestimate the 1.5-mile ascent to the peak of the ridge. The climb is grueling and the trail arduous. Be sure to hydrate well and to give yourself plenty of time. Once back at the intersection with the Massanutten/Tuscarora Trail, turn right and descend the mountain. Be alert for wildlife, as many animals, including black bears, call this mixed hardwood and pine forest home.

Options

For a shorter descent down the mountain, proceed 25 yards past the turnoff to the Massanutten/Tuscarora Trail, and then turn right onto the trail that you passed over twice on the way up. This trail runs straight down the mountain, so it's significantly shorter, but much steeper. Additionally, loose rock makes footing tricky, and this trail isn't maintained, so fallen trees, deep leaves, and other debris can cause difficulties.

Directions

Take I-495 to westbound I-66. Drive 58 miles, and then take exit 6, turning left onto southbound U.S. 340. After 1.2 miles, turn right onto Route 55 and drive 5.1 miles. Turn left onto Fort Valley Road, drive 4.0 miles, and then turn left into the Elizabeth Furnace picnic area. Proceed to the back lot.

Information and Contact

There is no fee. Dogs on leash are allowed. Map G from the Potomac Appalachian Trail Club covers this region and can be purchased at www.patc.net. For more information, contact the Lee Ranger District, 95 Railroad Avenue, Edinburg, VA 22824, 540/984-4101, www.fs.fed.us/r8/gwj.

6 SIGNAL KNOB   BEST ☾

George Washington National Forest

🏕 🦌 🐕

Level: Butt-Kicker   **Total Distance:** 10.7 miles round-trip

Hiking Time: 6 hours   **Elevation Gain:** 2,680 feet

Summary: Pass through a series of overlooks as you cross over the ridge of Meneka Peak.

Scenic vistas are a signature feature of the George Washington National Forest, and those along the Signal Knob hike don't disappoint. In winter, the views stretch for miles because there's no foliage to obstruct your sight line, but even in summer when the trees are fully dressed, the panoramas are broad. In autumn, expect to see a symphony of colors painting the mountainside, and spring, refusing to be outdone, boasts views framed by the white flowers of mountain laurel.

To enjoy these vistas, however, you're going to have to put in some hard work, because this hike features two serious ascents as well as tough trails covered in parts by scree and in other parts by sharp boulders. Start your hike on orange-blazed Massanutten Trail. As you begin to ascend, you'll pass an old stone Forest Service house on your left and then cross a spring-fed stream. The stream, which runs to your right, is neither deep nor wide, and in all but the wettest periods, it will be nearly dry where you cross it.

After 1.5 miles of winding uphill around the mountain, you'll reach Buzzard Rock Overlook. The trail makes a hairpin turn past the overlook, passes a primitive campsite, and then continues along an intermediate ridge. Multiple rockslides have covered the trail in this stretch, and you'll spend much of your time crossing boulder fields. After 0.7 mile, you'll reach the hike's second viewpoint, Fort Valley Overlook, which is marked with a sign. A log bench provides a resting spot from which to gaze down on the valley framed by high mountain ridges.

SIGNAL KNOB

Signal Knob

Richardson Knob 1,660 ft

BUZZARD ROCK OVERLOOK

678

Massanutten Trail

Meneka Peak 2,393 ft

Meneka Peak Trail

FORT VALLEY OVERLOOK

Start/Finish

George Washington National Forest

Green Mountain

Tuscarora Trail

Sidewinder Trail

B

678

0   400 yds
0   400 m

© AVALON TRAVEL

© THERESA DOWELL BLACKINTON

The Signal Knob hike offers multiple vistas, including this one out over town.

Continue ascending. As you approach the ridge, the grade of the trail lessens, and you'll pass two campsites before reaching a junction with Meneka Peak Trail 1.2 miles past Fort Valley Overlook. Stay straight, crossing over the ridge and descending gently to a transmission tower after about 1.1 miles. There's a partial view to the right of the noisy tower, but for the best panorama, proceed straight to where Massanutten Trail turns into a service road. Immediately turn right off the service road to reach Signal Knob; from there you have views of the town of Strasburg and its environs.

This spur trail to Signal Knob loops back to the orange-blazed service road, onto which you will turn right. After descending for 1.3 miles, you'll reach a junction with blue-blazed Tuscarora Trail. Turn left onto this trail, crossing a small creek and then beginning the most strenuous climb of the hike. For 0.8 mile, you'll navigate a series of switchbacks. The section after the second switchback is the most difficult because it is both steep and long. After the fourth switchback, you'll reach the other end of Meneka Peak Trail. Stay on the blue-blazed trail as it heads left. The trail snakes around the mountain for 1.9 miles, descending very slowly at first, and at points even ascending. The mixed hardwood and conifer forest in this section is older than it is in other areas. Keep an eye out for wildlife including deer, bears, and snakes.

After passing pink-blazed Sidewinder Trail on your right, you begin the true descent, which lasts for about 0.9 mile, at which point you will cross a stream. Remain on the blue-blazed trail for another 0.8 mile until it joins with the orange-blazed trail. The combined trail heads off to the right, but you'll want to stay straight on the now orange-blazed trail. You'll soon parallel Route 678, then arrive back at the parking lot about 0.5 mile past the split.

Options

You can shorten the hike, avoiding the stretch on the service road and the most strenuous uphill section, by turning left onto white-blazed Meneka Peak Trail, which you meet 1.2 miles past the Fort Valley Overlook. This trail will lead you along the ridge for 1.25 miles before meeting up with Tuscarora Trail. You will, however, miss the Signal Knob overlook, though you could make a detour to it.

Directions

Take I-495 to westbound I-66. Drive 58 miles, and then take exit 6, turning left onto southbound U.S. 340. After 1.2 miles, turn right onto Route 55 and drive 5.1 miles. Turn left onto Fort Valley Road, drive 3.3 miles, and then turn right into the Signal Knob parking lot. Park in the lot on your right. The trailhead is at the far end of this parking lot.

Information and Contact

There is no fee. Dogs on leash are allowed. Map G from the Potomac Appalachian Trail Club covers this region and can be purchased at www.patc.net. For more information, contact the Lee Ranger District, 95 Railroad Avenue, Edinburg, VA 22824, 540/984-4101, www.fs.fed.us/r8/gwj.

7 DICKEY RIDGE   BEST ◖

Shenandoah National Park

Level: Easy/Moderate   **Total Distance:** 5.2 miles round-trip

Hiking Time: 2.5 hours   **Elevation Gain:** 850 feet

Summary: On this circuit hike, play witness to Shenandoah's history as a settled region prior to its current existence as a national park.

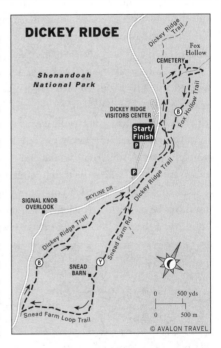

Less than a century ago, the area that is now Shenandoah National Park was more than a stretch of mountain and valley treasured for its natural beauty; it was a region that many called home. Before Shenandoah was established as a national park in the 1930s, homesteaders cleared much of the land, chopping down trees and removing stones in attempts to make the land suitable for farms and orchards. Houses, wells, barns, root cellars, and cemeteries dotted the land. Very few of these vestiges of human life remain, with much of it removed by the Civilian Conservation Corps (CCC) members tasked with returning Shenandoah to its natural state. On this circuit hike, however, you can find some evidence of the men and women who once lived here.

The hike begins in the field opposite Dickey Ridge Visitors Center. From the flagpole, cross Skyland Drive via the crosswalk and turn left at the informational sign onto blue-blazed Dickey Ridge Trail. The trail promptly enters a wooded area, but as the many vines remind you, this isn't old forest. Instead, this area is in an intermediate stage of succession as field returns to forest. After 0.2 mile, turn right at the post onto blue-blazed Fox Hollow Trail. As you descend into the hollow, notice the sections of stone fence constructed by the Fox family.

Following a brief uphill stretch, you'll begin to descend again, passing the small family cemetery on your left. Only two stones remain standing and legible, the tallest marking the resting place of Lemuel L. Fox, who died in 1916 at the age of 78. At mile 1.2, Fox Hollow Trail intersects Dickey Ridge Trail after a short ascent. Turn left onto Dickey Ridge Trail, which will lead you through more vine-covered forest and under a few cherry trees until it intersects with Snead Farm Road after 0.6 mile. You'll turn left onto this broad road, remaining on it through three forks. Stay to the left through the first fork, to the right through the second fork, and to the left through the third.

At the end of your 0.7-mile walk down Snead Farm Road, you'll reach the Snead Farm clearing. The most obvious fixture is the white barn that remains largely intact. If you scout around a bit, you'll also find a root cellar and the foundations of other structures. Post-exploration, turn left from the clearing onto blue-blazed Snead Farm Loop Trail, which will ascend for 0.7 mile to a junction with Dickey Ridge Trail. You'll tackle the majority of the hike's elevation gain on this section.

At the intersection with Dickey Ridge Trail, turn right. You'll be walking parallel to and only about 50 yards from Skyline Drive for a short period before the trail begins to climb well above the road. Just as you reach the end of the ascent, the forest will clear, and you'll have a good view of Signal Knob in the George Washington National Forest to your left. Hang gliders use the outcrop above you as a launch site. You'll make one more short ascent, and then begin a long downhill hike to where the trail intersects with Snead Farm Road after 1.2 miles.

Pick up Dickey Ridge Trail on the opposite side of the road, retracing your path for 0.6 mile to the intersection with Fox Hollow Trail. Turn left, proceeding 0.2 mile along the side of the field before arriving back at the trailhead.

The Snead Farm barn still stands, reminding visitors of the people who lived and worked the land before it became a park.

Options

This hike can be broken down into two individual loops—the 1.2-mile Fox Hollow Loop and the 3.4-mile Snead Farm Loop.

Directions

Take I-495 to westbound I-66. Drive 51.4 miles to exit 13. Turn left on Route 79, and after 0.2 mile, turn right on Route 55. Drive 5.2 miles, and then turn left on U.S. 340. After 0.5 mile, turn left on Skyline Drive and enter the park. Proceed to Dickey Ridge Visitors Center on your right at mile 4.6.

Information and Contact

There is a fee of $15 per vehicle, Mar.–Nov.; $10, Dec.–Feb., which covers admission for seven consecutive days. A $30 annual pass to Shenandoah is available. America the Beautiful passes accepted. Dogs are not allowed on Fox Hollow Trail. The park is open 24 hours daily. Maps are available at the visitors centers, or download the Dickey Ridge Area map from the park's website. For more information, contact Shenandoah National Park, 3655 Highway 211 East, Luray, VA 22835, 540/999-3500, www.nps.gov/shen.

8 BIG DEVILS STAIRS
Shenandoah National Park

Level: Easy/Moderate

Hiking Time: 2 hours

Total Distance: 4.7 miles round-trip

Elevation Gain: 600 feet

Summary: Hike to the edge of a steep, narrow canyon and gaze out at the mountains beyond.

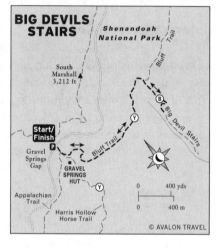

Though the multiple overlooks along Skyline Drive offer spectacular views to those who would rather not leave the comfort of the car, not one of them can compete with the vista from Big Devils Stairs. From a precarious spot on the canyon's edge you can peer down 100-foot cliffs, look out upon a farm valley, and admire the mountains in the distance.

Begin your hike on the white-blazed Appalachian Trail, which you pick up at the back of the parking lot. The trailhead lies to the right of Gravel Springs Gap Fire Road, which will actually lead you to the same place should you somehow end up on it instead. After just 0.1 mile, leave the Appalachian Trail behind and go left on blue-blazed Bluff Trail. After about 0.3 mile of switchbacks, you'll emerge in a clearing. A spring is directly in front of you, and to your right is Gravel Springs Hut, a trail shelter used by long-distance hikers. You might find an Appalachian Trail through-hiker sleeping here or having a meal. Take a minute to flip through the log book for some interesting observations from those who have passed through the area.

From the shelter, continue on Bluff Trail as it passes back near the spring and then turns right. You'll pass through junctions with Harris Hollow Horse Trail as you make a series of switchbacks. Stay on Bluff Trail, which is now marked with yellow blazes, indicating that both horses and humans are allowed to use it. Bluff Trail has multiple small ups and downs but overall is rather level as it runs along Mount Marshall. The forest here is mature, with tall trees and little undergrowth, though you will find large boulders littering the forest floor.

At about mile 1.1, the land to your right falls away, and you begin to have

There's more to see than the view on Big Devils Stairs, such as this great spangled fritillary butterfly.

partial views. Shortly after the forest clears, you'll have to cross a number of small spring branches, though they're likely to be dry during the hottest months of the year unless there's been a recent rain. You'll reach the very first hint of the gorge at about mile 1.75 as you climb up a boulder and then cross over a small stream. It doesn't seem like much, which means you'll be all the more shocked when you get the full view of the gorge and realize what this stream carved out.

Shortly past the crossing, you'll reach the junction with blue-blazed Big Devils Stairs Trail. Turn right at the concrete marker. Mountain laurels line the trail, and pines become more dominant overhead. Descend via switchback along the eastern rim of the gorge. After making a distinct right turn, you'll arrive at the first viewpoint at about mile 2.25. Continue to descend for about 0.1 mile to additional outcrops that provide smaller viewing platforms than the first but offer more extensive vistas. Find a safe perch and take in the entire panorama, including the hawks flying overhead. In autumn, the landscape is painted orange, yellow, and red. Be extremely careful because the drop-off is severe and there's nothing to prevent you from falling except your own common sense. When ready, return to the parking lot via the same series of trails.

Options

From the overlook, you can continue along Big Devils Stairs Trail, descending to the bottom of the canyon and the park boundary. This is a difficult descent of 1.25

miles. There is no other option for the return, so if you choose to descend past the overlook, be sure that you have enough energy, water, and food to make it back.

Directions

Take I-495 to westbound I-66. Drive 51.4 miles to exit 13. Turn left on Route 79, and after 0.2 mile, turn right on Route 55. Drive 5.2 miles, and then turn left on U.S. 340. After 0.5 mile, turn left on Skyline Drive and enter the park. Proceed to the Gravel Springs Gap parking area on your left at mile 17.6.

Information and Contact

There is a fee of $15 per vehicle, Mar.–Nov.; $10, Dec.–Feb., which covers admission for seven consecutive days. A $30 annual pass to Shenandoah is available. America the Beautiful passes accepted. Dogs on leash are allowed. The park is open 24 hours daily. Map 9 from the Potomac Appalachian Trail Club covers this region and can be purchased at www.patc.net. For more information, contact Shenandoah National Park, 3655 Highway 211 East, Luray, VA 22835, 540/999-3500, www.nps.gov/shen.

9 OVERALL RUN FALLS
Shenandoah National Park

Level: Moderate

Total Distance: 6.4 miles round-trip

Hiking Time: 3 hours

Elevation Gain: 1,100 feet

Summary: Enjoy a sweeping view that takes in Shenandoah's highest waterfall as well as rolling valleys and soaring mountains.

With a drop of 93 feet, Overall Run Falls is Shenandoah's highest waterfall. Few, however, would call it the park's most impressive waterfall, as it's more of a thin stream—reduced even further by summer droughts—than a heavy rush. It's still certainly worthy of a visit, however; the hike is pleasing, and if the waterfall fails to impress, the view will deliver.

The striking feature of the first section of this hike, which begins from the south side of the parking lot on the white-blazed Appalachian Trail, is the sheer abundance of ferns. They grow dense on both sides of the trail, interrupted only by a scattering of tree trunks. You may also find clusters of fly poison intermixed with the ferns, as well as the occasional wild columbine. Though fly poison doesn't sound pleasant, it's actually a very lovely member of the lily family. From grassy leaves, a tall stalk extends and produces tear-shaped clusters of tiny white flowers. The plant is toxic to animals, however, thus its name.

For 0.4 mile, you'll continue along the Appalachian Trail before reaching a fork marked with a concrete trail post. Turn right onto blue-blazed Tuscarora Trail. You'll weave your way downhill through hardwood forest, passing large rocks on both sides and maybe spotting a few Virginia bluebells. At mile 1.2, you'll reach another intersection. Turn right to stay on Tuscarora Trail. After about 0.1 mile, you'll proceed past a very large boulder on your left, and then begin a more noticeable descent down Hogback Mountain into the Overall Run watershed. You'll have to step over a few draws, although in summer, they're often dried up.

At mile 2.7, continue straight through an intersection with Mathews Arm

© THERESA DOWELL BLACKINTON

In summer, Overall Run Falls doesn't gush, but it still makes a splash as it drops 93 feet.

Trail. Mountain laurel appears here as you stair-step your way down toward the falls, reaching the top of a 29-foot, double-streamed waterfall at mile 2.9. From a small outcrop, you can gaze down at the rushing water. This is only a preview of the falls at the hike's turn-around point, so continue down through the canyon. You'll notice the forest clearing in front of you, and at mile 3.2, you'll arrive at the Overall Run Falls overlook. Peer out at the falls dropping rapidly into the river below. Try out the multiple rocky precipices to determine which offers the view you like best. After you've taken in the falls, turn your eyes to the west to see the landscape roll out in front of you.

You're looking at Page Valley, Massanutten Mountain, and, in the distance, the Alleghenies.

Though you won't tire of the view, you'll just have to decide to turn away from it at some point and proceed back to the trailhead the way you came. You'll gain all of your elevation on the return.

Options

If you'd like to extend your hike, continue along the Tuscarora–Overall Run Trail, descending steeply from the falls overlook to Overall Run, which you'll follow along and repeatedly cross. After 2.0 miles, Tuscarora Trail will split to the right; stay straight on Overall Run Trail. Continue an additional 1.2 miles before reaching an intersection with Beecher Ridge Trail. Turn left and follow this yellow-blazed trail uphill for 2.4 miles. Odds are good for spotting a black bear in this area. At the intersection with yellow-blazed Mathews Arm Trail, turn left and hike 0.5 mile back to Tuscarora Trail. Turn right and make the 2.7-mile hike back to the parking lot. Your total distance will be 12.0 miles.

Directions

Take I-495 to westbound I-66. Drive 51.4 miles to exit 13. Turn left on Route 79, and after 0.2 mile, turn right on Route 55. Drive 5.2 miles, and then turn left on U.S. 340. After 0.5 mile, turn left on Skyline Drive and enter the park. Proceed to the parking lot on your right at mile 21.1, just past Hogback Overlook.

Information and Contact

There is a fee of $15 per vehicle, Mar.–Nov.; $10, Dec.–Feb., which covers admission for seven consecutive days. A $30 annual pass to Shenandoah is available. America the Beautiful passes accepted. Dogs on leash are allowed. The park is open 24 hours daily. Maps are available at the visitors centers, or download the Mathews Arm and Elkwallow Area map from the website. For more information, contact Shenandoah National Park, 3655 Highway 211 East, Luray, VA 22835, 540/999-3500, www.nps.gov/shen.

10 PINEY RIVER FALLS   BEST C

Shenandoah National Park

Level: Moderate   **Total Distance:** 6.8 miles round-trip

Hiking Time: 3.25 hours   **Elevation Gain:** 1,300 feet

Summary: Splash around in a waterfall bypassed by most visitors to Shenandoah.

It must be the trailhead location that keeps Piney Branch Trail from being crowded. Instead of being located right on Skyline Drive, the trailhead is tucked away in an administrative area, which most people must mistakenly assume to be off-limits. What this means for you is a quiet hike through pretty woods and maybe even some solitude at a waterfall that invites you to splash around.

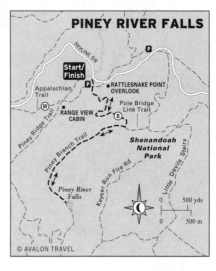

From the parking area, walk back in the direction of Skyline Drive, passing a signboard revealing the history of this location as a CCC camp. The Piney Branch trailhead is marked with a concrete post accompanied by a large map on display. The forest here is young, primarily composed of berry bushes and black locust trees reclaiming a field. After just 0.1 mile, you'll cross over the Appalachian Trail, continuing straight on blue-blazed Piney Branch Trail. You'll make gentle switchbacks as the trail meanders down into the valley. At mile 1.3, you'll approach the upper reaches of Piney River, which seems to be filled more with rocks than water during all but the wettest times of the year.

Over the next 0.1 mile, you'll cross multiple feeder streams, most of which can be traversed with one big step or via strategically placed rocks or logs, before arriving at a junction with Pole Bridge Link Trail. Turn right to stay on Piney Branch Trail, which passes through known bear country. In fact, the Park Service does surveys of the black bear population in this area, so keep your eyes open and make a little noise as you go. If you're lucky, you may spot one lumbering through the forest. You have a better chance, however, of sighting deer, raccoons, foxes, and skunks, as well as the common chipmunk, which despite its small size seems to create more noise as it moves than a 500-pound bear.

Though narrow, this section of Piney Branch Trail used to be an old road, and it retains a road's easy grade, making for a gradual descent. You can hear Piney River, which runs parallel to the trail but is far below it. From the junction with Piney Branch Trail, you must still hike 1.6 miles to reach the riverbank.

Piney River Falls makes for a pleasant and often quiet spot for relaxing.

Upon reaching the river at mile 3.0, cross to the western bank by way of stepping stones. Follow the cascading river through a forest of maple, birch, basswood, and hemlock. You may notice that some of the hemlocks have fallen victim to the wooly adelgid, an aphidlike invasive species that Shenandoah staff has been actively battling since identifying it in the park in the late 1980s.

Only 0.2 mile after crossing Piney River, you'll pass two huge rock formations on your left. At this point, you need to proceed carefully. The turnoff to the falls, which is unmarked and very easy to pass, is reached in an additional 0.2 mile. As the sound of rushing water grows, look for a narrow footpath on your left leading down to the river. If you reach a set of downhill switchbacks, you've gone too far, so retrace your steps. Take the trail down to the river, where you'll be treated to a three-tiered waterfall that drops a total of 25 feet. Large, mossy rocks make excellent seats from which you can dip your toes into the crisp water. Small pools are located at the bottom of each tier and are especially refreshing on a hot day. You will, however, want to tread carefully as the rocks can be rather slippery. Head back on the return trip before you've tired yourself out with too much frolicking, because, as with many hikes in Shenandoah, you have an uphill hike ahead of you.

Options

Create an 8.3-mile circuit by continuing along the Piney Branch Trail for about 0.5 mile to the intersection with blue-blazed Piney Ridge Trail. Turn right, hiking about 1.0 mile to a T junction. Turn right to remain on Piney Ridge Trail. You'll pass unmaintained Dwyer Cemetery on your left and then ascend for about 2.0 miles. At the intersection with the Appalachian Trail, turn right. Pass Range View Cabin, owned by the Potomac Appalachian Trail Club, and then turn left at the intersection with Piney Branch Trail. You'll arrive back at the parking area in 0.1 mile.

Directions

Take I-495 to westbound I-66. Drive 51.4 miles to exit 13. Turn left on Route 79, and after 0.2 mile, turn right on Route 55. Drive 5.2 miles, and then turn left on U.S. 340. After 0.5 mile, turn left on Skyline Drive and enter the park. Proceed to mile 22.1, then make a left turn on the road leading into the Piney River Developed Area. The visitor parking area is on your left.

Information and Contact

There is a fee of $15 per vehicle, Mar.–Nov.; $10, Dec.–Feb., which covers admission for seven consecutive days. A $30 annual pass to Shenandoah is available. America the Beautiful passes accepted. Dogs on leash are allowed. The park is open 24 hours daily. Maps are available at the visitors centers, or download the Mathews Arm and Elkwallow Area map from the park's website. For more information, contact Shenandoah National Park, 3655 Highway 211 East, Luray, VA 22835, 540/999-3500, www.nps.gov/shen.

11 LITTLE DEVILS STAIRS

BEST [

Shenandoah National Park

Level: Strenuous

Total Distance: 5.5 miles round-trip

Hiking Time: 2.75 hours

Elevation Gain: 1,500 feet

Summary: A steep boulder climb up a narrow gorge gives meaning to this trail's name.

Although the climb through the gorge that makes this hike so appealing is worth doing any time of year, if you can, plan to hit the trail in the spring before the summer droughts set in. The spring rains not only cause the wildflowers and trees to burst into bloom, but they also fill the creek and create cascading waterfalls. Throughout the gorge section of this hike, Keyser Run flows alongside the trail, kisses it and then turns away, and frequently cuts across it. You'll get your boots wet at least a time or two.

From the parking lot, follow blue-blazed Little Devils Stairs Trail through the gorge, which starts out wide but quickly becomes narrower and steeper. In fact, almost all of the trail's elevation is gained in a stretch of less than 2.0 miles. After 0.9 mile, the trail really begins to climb, and you'll find yourself crisscrossing the creek often. As you haul yourself over and around the boulders, the trail can be hard to find, but look for the blazes, and don't worry too much. It's quite difficult to get very far off course.

Be sure to pause once in a while to enjoy the waterfalls and the forest of red maples, yellow birches, and tulip poplars that surrounds you. If you take a break on one of the rocks—definitely recommended—closely observe the world around you, as you'll likely see stick bugs, newts, frogs, and other small creatures. At about 1.7 miles you'll make the final crossing of Keyser Run, and the uphill ascent will relent to a series of switchbacks. After an additional 0.3 mile, the trail will reach an intersection with Keyser Run Fire Road.

Turn left onto the yellow-blazed fire road, which is broad and covered in gravel. Goldenrod and other wildflowers grow thick, stretching out into the

© THERESA DOWELL BLACKINTON

Hiking out of the gorge is hard work, but the scenery makes the effort worthwhile.

road. In autumn, the overhead foliage turns red and orange, and where trees grow less densely you can peek through and see a kaleidoscope of colors on the slopes of the surrounding mountains. The road runs downhill, and in the forest to the right you may spot deer or even black bears, which are known to frequent this area.

After 1.8 miles on the fire road, you'll pass under a power line, and the trail will flatten out for a stretch. Just before you reach a junction with the Hull School Trail on your left at mile 4.4, you'll pass Bolen Cemetery, which is worth a few minutes of exploration. A small monument pays tribute to those families who were forced to give up their land for the creation of the park. After honoring their sacrifice, descend through the hemlocks that line the fire road until you reach the parking lot and complete the circuit.

Options

For a longer hike, continue straight across the fire road onto blue-blazed Pole Bridge Trail, which you'll follow for a little less than a mile before turning left onto blue-blazed Piney Branch trail. Piney Branch Trail extends for 2.8 miles before running into yellow-blazed Hull School Trail, at which point you'll turn left and head back toward the fire road. Turn right onto Keyser Run Fire Road to complete the hike.

Directions

Take I-495 to westbound I-66. Drive 21.7 miles, and then take exit 43A to merge onto southbound U.S. 29. After 11.5 miles, merge onto westbound U.S. 211. Continue for 26.6 miles, then turn right on Gidbrown Hollow Road. After 1.9 miles, turn left on Keyser Run Road, which will turn into a gravel road that ends at the trailhead after 3.1 miles.

Information and Contact

There is a fee of $15 per vehicle, Mar.–Nov.; $10, Dec.–Feb., which covers admission for seven consecutive days. A $30 annual pass to Shenandoah is available.

America the Beautiful passes accepted. Dogs on leash are allowed. The park is open 24 hours daily. A trail map is available at the visitors centers, or download the Mathews Arm and Elkwallow Area map from the park's website. For more information, contact Shenandoah National Park, 3655 U.S. Highway 211 East, Luray, VA 22835, 540/999-3500, www.nps.gov/shen.

12 BUCK RIDGE–BUCK HOLLOW CIRCUIT

BEST ◖

Shenandoah National Park

Level: Strenuous

Hiking Time: 2.5 hours

Total Distance: 5.6 miles round-trip

Elevation Gain: 1,800 feet

Summary: Keep an eye out for bears and other wildlife on this hike through seldom-traveled wilderness.

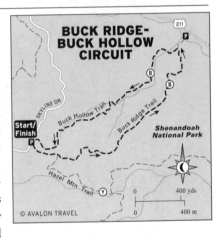

This hike begins along the same fire road as the Hazel River Falls hike, but beyond that, the two hikes share very few traits. While the trails to Hazel River Falls remain at a moderate grade for their entirety, the Buck Ridge–Buck Hollow circuit leads you along a ridge before plunging you down into a hollow and then carrying you back up. This hike doesn't have a distinct featured destination; rather, it provides the opportunity to spend time on very lightly traversed trails that feel wild and offer a better-than-average chance at spotting one of Shenandoah's black bears.

From the south corner of the parking lot, begin your hike with a 0.5-mile walk down yellow-blazed Hazel Mountain Fire Road. Buck Hollow Trail immediately splits off from the left, but you'll bypass it for now, as this is your return route. For the outbound part of the hike, you'll turn left onto blue-blazed Buck Ridge Trail, which is marked with a post. It's immediately obvious that this route sees little traffic, as heavy, tangled undergrowth invades the trail, leaving only a narrow footpath. Take a moment to examine the growth in this area. You'll notice an abundance of vines, berry bushes, and ferns but very few trees. In fact, nothing grows more than about 15 or 20 feet overhead. This area was ravaged by a 24,000-acre fire in 2000 and is currently in the early stages of regrowth.

After about 0.7 mile on Buck Ridge Trail, the trail drops steeply and mountain laurel dominates. Here you begin to get views to your left of Pass Mountain. Notice the denuded trees that stand out amid the healthy trees. Shenandoah Park staff and volunteers are in a constant battle against insects and disease. Beyond this first view, steep boulder-ridden downhills are moderated by short, flat stretches

The encroaching forest at the start of Buck Hollow Trail is evidence that this hike remains off most visitors' radars.

before the trail levels off and you have an easy walk along the ridge where the forest is much more mature. Don't be surprised if you see one of the park's hundreds of black bears hanging out in this area.

Your leisurely walk ends abruptly as the trail plunges down to Buck Hollow Trail. The descent is extremely steep over very loose rock, so be cautious and take your time. At mile 2.8, you'll reach the creek that cuts through Buck Hollow. Rock-hop across the water to blue-blazed Buck Hollow Trail, turning left onto it and walking along the creek bank. You immediately begin your ascent out of the hollow, although it is very gentle at first as the trail crosses over a number of small feeders. After about 0.8 mile, you'll cross back over to the other side of the creek, this time via very large boulders that keep you high above the water. The trail begins to climb noticeably through a hardwood forest of beeches, birches, maples, and oaks. A hard left turn after just about 0.3 mile leads you away from the water and marks the beginning of the most pronounced part of the ascent. It's a constant uphill hike at this point.

The hike nears completion as you make one final crossing over the upper section of the creek and finish the ascent. Just before you return to the trailhead, the trail levels out and changes from dirt track to grass. At the end of 2.8-mile Buck Hollow Trail, turn right and return to the parking lot.

Options

The Hazel Falls hike leaves from the same parking area. For a full day of hiking, you could do both trails, with the pools on the Hazel River offering a nice way to relax after all that exertion.

Directions

Take I-495 to westbound I-66. Drive 21.7 miles to exit 43A and merge onto southbound U.S. 29. Proceed 11.5 miles to westbound U.S. 211. Drive 35.9 miles, exiting toward Shenandoah National Park at Skyline Drive. Go through the entrance station and then keep left to proceed south on Skyline Drive. Continue to the Meadow Spring parking area on your left at mile 33.5.

Information and Contact

There is a fee of $15 per vehicle, Mar.–Nov.; $10, Dec.–Feb., which covers admission for seven consecutive days. A $30 annual pass to Shenandoah is available. America the Beautiful passes accepted. Dogs on leash are allowed. The park is open 24 hours daily. Maps are available at the visitors centers, or download the Panorama Area map from the park's website. For more information, contact Shenandoah National Park, 3655 Highway 211 East, Luray, VA 22835, 540/999-3500, www.nps.gov/shen.

13 HAZEL RIVER FALLS

BEST (

Shenandoah National Park

Level: Easy/Moderate

Total Distance: 5.4 miles round-trip

Hiking Time: 2.5 hours

Elevation Gain: 800 feet

Summary: An undemanding hike leads to a natural water park with pools, falls, and caves to explore.

Often great reward comes only at great cost. The hike to Hazel Falls, however, defies conventional wisdom, demanding little in exchange for a gorgeous series of waterfalls complete with pools perfect for playing in as well as a natural cave ideal for picnicking. Though it's easy to do this hike in a couple of hours, you may want to free up your entire day. Once you get to the falls, you're not going to want to leave.

Your hike begins on yellow-blazed Hazel Mountain Fire Road, which has its trailhead in the south corner of the parking area. Buck Hollow Trail splits off immediately, but you'll want to follow the broad road straight, reaching an intersection with Buck Ridge Trail at 0.5 mile. Stay to the right to follow yellow-blazed Hazel Mountain Trail. Though you are descending here, the grade is almost imperceptible. Multiple branches of a spring cut across the path, but they're small and easily crossed.

At mile 1.6, Hazel Mountain Trail reaches a junction with yellow-blazed White Rocks Trail. Turn left and follow this trail as it ascends slightly. You'll notice that there are very few mature trees along White Rocks Trail, and, in fact, there isn't much midlevel growth either. This area was devastated by several fires that raged in Shenandoah in the past few decades. One of the most recent, a fire that began in October 2000, burned 24,000 acres. Seeing the burned trunks of the remaining trees as well as the many stumps and snags is sobering. You will, however, find hope in the knee-high beech, sassafras, oak, and poplar trees that will one day reforest the land.

After 0.9 mile on White Rocks Trail, you'll reach a concrete post, indicating the falls and cave are 0.2 mile down the narrow footpath on your right. In the short stretch before this marker, you may notice a few other faint trails on your right. These are bushwhacked paths that lead down to the water, but most are extremely steep and don't provide access to the best sections of the falls. Even on the official trail, it's a tough descent, but rather than slipping down a steep embankment, you're stepping from one large, flat stone to another. Upon reaching the end of this natural staircase, turn right. You'll immediately reach the first pool and waterfall, which snakes down the rocks. Continue to your right, where you'll find another cascade, and then the largest of the waterfalls, which drops down a 30-foot chute into a deep pool.

The large cave, which is about 10 feet deep, 30 feet wide, and 8 feet high, is to the right of the pool. Climb up past this cave to a smaller opening in the rocks, through which you can access the base of the falls. Scramble around, and you'll find similar caves in the surrounding rocks. Pick your favorite spot and set yourself up for a day at the pool. When you're ready to leave, return the way you came.

Options

Really earn the right to enjoy the falls on a 10.3-mile loop with over 2,100 feet of elevation gain. Begin the hike as previously described, but at the intersection with White Rocks Trail, stay right on Hazel Mountain Trail and continue for another 1.4 miles to a junction with blue-blazed Sam's Ridge Trail. Turn left and proceed for almost 2.0 miles. At the junction with yellow-blazed Hazel River Trail, turn left, walking upstream and crossing the river multiple times as you hike 1.3 miles to the junction with White Rocks Trail. Turn right and hike 1.3 miles, much of it on a steep uphill, to the falls and cave trail intersection. Visit the falls, and then finish the hike with the 2.7 miles outlined in the main listing.

Directions

Take I-495 to westbound I-66. Drive 21.7 miles to exit 43A and merge onto southbound U.S. 29. Proceed 11.5 miles to westbound U.S. 211. Drive 35.9 miles, exiting toward Shenandoah National Park at Skyline Drive. Go through the entrance station, and then keep left to proceed south on Skyline Drive. Continue to the Meadow Spring parking area on your left at mile 33.5.

© THERESA DOWELL BLACKINTON

The first of three cascades on this hike slides down into a pool.

Information and Contact

There is a fee of $15 per vehicle, Mar.–Nov.; $10, Dec.–Feb., which covers admission for seven consecutive days. A $30 annual pass to Shenandoah is available. America the Beautiful passes accepted. Dogs on leash are allowed. The park is open 24 hours daily. Maps are available at the visitors centers, or download a Panorama Area map from the park website. For more information, contact Shenandoah National Park, 3655 Highway 211 East, Luray, VA 22835, 540/999-3500, www.nps.gov/shen.

14 MARY'S ROCK

Shenandoah National Park

Level: Moderate	**Total Distance:** 6.8 miles round-trip
Hiking Time: 3 hours	**Elevation Gain:** 950 feet

Summary: Take a scenic walk along the Appalachian Trail, passing multiple westward overlooks on the way to a 3,514-foot summit that challenges other peaks for the claim to Shenandoah's best views.

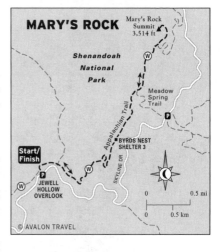

One hundred one miles of the Appalachian Trail wind through Shenandoah National Park, passing overviews, running alongside tumbling creeks, and threading through wilderness, but the 3.4 miles of the trail that you'll cover on this hike might just be the most rewarding. The trail is not difficult here, but it offers vistas that rank among the park's most splendid.

From the back end of the parking lot, hike 50 feet up the spur trail that connects you to the white-blazed Appalachian Trail. Turn right, heading south for a short distance before making a switchback that will send you north. You'll pass below the overlook and then through a meadow with views to the left. Continue straight as Leading Ridge Trail branches off to your left. Ferns and berry bushes quickly give way to a dense thicket of mountain laurel as you proceed gently uphill. In June you'll be treated to the elegant white flowers of the laurel along with the delightful red-and-yellow blooms of wild columbine.

The trail gradually grows rockier until you're walking between huge lichen-covered boulders. Ascend through the boulders to an overlook at mile 1.0 known as the Pinnacle. At 3,730 feet, it offers wide views of the mountains and valleys to the west. From here, the trail descends via switchback to Byrds Nest Shelter #3 at mile 2.0. This shelter is for day use only, providing a resting spot for Appalachian Trail through-hikers, a picnic spot for those who like to take their lunch on the trail, and a protective spot for anyone caught in one of Shenandoah's sudden storms.

Beyond the shelter, a service road veers to the right, but you'll want to stay on the Appalachian Trail, which again climbs, though not steeply. About 0.4 mile

© THERESA DOWELL BLACKINTON

A nearly 360-degree view awaits atop Mary's Rock.

past the shelter, just as the trail makes a right turn, an overlook offers a view to the west. Another overlook lies just 0.2 mile farther down the trail, and 0.2 mile past it you'll pass a junction on your right with Meadow Spring Trail. At this point, the trail begins its most noticeable ascent, climbing 0.3 mile over rocky terrain.

Beyond this ascent, an additional 0.3 mile of gentle up and down hiking leads to Mary's Rock. Along the way, westward vistas follow one after another. Multiple rock promontories appear ahead of you, but when you reach Mary's Rock, you'll know it. It looks like a structure that deserves a name. The trail curves around the back of this massive rock before reaching a marked juncture on your left. This spur trail leads to a panorama that is hard to beat. To the north, the peaks of the Blue Ridge Mountains rise and fall. To the west, you can see the town of Luray in one of the many valleys of the Shenandoah. Climb to the highest boulders of this 3,514-foot summit to get a near-360-degree view of this great national park and its environs. Then return via the same stretch of Appalachian Trail.

Options

For a short trek to the summit, park at the Meadow Spring lot at mile 33.5. Then cross Skyline Drive and hike 0.7 mile up blue-blazed Meadow Spring Trail, which passes by the remains of a mountain cabin that was destroyed by fire in the 1940s. At the intersection with the Appalachian Trail, turn right and proceed to Mary's Rock via the route in the preceding description.

Directions

Take I-495 to westbound I-66. Drive 21.7 miles to exit 43A and merge onto southbound U.S. 29. Proceed 11.5 miles to westbound U.S. 211. Drive 35.9 miles, exiting toward Shenandoah National Park at Skyline Drive. Go through the entrance station, and then keep left to proceed south on Skyline Drive. Continue to the Jewell Hollow Overlook on your right at mile 36.4 and park in the lot at the far end of the overlook.

Information and Contact

There is a fee of $15 per vehicle, Mar.–Nov.; $10, Dec.–Feb., which covers admission for seven consecutive days. A $30 annual pass to Shenandoah is available. America the Beautiful passes accepted. Dogs on leash are allowed. The park is open 24 hours daily. Maps are available at the visitors centers, or download a copy of the Panorama Area map from the park's website. For more information, contact Shenandoah National Park, 3655 Highway 211 East, Luray, VA 22835, 540/999-3500, www.nps.gov/shen.

15 CORBIN CABIN CIRCUIT
Shenandoah National Park

Level: Moderate

Hiking Time: 2 hours

Total Distance: 4.0 miles round-trip

Elevation Gain: 1,190 feet

Summary: Imagine life as an early settler on a visit to the only remaining intact mountain cabin in Shenandoah.

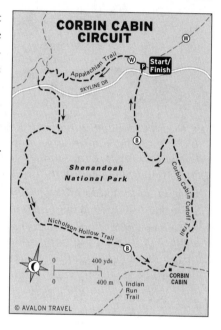

In the decades before Skyline Drive cut through this swath of the Blue Ridge Mountains, turning the area into a beloved national park, Shenandoah was settled by farmers and mountain folk. Intrepid men and women tamed portions of the wilderness and sustained themselves on its bounty and their hard work. Today little evidence remains of their history. In fact, Corbin Cabin, the highlight of this hike, is the only intact example of a mountain cabin within Shenandoah National Park.

To make this hike into a circuit, begin by walking south (left) along the white-blazed Appalachian Trail, which has a trailhead in the southeast end of the parking area. For 0.7 mile, you'll make mild ascents and descents as you hike along a ridge. Upon reaching a trail intersection marked with a post, turn left onto Crusher Ridge Trail to travel 0.1 mile back toward Skyline Drive. Turn left at the second post, from which Skyline Drive is only 50 yards away. You'll cross the road here, turning left and walking 100 yards to Nicholson Hollow Trail on your right.

Follow this blue-blazed trail as it leads down into the valley, where wild columbine and fly poison thrive in the summer months. You'll pass over a spring and then cross Indian Run. Just over the water, Indian Run Trail runs off to your right. Stay straight for another 0.1 mile, arriving at Corbin Cabin after 1.8 miles on Nicholson Hollow Trail. This traditional mountain cabin on the banks of the Hughes River was built in 1909 by George Corbin. He lived in the simple log structure until 1938, when he was forced to vacate the land so that his homestead

© THERESA DOWELL BLACKINTON

Built in 1909 by George Corbin, who was forced to abandon it in 1938 for the creation of the park, Corbin Cabin remains in remarkably good shape.

could become part of Shenandoah National Park. In 1954, the Potomac Appalachian Trail Club renovated the cabin, repairing what had deteriorated in the years it was unoccupied while maintaining its historical integrity. Though you're free to take a look around the outside of the cabin, the inside is off-limits except to those who rent it for an overnight stay.

After you've taken a look at the cabin, cross the Hughes River at the concrete trail post, turning left onto blue-blazed Corbin Cabin Cutoff Trail. From here, it is 1.4 miles back to Skyline Drive. Just after crossing the river via large boulders, you'll spot another cabin to your left. This was part of the Corbin homestead, but unlike the main cabin, it is in poor condition. Explore it if you wish, and then continue up the trail. After about 0.1 mile, a side trail on your left leads to an old cemetery, though only a few uninscribed headstones remain.

The entire return hike is uphill, with the last 0.9 mile steeper than the first 0.5 mile. You'll emerge from the trail at Skyline Drive, directly opposite the parking lot. Carefully cross the road to return to your car.

Options

Want to spend a night or two living in the manner of early Shenandoah settlers? Then make plans to stay overnight at Corbin Cabin. Reservations can be made through the Potomac Appalachian Trail Club (www.patc.net). The cabin is primitive, without electricity or running water. The PATC takes reservations up to two months in advance. The cabin is popular, so plan in advance.

Directions

Take I-495 to westbound I-66. Drive 21.7 miles to exit 43A to merge onto southbound U.S. 29. Proceed 11.5 miles to westbound U.S. 211. Drive 35.9 miles, exiting toward Shenandoah National Park at Skyline Drive. Go through the entrance station, and then keep left to proceed south on Skyline Drive to the parking area on the right at mile 37.9.

Information and Contact

There is a fee of $15 per vehicle, Mar.–Nov.; $10, Dec.–Feb., which covers admission for seven consecutive days. A $30 annual pass to Shenandoah is available. America the Beautiful passes accepted. Dogs on leash are allowed. The park is open 24 hours daily. Maps are available at the visitors centers, or download the Skyland Area map from the park's website. For more information, contact Shenandoah National Park, 3655 Highway 211 East, Luray, VA 22835, 540/999-3500, www.nps.gov/shen.

16 STONY MAN MOUNTAIN
Shenandoah National Park

Level: Easy/Moderate

Hiking Time: 1.5 hours

Total Distance: 3.3 miles round-trip

Elevation Gain: 860 feet

Summary: Westward views abound on this hike that leads to Shenandoah's second-highest peak.

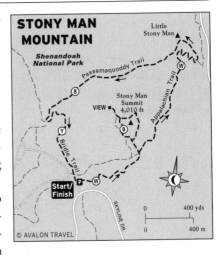

Stony Man Mountain, with a height of 4,010 feet, boasts the second-highest peak in Shenandoah. Close to the Skyland complex, which offers lodging and dining, Stony Man is a popular destination for casual visitors to the park. More experienced hikers also appreciate the hike, which incorporates the Appalachian Trail and offers outstanding summit views.

Begin at the trailhead near the map posted in the right corner of the parking lot. Here you can purchase a brochure for $1 that provides information about marked points along the trail. For the first 0.4 mile of this hike, you'll stroll through a pleasant hardwood forest on the white-blazed Appalachian Trail. In May, pink azalea blossoms line the trail; the white flowers of mountain laurel appear in June. The first junction you reach will be a four-way intersection. To your left is a connector trail that leads to a popular bridle trail. The Appalachian Trail continues to your right. At 3,837 feet, this intersection marks the highest point of the Appalachian Trail in Shenandoah. Straight ahead is the blue-blazed Stony Man Trail, the trail you want to follow as it climbs 0.3 mile to the summit.

Stony Man Trail quickly branches; stay to the right to create a short loop. You'll rise over the Stony Man summit and then reach an intersection with a spur trail. Turn right to venture out to a rocky precipice where you have a 180-degree view of the western part of the region. Proceed back down the spur trail, and then follow the blue blazes to your right. A yellow-blazed trail also departs from here, so make sure you have the correct trail, which will lead you back to the start of the loop. Stay straight to return to the four-way intersection, then turn left onto the Appalachian Trail.

© THERESA DOWELL BLACKINTON

The Little Stony Man overlook is the second of two prime vistas on this hike.

After 0.6 mile on the Appalachian Trail, which descends at a light clip, you will reach the Little Stony Man overlook. From the rock ledge dotted with vernal pools, look up and to your left to see the Stony Man summit and down and to your right to watch cars pass on Skyline Drive.

Continue past Little Stony Man on the Appalachian Trail, which switchbacks down the mountain. It will lead all the way down to Skyline Drive, but you won't go that far. Instead, after 0.2 mile, in the middle of a bend, stay straight onto blue-blazed Passamaquoddy Trail, which is marked with a concrete post. This narrow, rocky footpath travels for 1.0 mile on a ridge that passes below Little Stony Man and Stony Man. Intermittent views open to your right. Just after you pass under power lines, Passamaquoddy Trail ends at a junction with Skyland Fire Road. Make a hard left, following the yellow-blazed bridle trail. In late spring, look for foxglove, a plant with tall stalks, tubular purple flowers, and medicinal properties (extract from foxglove is used in heart medicines). Finish the hike by walking 0.5 mile through a quiet evergreen forest, emerging at the opposite end of the parking lot from where you began.

Options

For a short hike to the Stony Man summit and back, proceed to the Stony Man summit as outlined here, but rather than retracing your steps on the return trip, take the yellow-blazed bridle trail, which branches off from the end of the spur trail leading to the overview. This trail runs parallel to the Appalachian Trail and will lead you back to the parking lot.

Directions

Take I-495 to westbound I-66. Drive 21.7 miles to exit 43A and merge onto southbound U.S. 29. Proceed 11.5 miles to westbound U.S. 211. Drive 35.9 miles, exiting toward Shenandoah National Park at Skyline Drive. Go through the entrance station, and then keep left to proceed south on Skyline Drive. Continue to mile 41.7, turn right into the north entrance of Skyland, and then turn immediately right into the Stony Man parking lot.

Information and Contact

There is a fee of $15 per vehicle, Mar.–Nov.; $10, Dec.–Feb., which covers admission for seven consecutive days. A $30 annual pass to Shenandoah is available. America the Beautiful passes accepted. Dogs are not allowed on the Stony Man Trail. The park is open 24 hours daily. Maps are available at the visitors centers, or download the Skyland Area map from the park's website. For more information, contact Shenandoah National Park, 3655 Highway 211 East, Luray, VA 22835, 540/999-3500, www.nps.gov/shen.

17 WHITEOAK CANYON FALLS   BEST ◖

Shenandoah National Park

Level: Butt-Kicker

Total Distance: 7.3 miles round-trip

Hiking Time: 4 hours

Elevation Gain: 2,300 feet

Summary: Shenandoah's second-highest waterfall is impressive, but it's only one of six falls you'll see on this hike.

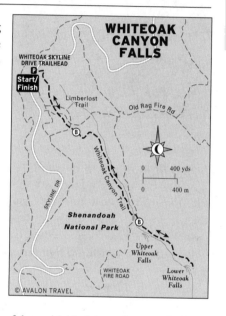

Whiteoak Run, which you will hug for the majority of this hike, has more waterfalls per mile than any other waterway in Shenandoah National Park. In fact, you will pass six waterfalls on the final 1.3-mile section of this out-and-back trail. Not all of them are accessible, however; some you can only view from a distance, while others have pools you can soak in.

Popular Whiteoak Canyon Trail begins as a broad, blue-blazed gravel path through mountain laurel with a nice canopy of mature trees providing shade. Though this area is well traveled and close to Skyline Drive, there's still a good chance of spotting wildlife. Deer are abundant, and you may even spy one of the park's black bears foraging for food.

At about 0.3 mile, you'll cross a footbridge over a creek and then reach an intersection with Limberlost Trail. Stay straight through the intersection and continue another 0.2 mile to Old Rag Fire Road. Note the post at the fire road intersection, which tells you that it's 1.9 miles to the upper falls, then continue straight. In this stretch you will notice an abundance of fallen trees, victims of Tropical Storm Fran in 1996.

Shortly after crossing over another section of Limberlost Trail, the trail meets up with a branch of Whiteoak Run. For a brief distance, you'll follow this branch as it flows to your right. Near where the branch meets the main creek, you'll cross the branch via a footbridge and then follow Whiteoak Run, which will be on your left. The trail begins to descend more noticeably at this point, and large boulders appear trailside. About 1.6 miles after you cross Old Rag Fire Road, you'll reach

For much of its length, this hike follows Whiteoak Run, which boasts six waterfalls.

another footbridge, which will allow you to cross to the opposite bank of Whiteoak Run. Once across the bridge, turn right, passing Whiteoak Fire Road on your left. About 0.3 mile beyond the bridge, you'll reach a viewpoint from where you can peer into the canyon and at the first of the falls. This 86-foot waterfall is the second-highest waterfall in the park, only 7 feet shorter than Overall Run Falls.

Beyond this overview, the trail becomes significantly more difficult. To reach the second waterfall, you must step your way down a steep stone staircase, passing giant boulders and sheer cliff faces. For your effort, the second waterfall rewards with an accessible pool, ideal for cooling off on a hot summer day. A combination of switchbacks and stone steps leads you farther down the trail, with multiple overlooks providing glimpses of waterfalls roaring down the canyon.

You'll return to water level at the last of the six falls, with the trail carrying you directly to another pool that invites swimmers. Continue just a bit farther down the trail to a spot marked with a sign that says Lower Falls. Climb on one of the creekside boulders here for a good look back at the falls. When you're ready, make the return hike, which isn't easy. The 1.35-mile climb back to the first waterfall is the most difficult part: You gain 1,100 feet of elevation in this section. The remaining elevation gain of 1,200 feet seems much easier because it's spread over 2.3 miles.

Options

To avoid the most strenuous part of this hike, proceed only to the first falls, where you can enjoy a splendid view of Shenandoah's second-highest falls along with an expansive look at Whiteoak Canyon. If you turn around here, you will reduce your distance to 4.6 miles and cut the elevation gain in half.

Directions

Take I-495 to westbound I-66. Drive 21.7 miles to exit 43A and merge onto southbound U.S. 29. Proceed 11.5 miles to westbound U.S. 211. Drive 35.9 miles, exiting toward Shenandoah National Park at Skyline Drive. Go through the entrance station, and then keep left to proceed south on Skyline Drive. Continue to the parking lot on your left at mile 42.6.

Information and Contact

There is a fee of $15 per vehicle, Mar.–Nov.; $10, Dec.–Feb., which covers admission for seven consecutive days. A $30 annual pass to Shenandoah is available. America the Beautiful passes accepted. Dogs on leash are allowed. The park is open 24 hours daily. Maps are available at the visitors centers, or download the Whiteoak Canyon Area map from the park's website. For more information, contact Shenandoah National Park, 3655 Highway 211 East, Luray, VA 22835, 540/999-3500, www.nps.gov/shen.

18 LIMBERLOST TRAIL
Shenandoah National Park

Level: Easy

Hiking Time: 0.75 hour

Total Distance: 1.3 miles round-trip

Elevation Gain: 130 feet

Summary: This wheelchair-accessible trail winds through Shenandoah's most enchanting display of mountain laurels.

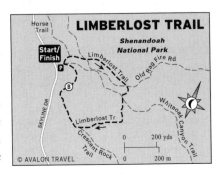

A crushed greenstone surface and a lack of any significant elevation change mean that Limberlost Trail meets ADA standards for wheelchair accessibility. It's not by any means restricted, however, to those with disabilities. The trail is also ideal for young children and those just starting out hiking because it's an easy-to-traverse trail with attractive natural features.

Begin this blue-blazed loop trail at the signboard, and then proceed in a clockwise direction. You'll immediately cross a yellow-blazed horse trail. Overhead you'll notice white pine, birch, and maple trees. Oaks mingle with these other hardwoods, but as you may observe, they've been fighting a difficult battle with the gypsy moth, an invasive species that strips the trees. On the forest floor, where mushrooms thrive and fly poison plants bloom, you'll see the remains of the many hemlock trees that once stood tall in this area. Some of the trees were more than 400 years old, but these ancient wonders fell victim to the wooly adelgid insect, which kills the trees by sucking the food from the hemlock needles. These invaders have done damage throughout Shenandoah, but it really stands out along this trail.

Though these losses are tragic, you'll notice much to rejoice over as you continue your walk. Because the oldest of the trees in this area have come down, new growth is springing forth, allowing you to witness the way in which a forest rejuvenates. Take a seat on one of the many benches along this trail to reflect on the changing forest. You may also want to simply sit and watch for birds (such as ovenbirds, red-eyed vireos, gray catbirds, scarlet tanagers, eastern towhees, and dark-eyed juncos) and wildlife (such as deer, chipmunks, salamanders, and snakes). Or just linger and enjoy the mountain laurels that dominate the path. In June, it's a pure delight to walk amid the

© THERESA DOWELL BLACKINTON

A bench welcomes hikers to enjoy the bountiful blooms along the trail.

blooms. There may not be a better trail in the park for enjoying these flowers, which last for only a short period.

As Limberlost Trail progresses, it passes over Whiteoak Canyon Trail, Old Rag Fire Road, and again Whiteoak Canyon Trail. At this second Whiteoak intersection, look to your left to see a rock formation that appears as if it were sculpted by an artist's hand rather than Mother Nature. Shortly past here, you'll cross a stream via a bridge. In this area, look for red spruce trees, one of which is thought to be more than 250 years old. You may also notice downed trees, the result of Tropical Storm Fran, which passed through in 1996 and caused much damage to the trail and surrounding forest.

Crescent Rock Trail junctions with Limberlost Trail on your left at mile 0.9; stay right. A boardwalk leads over a marshy area just past this junction, and then you pass through what might be the best of the mountain laurel. It's dense and hugs the trail, creating a walkway of blooms; you can savor it until you reach the trail's end at 1.3 miles, thus completing the loop.

Options

Turn left off Limberlost Trail onto Crescent Rock Trail and hike 1.1 miles to the Crescent Rock Overlook, which offers views of Hawksbill Mountain. Then return the same 1.1 miles to reconnect to Limberlost Trail and complete the hike as described. Crescent Rock Trail is easy, with an elevation change of only 320 feet, but it is not wheelchair accessible.

Directions

Take I-495 to westbound I-66. Drive 21.7 miles to exit 43A and merge onto southbound U.S. 29. Proceed 11.5 miles to westbound U.S. 211. Drive 35.9 miles, exiting toward Shenandoah National Park at Skyline Drive. Go through the entrance station, and then keep left to proceed south on Skyline Drive. Continue to mile 43.0, turning left on the short drive that leads you to the Limberlost parking lot.

Information and Contact

There is a fee of $15 per vehicle, Mar.–Nov.; $10, Dec.–Feb., which covers admission for seven consecutive days. A $30 annual pass to Shenandoah is available. America the Beautiful passes accepted. Dogs are not allowed on Limberlost Trail. The park is open 24 hours daily. Maps are available at the visitors centers, or download a copy of the Skyland Area map from the park's website. For more information, contact Shenandoah National Park, 3655 Highway 211 East, Luray, VA 22835, 540/999-3500, www.nps.gov/shen.

19 ROBERTSON MOUNTAIN
Shenandoah National Park

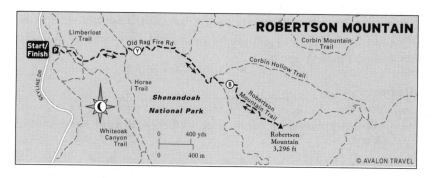

Level: Moderate

Hiking Time: 3 hours

Total Distance: 6.2 miles round-trip

Elevation Gain: 1,300 feet

Summary: A seldom-traveled trail leads to one of Shenandoah's most underrecognized peaks.

It's rare that you can stand atop a peak in Shenandoah in only the company of butterflies and songbirds. Atop 3,296-foot Robertson Mountain, however, your chances are good of having a moment's solitude to drink in the beauty of the Blue Ridge.

The majority of this hike is spent traveling down yellow-blazed Old Rag Fire Road, which leaves from the end of the Limberlost parking lot. The road is broad, gravel, and nearly level for the first stretch as it passes intersections with Whiteoak Canyon Trail and Limberlost Trail. Beyond here, you begin to descend, though because you're on a fire road, the grade is gentle.

The thick branches of mature hardwood trees extend over the road, and the ground is a patchwork of sun and shade. Roadside you'll find red-and-yellow wild columbine, the white teardrop-shaped flower clusters of fly poison, cheery stalks of bluebells, and the feathery petals of fleabane and other asters. Bridle paths will branch off, but stay straight along the fire road, passing by a ranger station on your right after 1.0 mile.

After another 0.7 mile down Old Rag Fire Road, you'll pass Corbin Mountain Trail on your left; in another 0.5 mile, you'll pass its sister trail, Corbin Hollow Trail. From the post marking Corbin Hollow Trail, look down the fire road and notice that just ahead the road turns to the right. Before you reach this turn, you'll come to a post on your left indicating the turnoff to blue-blazed Robertson

Mountain laurels frame the view from the summit of Robertson Mountain.

Mountain Trail. Take this turnoff; from there it is 0.8 mile to the summit of the mountain.

The first section of Robertson Mountain Trail is dense with mountain laurel, and thick ground cover threatens to overrun the footpath. After about 0.25 mile, the trail becomes both rockier and more steeply graded uphill. Listen for movement, and you might spot a ruffed grouse emerging from the underbrush. Continue switchbacking your way up the mountain via the narrow footpath until the trail plateaus. At this point, look for the unmarked summit trail on your right. This will lead up to a grassy patch and then turn right to proceed to a rocky summit. Scamper up one of the boulders for a near-360-degree view. Look down into Whiteoak Canyon and out toward Hawksbill Mountain, the peak to the southwest. If you look closely, you may also be able to see the faint line that is Skyline Drive. You should also take a moment to notice the variation in plant life from below. Here, thanks to the elevation, the mountain laurel blooms later, while the trees erupt into fall color earlier. When you're ready, follow your footprints in reverse to return to the trailhead.

Options

Make this hike into an 8.8-mile circuit by continuing along the ridge of Robertson Mountain and then down the eastern slope, reaching Weakley Hollow Fire Road after 1.5 miles. Turn left and walk a short distance before turning left onto blue-blazed Corbin Hollow Trail, which travels about 2.0 miles before reconnecting with Old Rag Fire Road. Turn right onto the fire road and hike 2.2 miles back to the trailhead.

Directions

Take I-495 to westbound I-66. Drive 21.7 miles to exit 43A and merge onto southbound U.S. 29. Proceed 11.5 miles to westbound U.S. 211. Drive 35.9 miles, exiting toward Shenandoah National Park at Skyline Drive. Go through the entrance station, and then keep left to proceed south on Skyline Drive. Continue to mile 43.0; turn left at the sign marked Limberlost and proceed down the short drive to the parking lot.

Information and Contact

There is a fee of $15 per vehicle, Mar.–Nov.; $10, Dec.–Feb., which covers admission for seven consecutive days. A $30 annual pass to Shenandoah is available. America the Beautiful passes accepted. Dogs on leash are allowed. The park is open 24 hours daily. Maps are available at the visitors centers, or download the Whiteoak Canyon Area map from the park's website. For more information, contact Shenandoah National Park, 3655 Highway 211 East, Luray, VA 22835, 540/999-3500, www.nps.gov/shen.

20 OLD RAG

BEST (

Shenandoah National Park

Ⓐ 🦌 🌾

Level: Butt-Kicker

Hiking Time: 5 hours

Total Distance: 7.2-8.8 miles round-trip

Elevation Gain: 2,510 feet

Summary: Discover why Old Rag is the most popular hike in the mid-Atlantic on this strenuous rock scramble.

Just as you can't go to Yellowstone without seeing Old Faithful, you can't hike Shenandoah without summiting Old Rag at least once. Many people consider this the region's best hike, and the full parking lots attest to its popularity. If possible, do this hike on a weekday, when crowds are down. Without hordes hustling you along, you can take your time on the long switchbacks, ponder all the possible options for hauling yourself up and around boulders, and enjoy in peace as many of the mountain's views as you'd like.

The trailhead for blue-blazed Ridge Trail, the starting point for this hike, is on the left side of the upper parking lot. You'll be climbing for the first 2.7 miles to the summit, although the ascent begins gently with the trail leading through a hemlock forest through which sunshine streams and butterflies dance. Around 0.75 mile, the trail narrows into a rocky path, and large boulders scattered through the forest hint at what is to come. Soon the ascent is steep enough to demand switchbacks, which are lined with mountain laurel.

As you reach the 2,800-foot elevation mark, designated by a No Camping sign, you leave the rock-studded trail behind for a path composed entirely of granite. At first you must simply step up boulder to boulder, but after you pass a broad slab providing your first vista, the real adventure begins. You must now climb, crawl, creep, scramble, and shimmy your way west for a mile across a playground of granite. Take it slow and always look for the next blue blaze before making a move. At times, you'll have to drop into crevices, crouch through caves, leap over cracks, and push yourself up onto ledges. This is not a trail for the faint of heart. Potential hikers should also be aware that some of the passes are rather narrow, creating tight squeezes for even an average-size adult.

At about 2.4 miles, you'll emerge from the first part of the rock labyrinth onto the minor summit, a large flat area with views in all directions. From here, the rock scramble continues, but it's not quite as intense, and after 0.3 mile, you'll reach the 3,284-foot summit of Old Rag, marked by one of Shenandoah's ubiquitous concrete posts. Scramble up one of the rock piles to your right to reach the highest point.

Duck walking and other acts of physical contortion are required if you want to hike Old Rag.

Go ahead and bask in the glory of having achieved the peak and conquered the hike's toughest parts; the remaining 4.5 miles are much easier. From the summit, continue your circuit on blue-blazed Saddle Trail, a dirt path that leads down from the peak. After 0.4 mile, you'll pass Byrds Nest Shelter #1, and after another 1.1 miles of switchbacks through heavy forest, you'll reach Old Rag Shelter.

Continue the downhill trek, turning right onto Weakley Hollow Fire Road after an additional 0.4 mile. For 2.6 miles, you'll enjoy a well-deserved easy walk through lush forest. You'll pass Robertson Mountain and Corbin Hollow trails after about 1.0 mile, make multiple crossings over Brokenback Run, and then parallel the Hughes River the rest of the way back to the upper lot. Along the way, look for wild columbine, white-tailed deer, and maybe even a black bear.

Options

If you love the rock scramble, you can make this an out-and-back hike rather than a loop. If you'd like to reach the summit but don't think you'd enjoy the rock scramble, start on Weakley Hollow Fire Road and then ascend via Saddle Trail. You can then come back down the same way.

Directions

Take I-495 to westbound I-66. After 21.7 miles, take exit 43A to southbound U.S. 29. Drive 11.5 miles, then exit onto westbound U.S. 211. After 29 miles, turn left on U.S. 522, driving 0.8 mile before turning right on Route 231. Drive 7.3 miles, turn right on Sharp Rock Road, proceed 1.2 miles, and then turn right on Nethers Road. After about 2.2 miles, you'll reach the lower lot and fee station. The upper lot, which has only eight spots, is 0.8 mile farther down the road. If you have to park in the lower lot, turn left and walk the 0.8 mile up Nethers Road to the trailhead.

Information and Contact

There is a fee of $15 per vehicle, Mar.–Nov.; $10, Dec.–Feb., which covers admission for seven consecutive days. A $30 annual pass to Shenandoah is available. America the Beautiful passes accepted. Dogs are not allowed. The park is open 24 hours daily. Maps are available at the fee station in the lower parking lot, or download a copy of the Old Rag Area map from the park's website. For more information, contact Shenandoah National Park, 3655 Highway 211 East, Luray, VA 22835, 540/999-3500, www.nps.gov/shen.

21 CATLETT MOUNTAIN

BEST ◖

Shenandoah National Park

Level: Butt-Kicker

Total Distance: 10.5 miles round-trip

Hiking Time: 6 hours

Elevation Gain: 2,010 feet

Summary: Seek out solitude in the outer regions of Shenandoah on this tough mountain hike.

Though Catlett Mountain shares a parking lot with Old Rag, it doesn't share that famed trail's popularity. Here you can amble alongside the cascading Hughes River, ramble among the ruins of mountain homes, claw your way up the steepest 0.25-mile section of trail in Shenandoah, and marvel at the autumn explosion of color atop the mountain with little human company.

From the parking lot, turn left and walk 0.3 mile to the gravel turnoff to Nicholson Hollow Trail. The actual trail branches off to the right just before a gate. Note the sign indicating that part of this hike passes through private property, and be respectful of the landowners' rights. The blue-blazed trail promptly leads over the Hughes River and Brokenback Run, both crossed via large boulders. Tall hardwoods tower overhead, while smaller evergreens and mountain laurel dominate the lower levels. You'll walk against the flow of the Hughes River, which

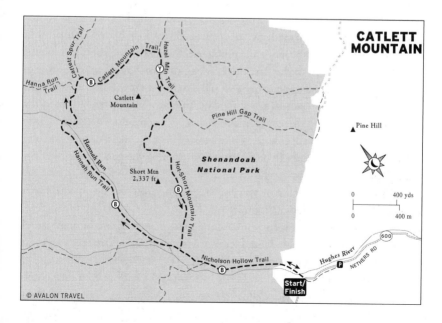

A splash in the Hughes River is well deserved after completing this hike.

runs to your left and is a favorite of trout anglers. After 0.3 mile, a sign indicates that you are now entering Shenandoah National Park.

A mile past the sign, just as the trail returns to the river after arcing away from it, you'll reach a trail junction. Turn right to continue along Nicholson Hollow Trail. After another 0.3 mile, pass Hot-Short Mountain Trail on your right. This will be your return route, but for now stay straight to begin the loop portion of the hike. Cross Hannah Run, reaching an intersection with blue-blazed Hannah Run Trail after 0.2 mile. Turn right and commence the ascent up Catlett Mountain.

It's a 1.5-mile climb to the first ridge. Along the way you'll pass the ruins of old homes. The most distinct ruin is an old chimney that will be on your right after you make the steepest climb of the hike thus far. Beyond the chimney, the trail flattens for a brief stretch, then climbs steeply again before descending into a gulch and leading you over water. Once across the water, take a deep breath and then begin what is thought to be the steepest 0.25 mile you can hike in Shenandoah. The trail is nearly straight up, with no switchbacks to temper it, and the loose dirt and rock make it hard to get good footing. You may be on all fours at points; fortunately, it's only 0.25 mile.

Upon summiting, hike for 0.4 mile along a ridge lined with mountain laurel to the intersection with blue-blazed Catlett Mountain Trail. Turn right onto it, staying right at the junction with Catlett Spur Trail in 70 yards. Over the next mile, you'll descend into a hollow. Cross a stream at the bottom, and then climb 0.2 mile to the junction with yellow-blazed Hazel Mountain Trail. Turn right and follow this pine-needled path for 0.5 mile to the junction with blue-blazed Hot-Short Mountain Trail. The marker for this trail is set back a few yards, so be on the lookout for the turnoff. From here, it is 2.2 miles of downhill hiking to return to Nicholson Hollow Trail. Some of the descent is quite steep. Enjoy intermittent views of Old Rag, and keep an eye out for signs of bears, such as scat or claw marks on trunks. You may even spot a bear clambering through the undergrowth or up a tree. Should you see one ascend or descend a tree, you'll immediately understand why you're not advised to climb a tree if you encounter a bear! Once back at the intersection with the Nicholson Hollow Trail, turn left to return to the trailhead.

Options

Consider a backcountry camping trip in this area. There are many nice sites along the Hughes River for pitching a tent, and you can connect to multiple other trails in this area. For instance, if you continue straight along Nicholson Hollow Trail, you can reach Corbin Cabin, and then loop around on Indian Run Trail and Corbin Mountain Trail to explore more of Shenandoah.

Directions

Take I-495 to westbound I-66. After 21.7 miles, take exit 49A to southbound U.S. 29. Drive 11.5 miles, then exit onto westbound U.S. 211. After 29 miles, turn left on U.S. 522, driving 0.8 mile before turning right on Route 231. Drive 7.3 miles, turn right on Sharp Rock Road, proceed 1.2 miles, and then turn right on Nethers Road. After about 2.2 miles, you'll reach the parking lot and fee station.

Information and Contact

There is a fee of $15 per vehicle, Mar.–Nov.; $10, Dec.–Feb., which covers admission for seven consecutive days. A $30 annual pass to Shenandoah is available. America the Beautiful passes accepted. Dogs are not allowed. The park is open 24 hours daily. Map 10 from the Potomac Appalachian Trail Club covers this region and can be purchased at www.patc.net. For more information, contact Shenandoah National Park, 3655 Highway 211 East, Luray, VA 22835, 540/999-3500, www.nps.gov/shen.

22 CEDAR RUN FALLS

BEST **(**

Shenandoah National Park

Level: Strenuous

Total Distance: 3.4 miles round-trip

Hiking Time: 2 hours

Elevation Gain: 1,600 feet

Summary: Follow a steep, rocky trail alongside a cascading creek to a natural waterslide and a plunging waterfall.

CEDAR RUN FALLS

The Blue Ridge is marked not just by soaring mountains, but also by deep canyons, and the canyon through which Cedar Run cuts is one of the most scenic in the park. It is not a gradual cut, but rather a quick one that causes the creek to constantly cascade and the trail to run rough.

Immediately after you begin your hike down blue-blazed Cedar Run Trail, you'll pass a junction on your right with a yellow-blazed bridle trail. Stay straight through both this junction and another one on your left, and begin what will be almost a constant descent to the falls. The trail, which weaves through a mature forest of large oaks as well as other hardwoods, is very rocky, and you have to step carefully, especially when the trail is wet because the stones become extremely slippery. Don't keep your eyes strictly on the ground, however, as you might miss seeing a bear scavenging for berries.

The trail soon meets Cedar Run, and you'll continue down into the canyon with the creek on your right. At points you're right along the cascading water, while at other times you're above it. The descent becomes steeper as you encounter a rugged rock bluff on your left side. Beyond these massive formations, the trail levels before reaching another stone-wall section where it again drops quickly.

The steep, rocky trail makes for slow going, but that's not a negative. The creek environment here is a popular habitat for Shenandoah wildlife, and if you walk slowly and quietly down the trail, you may be treated to a wide array of park inhabitants. Snakes sunbathe on rocks, while skinks and salamanders scurry along downed tree trunks. White-tailed deer feed, their ears perked to danger. Skunks, raccoons, foxes, and chipmunks crunch through the underbrush. And bobcats and coyotes linger, though they remain out of sight of all but the luckiest visitors.

At about 1.5 miles, you'll pass a particularly lovely cascade, where the water

© THERESA DOWELL BLACKINTON

Cedar Run is rightly popular for its water features.

drops about three feet into a small pool and then washes over rocks back into the rushing creek. Ahead you'll see a large boulder field. This is the point where the trail crosses to the other bank of Cedar Run. Look across the creek, and you'll see a blue blaze and the continuation of the trail. Hopscotch over the rocks strewn across the creek, and then make a brief ascent before descending to the falls.

What you'll first encounter is nature's own water park. Cedar Run flows down a smooth rock formation, creating a waterslide. Climb up and slip and slide your way down into a plunge pool. You can lie on the large, smooth boulders and soak up some sun after your icy dip. Just below this slide is 34-foot Cedar Run Falls, so continue descending on the trail and then carefully scramble down to the side of the creek. It's a steep and slippery descent, so be careful. You can climb out on the rocks or wade into the water to get a better view of the waterfall, which plunges between jagged rocks. Remember that the return trip, a retracing of your steps, is almost entirely uphill, so plan your time accordingly.

Options

For the waterfall aficionado, there's not a better hike in the park than the 8.2-mile circuit that takes in both the Cedar Run and Whiteoak Canyon waterfalls. Continue to follow Cedar Run Trail past the falls, reaching another 12-foot waterfall before the trail turns left. Pick up Cedar Run Link Trail on your left, which will connect you to Whiteoak Canyon Trail. You'll then proceed uphill, passing six waterfalls. Just past the upper falls, turn left onto Whiteoak Fire Road, which leads back to Skyline Drive. Immediately before you reach Skyline Drive, however, you'll want to turn left onto the yellow-blazed bridle trail, which will take you back to the beginning of Cedar Run Trail and the parking lot where your car waits.

Directions

Take I-495 to westbound I-66. Drive 21.7 miles to exit 43A and merge onto southbound U.S. 29. Proceed 11.5 miles to westbound U.S. 211. Drive 35.9 miles, exiting toward Shenandoah National Park at Skyline Drive. Go through the entrance station, and then keep left to proceed south on Skyline Drive. Continue to the parking lot on your left at mile 45.6.

Information and Contact

There is a fee of $15 per vehicle, Mar.–Nov.; $10, Dec.–Feb., which covers admission for seven consecutive days. A $30 annual pass to Shenandoah is available. America the Beautiful passes accepted. Dogs on leash are allowed. The park is open 24 hours daily. Maps are available at the visitors centers, or download the Whiteoak Canyon Area map from the park's website. For more information, contact Shenandoah National Park, 3655 Highway 211 East, Luray, VA 22835, 540/999-3500, www.nps.gov/shen.

23 HAWKSBILL MOUNTAIN   BEST ☾
Shenandoah National Park

🏕 🐾 ✈ 🦌 👥

Level: Easy

Total Distance: 2.1 miles round-trip

Hiking Time: 1 hour

Elevation Gain: 400 feet

Summary: From Shenandoah's highest peak, search for soaring peregrine falcons and pick out the park's other mountains.

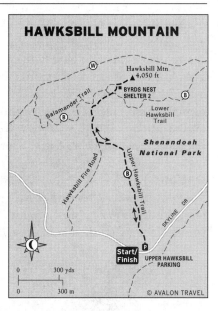

You would think that reaching the highest viewpoint in Shenandoah National Park would be difficult, but you'd be wrong. Though the observation platform is at 4,050 feet, from the parking lot to the 360-degree view, the hike is just over a mile, with very little elevation gain. Even the most novice hiker can enjoy this Shenandoah landmark.

Blue-blazed Upper Hawksbill Trail leaves from the middle of the parking lot. As you walk along the broad, gravel path under the shade of mature hardwoods, you'll likely see deer, as they like to graze here and show little concern for all the human traffic. The trail climbs in elevation for the first 0.4 mile, but the ascent is very gradual, and the most difficulty you face is stepping up over the logs laid across the trail to prevent erosion. Summer thunderstorms are a common occurrence in Shenandoah, and the heavy rains they bring can wipe out sections of trail. In the afternoon, especially, you should keep tuned in to the weather, as the last place you want to be during a storm is atop the park's highest peak.

After the initial ascent, the trail levels out and even descends a bit as it works its way toward Hawksbill Fire Road, which you'll reach at mile 0.6. Turn right onto this rocky road, which climbs through forest that gradually changes in character. By the time you reach a junction with Salamander Trail on your left at mile 0.9, you'll begin to notice balsam firs and red spruce. These boreal forest trees are the remainders of the cold-weather forest that covered Shenandoah thousands of years ago. Now these trees exist only in the highest reaches of the park.

Continue on the fire road, which leads to Byrds Nest Shelter #2, a day shelter just shy of the peak. Proceed past the shelter, ascending to the observation platform at the peak. Orient yourself using the metal plates inscribed with the cardinal points that are set into the walls of the stone platform, and take in the expanses of mountain and valley, wilderness and towns. See if you can pick out Old Rag to the south and Stony Man to the northeast.

In summer, if you're lucky you may also spot peregrine falcon chicks taking their first flights. These birds were nearly wiped out by DDT, but recovery efforts begun in the 1970s have helped bring them back. Unfortunately, however, the falcons have taken to nesting in buildings and bridges, which are often not high enough for fledgling birds, because they may need to free fall for hundreds of feet before getting the hang of flying. By relocating peregrine falcons to the highest cliffs of Shenandoah, experts hope to increase the chances of the young making it to adulthood. The probability of seeing chicks is highest in July, when they take practice flights; they leave in August, hopefully to return in future years to raise their own young. After you've identified as many landmarks as you can and maybe caught sight of a falcon, return to the trailhead via the same route.

Options

The Lower Hawksbill Trail, which has a trailhead in the parking lot at mile 45.6, provides a shorter route to the summit at 1.7 miles round-trip, but the path is much steeper. If you want a short but challenging hike, choose this route.

Mountains rise from behind the observation platform on Hawksbill Mountain.

© THERESA DOWELL BLACKINTON

Directions

Take I-495 to westbound I-66. Drive 21.7 miles to exit 43A and merge onto southbound U.S. 29. Proceed 11.5 miles to westbound U.S. 211. Drive 35.9 miles, exiting toward Shenandoah National Park at Skyline Drive. Go through the entrance station, and then keep left to proceed south on Skyline Drive. Continue to the parking lot on your right at mile 46.7.

Information and Contact

There is a fee of $15 per vehicle, Mar.–Nov.; $10, Dec.–Feb., which covers admission for seven consecutive days. A $30 annual pass to Shenandoah is available. America the Beautiful passes accepted. Dogs on leash are allowed. The park is open 24 hours daily. Maps are available at the visitors centers, or download the Hawksbill Mountain Area map from the park's website. For more information, contact Shenandoah National Park, 3655 Highway 211 East, Luray, VA 22835, 540/999-3500, www.nps.gov/shen.

24 ROSE RIVER FALLS BEST ◖

Shenandoah National Park

Level: Easy/Moderate   **Total Distance:** 4.0 miles round-trip

Hiking Time: 2 hours   **Elevation Gain:** 875 feet

Summary: A water lover's ideal outing, this trail offers idyllic swimming holes, picturesque cascades, and attractive waterfalls.

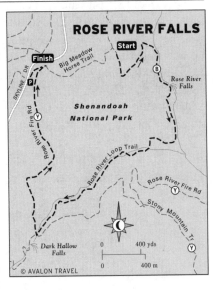

The Rose River Falls hike is among the prettiest in Shenandoah National Park. Though the hike takes its name from one specific waterfall, for the majority of the loop you'll be traveling alongside rivers rife with cascades and pools. The rush of water provides a soundtrack to your hike, and the lush landscape is a treat for your eyes.

Proceed past the chain across Rose River Fire Road and turn left onto yellow-blazed Skyland–Big Meadows Horse Trail, which is marked with one of the park's concrete posts. Follow this broad trail for 0.5 mile to blue-blazed Rose River Loop Trail, which continues straight from the path you've been traveling on, while the bridle trail turns off to the left. After the intersection, you begin a gentle descent moderated by a series of switchbacks. The forest is mature here, with tall trees and a floor that contains more large boulders than plants.

After about 0.4 mile on Rose River Loop Trail, you'll reach another post indicating that the falls are only 0.3 mile away. This won't surprise you because you'll already be able to hear the gurgling water. Shortly after this post, the trail approaches Rose River, and you begin to walk along its western bank. At mile 1.2, the trail leads directly to the top of Rose River Falls. Peek out over the edge as the water drops in one large fall plus multiple thin cascades over dark, mossy rocks into the pool below. Then scamper to the base of the falls. The pool invites you to take a plunge, but beware that the water is icy cold. If you have thick skin or the day is hot enough, then go for it.

Immediately beyond the falls, the trail climbs away from the river and then drops back down, following Rose River downstream past flutes, pools, and cascades. About 0.5 mile from the falls, another post interrupts the trail. Spur trails branch off to the left and straight ahead, leading to the water's edge, but you'll want to turn right, remaining on Rose River Loop Trail. You'll soon encounter a large concrete block in the middle of the path. The purpose of this is unclear, but it may have some relation to a copper mine, which was once located on the hill to your right. The trail then leads to a footbridge, which you'll use to cross Hogcamp Branch. From here until you reach Rose River Fire Road at mile 2.9, you'll be walking upstream along this delightful waterway. Ferns abound, and

This hike follows cascading water for most of its length, making it one of the prettiest hikes in Shenandoah.

you'll pass cascade after cascade. Pick your favorite, and enjoy a dip in one of the swimming holes or take a break perched atop a boulder on the bank.

Because you are walking upstream, you are also walking uphill, but it's not strenuous, and you'll probably be too busy taking in the sights to notice any exertion. Upon reaching Rose River Fire Road, turn right, passing a large waterfall on your left as you cross back over Hogcamp Branch via a bridge. Dark Hollow Falls Trail will be on your left after you cross the bridge. Continue straight along the yellow-blazed fire road, enjoying Indian pipe, three-leaved sedum, goldenrod, and the other summer wildflowers that grow alongside your path. After a gentle ascent of 1.1 miles, you'll return to Skyline Drive.

Options

Add on a side trip to Dark Hollow Falls by turning left at the trailhead just past the falls on Rose River Fire Road. Continue 0.2 mile to the bottom of Dark Hollow Falls, and add on another 0.1 mile to reach the top. You can then make the 0.3-mile return trip to the fire road to complete the hike.

Directions

Take I-495 to westbound I-66. Drive 21.7 miles to exit 43A, merging onto southbound U.S. 29. Proceed 11.5 miles to westbound U.S. 211. Drive 35.9 miles, exiting toward Shenandoah National Park at Skyline Drive. Go through the entrance station, and then keep left to proceed south on Skyline Drive. Continue to the parking area on the right at mile 49.4, just north of Fisher's Gap Overlook. The trailhead is across the road.

Information and Contact

There is a fee of $15 per vehicle, Mar.–Nov.; $10, Dec.–Feb., which covers admission for seven consecutive days. A $30 annual pass to Shenandoah is available. America the Beautiful passes accepted. Dogs on leash are allowed. The park is open 24 hours daily. Maps are available at the visitors centers, or download the Big Meadows Area map from the park's website. For more information, contact Shenandoah National Park, 3655 Highway 211 East, Luray, VA 22835, 540/999-3500, www.nps.gov/shen.

25 DARK HOLLOW FALLS
Shenandoah National Park

Level: Easy/Moderate

Hiking Time: 1 hour

Total Distance: 1.4 miles round-trip

Elevation Gain: 440 feet

Summary: Find out why Dark Hollow Falls Trail is Shenandoah National Park's most traveled trail on this short trip along a stream to a striking waterfall.

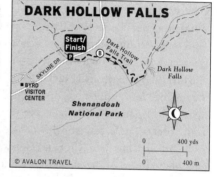

Showcasing the nearest waterfall to Skyline Drive and strategically located at about the midway point of Shenandoah, Dark Hollow Falls Trail is the most traveled path in the park. Unless you arrive in sync with the sunrise, you'll probably be sharing the trail with plenty of other waterfall aficionados, so though the trail is short, plan for more time than you think you'll need.

Moss, ferns, and liverwort line blue-blazed Dark Hollow Falls Trail, which begins with a stretch of pavement leading from the north end of the parking lot. The trail transitions to a broad gravel path that follows the course of Hogcamp Branch. This waterway drains Big Meadows Swamp and cuts through the valley, wearing away the mountain to create Dark Hollow. The trail proceeds downhill at a fairly consistent grade. In June, the mountain laurel that edges the trail sports white blossoms.

As you come closer to the falls, the trail turns left away from the stream before returning back to it. You'll notice that the stream is now moving with more force. Once more, you'll turn away from the water, this time reapproaching the stream just as it begins its 70-foot drop. Admire the spectacle from the upper viewing area, then continue on for 1,000 feet to the base of this tiered waterfall, which is a popular spot for water play. From here, Hogcamp Branch continues to cascade down, making small drops over rocks and then pooling before dropping again. If you'd like, you can continue on from the base of the falls, following the trail 0.2 mile as it parallels the rushing water down to Rose River Fire Road. Here Hogcamp Branch makes another large drop, creating a waterfall also seen from the Rose River Falls Loop.

From either the base of the main falls or from Rose River Fire Road, turn around and proceed back to the parking lot the same way you came. You'll be going uphill, so expect the return trip to take longer than the outbound trip. Though the overall elevation gain is only 440 feet, it all occurs in a short 0.7 mile, meaning you might want to take advantage of some of the large, smooth, trailside stones for a quick break.

Dark Hollow Falls is a popular place to get your feet wet in Shenandoah.

Options

Combine this trail with Rose River Loop Trail for a 7.2-mile hike. Continue past Dark Hollow Falls down to Rose River Fire Road and turn left. Hike uphill along the fire road for 1.1 miles before turning right onto Skyland–Big Meadows Horse Trail. After 0.5 mile, stay straight onto Rose River Loop Trail, which will lead you for 2.4 miles along Rose River and Hogcamp Branch, past one large waterfall and multiple cascades. At the end of Rose River Loop Trail, you'll turn onto Rose River Fire Road and reconnect with Dark Hollow Falls Trail at an intersection on your left.

Directions

Take I-495 to westbound I-66. Drive 21.7 miles to exit 43A and merge onto southbound U.S. 29. Proceed 11.5 miles to westbound U.S. 211. Drive 35.9 miles, exiting toward Shenandoah National Park at Skyline Drive. Go through the entrance station, and then keep left to proceed south on Skyline Drive. Continue to the parking lot on your left at mile 50.7.

Information and Contact

There is a fee of $15 per vehicle, Mar.–Nov.; $10, Dec.–Feb., which covers admission for seven consecutive days. A $30 annual pass to Shenandoah is available. America the Beautiful passes accepted. Dogs are not allowed on Dark Hollow Falls Trail. The park is open 24 hours daily. Maps are available at the visitors centers, or download the Big Meadows Area map from the park's website. For more information, contact Shenandoah National Park, 3655 Highway 211 East, Luray, VA 22835, 540/999-3500, www.nps.gov/shen.

26 LEWIS SPRING FALLS

Shenandoah National Park

Level: Moderate

Hiking Time: 1.5 hours

Total Distance: 3.3 miles round-trip

Elevation Gain: 800 feet

Summary: From a CCC-built overlook, gaze down upon an 81-foot waterfall.

Lewis Spring Falls is Shenandoah's fourth-highest waterfall at 81 feet. In times of high water, it makes a thunderous plunge, while in low water seasons, it may split into branches. It remains impressive, however, even in the driest times of the year and is thus always worth a visit.

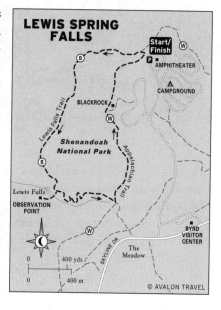

From the amphitheater, walk 75 yards down the white-blazed Appalachian Trail, turning left at the first post and right at the second post to reach blue-blazed Lewis Falls Trail. This trail leads directly downhill to the falls, but it's not an easy 1.3 miles; you'll have to watch your every step because the path is very rocky. If you do get a chance to take your eyes off the ground, you'll notice that hardwood trees border the path, and you may spot a deer. Unlike most deer, the ones in Shenandoah aren't very skittish and will likely not run away should they see you, though they will keep a wary eye on you.

The trail levels as you approach the falls, which you can hear well before you can see it. The first overlook you reach provides a look toward the mountains. The falls are just below you. Turn left from the overlook, crossing two streams as you move down toward the falls viewing area, a stone overlook constructed in the 1930s by members of the Civilian Conservation Corps (CCC). Though the warning signs near the falls appear comical with their stick-figure drawings, the message is serious: Falls can kill. Do not try to venture down to the falls from this point; instead enjoy the view from the safety of the overlook. The view may be best in winter when the trees are bare and your line of vision is less obstructed, though it's never possible to see the falls from top to bottom.

A sign at the top of the falls warns hikers not to venture off trail in an effort to get closer to the falls; by continuing to the trail's end, you can view the falls from an overlook.

From the Lewis Falls viewing area, backtrack to the first overlook, and then continue along the blue-blazed trail as it turns right uphill, running parallel to the creek that feeds the falls. You'll navigate a series of switchbacks and then continue climbing, reaching Lewis Spring Fire Road after 0.6 mile. Turn right onto the fire road, proceed about 70 yards, and then turn left onto the white-blazed Appalachian Trail.

For 1.4 miles you'll hike gently uphill along the Appalachian Trail. In the summer months, you may encounter a few through-hikers, those hearty souls making the 2,175-mile trip from Georgia to Maine along this famed trail. You'll certainly see fly poison, a lily common throughout Shenandoah, as well as mountain laurel, which peaks in June. A few views open to your left as you near the end of the hike, and you'll know you're about back to the trailhead when you see the accommodations of Big Meadows Lodge on your right.

Options

While you're in the area, take time to explore Big Meadows, which is across Skyline Drive from the Big Meadows complex. This 134-acre, prairielike habitat is unlike any other region of Shenandoah. Deer are abundant, as are a wide variety of wildflowers, berry bushes, and flowering shrubs. There is no official trail, though multiple footpaths course through the meadow, and you're free to explore at leisure. If you'd like your hike to have some structure, ask at the Byrd Visitors Center about ranger-guided walks, which occur frequently.

Directions

Take I-495 to westbound I-66. Drive 21.7 miles to exit 43A and merge onto southbound U.S. 29. Proceed 11.5 miles to westbound U.S. 211. Drive 35.9 miles, exiting toward Shenandoah National Park at Skyline Drive. Go through the entrance station, and then keep left to proceed south on Skyline Drive. Turn right into the Big Meadows complex at mile 51.2 and follow the signs to the amphitheater parking lot.

Information and Contact

There is a fee of $15 per vehicle, Mar.–Nov.; $10, Dec.–Feb., which covers admission for seven consecutive days. A $30 annual pass to Shenandoah is available. America the Beautiful passes accepted. Dogs on leash are allowed. The park is open 24 hours daily. Maps are available at the visitors centers, or download the Big Meadows Area map from the park's website. For more information, contact Shenandoah National Park, 3655 Highway 211 East, Luray, VA 22835, 540/999-3500, www.nps.gov/shen.

27 STONY MOUNTAIN
Shenandoah National Park

Level: Strenuous

Hiking Time: 5 hours

Total Distance: 10.1 miles round-trip

Elevation Gain: 1,840 feet

Summary: This hike winds through old forests and offers a respite from the crowds.

Unlike many of Shenandoah's trails, the Stony Mountain hike can't easily be summed up in a couple of words. It's not a waterfall hike or a hike to a scenic vista or a hike past historic ruins. The trail does spend some time along a picturesque river, and it does offer limited views if you're willing to scramble up a rock or two, but primarily the hike up and around Stony Mountain is simply a walk in the woods. Long and with some challenging uphill sections, this is a hike for quiet contemplation, for the observation of details, for the simple enjoyment of being out in a beautiful forest.

Begin your hike on yellow-blazed Rose River Fire Road, which is a rock-studded, rough road more akin to an off-road-vehicle trail than a fire road. Rose River runs to your right. Multiple spurs lead down to the river, and they're worth exploring, as the river offers cascades and clear pools that attract both swimmers and trout anglers. After 1.1 miles, you'll cross a steel bridge spanning Dark Hollow Creek as it runs down to meet Rose River. The fire road then turns left and begins ascending Stony Mountain.

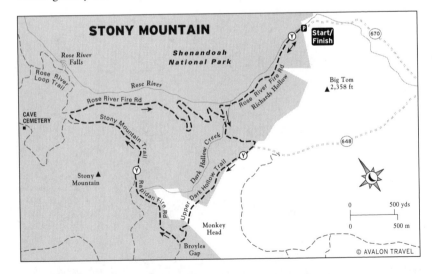

Rose River accompanies hikers for the first mile and last mile of the Stony Mountain hike.

About 0.2 mile past the bridge and just as the road begins to turn right, you'll reach the turnoff to Upper Dark Hollow Trail on your left. Transition to this yellow-blazed trail, which will climb Stony Mountain for 2.2 miles. The first 0.1 mile is easy; the next 0.5 mile is the most difficult, with loose dirt and rock making footwork tricky. Though you're unlikely to find many other hikers on this route, you may find horseback riders, to whom you should always yield. After 0.6 mile, the trail will split. Stay to the right. Near the split, you'll notice red blazes in addition to the yellow blazes. The red blazes mark the boundary of the Rapidan State Wildlife Management Area, which is enclosed within Shenandoah. You may spot deer, ground animals such as squirrel and chipmunk, and maybe even a bear.

The remaining 1.6 miles of Upper Dark Hollow Trail are uphill and require constant exertion, but the upper section of this trail isn't as difficult as the lower section. The trail ends at a junction with Rapidan Fire Road. Turn right onto this yellow-blazed road as it climbs at a moderate grade for 0.9 mile. In the winter, you'll have views to your right. When the trees are leafy, you can climb up on the rock outcrop at the midpoint of this section for partial views.

Upon reaching the junction with yellow-blazed Stony Mountain Trail, turn right and make a gentle ascent for 0.3 mile to the highest point of this hike. From here, descend for 0.8 mile along the ridge, passing multiple large outcrops. In winter, icicles sparkle against the dark stone. The trail ends at Rose River Fire Road, which you will follow for 4.7 miles as it makes long switchbacks down the mountain and back to the parking lot. Under 100-foot hardwoods, mayapples bloom in early spring and bear fruit in early summer. Asters line the road along with other wildflowers, and the occasional Turk's cap lily provides a burst of bright orange. On a hot summer day, it's hard to resist a swim in Rose River as you complete your hike.

Options

If you prefer a long but less steep ascent paired with a shorter but more severe descent, you can opt to do the route in reverse, traveling up the switchbacks of Rose River Fire Road and then down Upper Dark Hollow Trail.

Directions

Take I-495 to westbound I-66. After 21.7 miles, take exit 43A to southbound U.S. 29. Continue 44.9 miles, and then turn right on Hoover Road. Drive 9.4 miles, and then turn right on Route 231. After 0.6 mile, make a slight left onto Old Blue Ridge Turnpike. Follow the road for 6.7 miles until it ends at the parking lot at the Shenandoah National Park boundary.

Information and Contact

There is a fee of $15 per vehicle, Mar.–Nov.; $10, Dec.–Feb., which covers admission for seven consecutive days. A $30 annual pass to Shenandoah is available. America the Beautiful passes accepted. Dogs on leash are allowed. The park is open 24 hours daily. Map 10 from the Potomac Appalachian Trail Club covers this region and can be purchased at www.patc.net. For more information, contact Shenandoah National Park, 3655 Highway 211 East, Luray, VA 22835, 540/999-3500, www.nps.gov/shen.

28 THOMPSON WILDLIFE CIRCUIT BEST C
G. Richard Thompson Wildlife Management Area

Level: Moderate

Hiking Time: 3.5 hours

Summary: Bathe in the beauty of one of the region's best wildflower displays on this circuit hike.

Total Distance: 7.5 miles round-trip

Elevation Gain: 1,670 feet

The nearly 4,000 acres that make up the G. Richard Thompson Wildlife Management Area, stretching from lower-lying lands at about 700 feet to a 2,200-foot crest of the Blue Ridge, were donated to the state of Virginia by the man for whom the park is now named, with the intention that it be set aside for hunters. And while hunters certainly enjoy the hardwood forests and the animals that call it home— deer, turkey, grouse, woodcock, groundhog, and numerous other species—they aren't the only ones taking advantage of this parcel of land. Birders seek out wrens, vireos, towhees, warblers, pewees, and other forest birds. Anglers fish for trout, bass, sunfish,

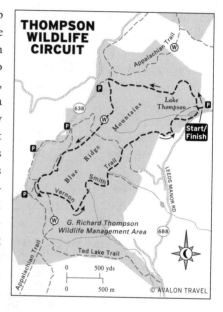

and catfish. Wildflower lovers gasp in awe at what might be the largest stand of trillium in the United States. And hikers take it all in on a labyrinth of trails.

Begin this long circuit around the perimeter of the preserve by walking up the gravel drive from the parking lot toward Lake Thompson. Turn right as you approach the lake, passing thistle, black-eyed Susans, and Queen Anne's lace where eastern tiger and spicebush swallowtail butterflies congregate in summer. At the end of the lake, veer right and begin the long ascent to the ridgeline. The trail is narrow and overgrown, so wearing pants and a long-sleeved shirt is highly recommended.

Stay on the trail as it curves left onto the lower reaches of the ridge, becoming a bit wider and less overgrown, but still ascending. In spring, trilliums bloom zealously in the higher reaches of the park. Joining the springtime show of beauty are bloodroot, yellow lady slipper, rue anemone, wild geranium, sweet cicely, and a variety of other species. Some plants grow only in small pockets, so look carefully and don't be afraid to venture down a spur trail in search of a rare find.

After 2.5 miles, you'll reach a four-way intersection with the white-blazed Appalachian Trail. Turn left onto this much better maintained pathway and proceed 0.6 mile to a dirt road. Turn left onto it and then right off of it to stay on the Appalachian Trail. Continue to climb through pawpaws and wild hydrangeas, staying to the left at a junction with a blue-blazed trail 0.3 mile past the road. You'll begin to descend shortly after this split. In summer, you'll find this section of the trail ablaze with Asiatic dayflowers, soapwort, and jewelweed, which butterflies and hummingbirds seem to love.

About 1.1 miles past the last trail split, you'll reach an intersection with the Vernon Smith Trail. Turn left onto it and stay straight as the Appalachian Trail bends off to the right. Pass through a cleared area on your right where great mullein grows tall. Stay right to edge the clearing, and then enter the woods on your left via an extremely overgrown path that can be hard to follow. The Vernon Smith Trail extends for 1.9 miles through dense underbrush and over two springs before ending at a dirt road. Turn right here; after 0.1 mile, stay left at the split. You'll proceed downhill, and as the trail turns to the left, you'll walk alongside private property. Barns, rolling hills, and even a vineyard make for a scenic stretch.

Upon reaching a split in the trail after 0.9 mile, follow the grassy path downhill

© THERESA DOWELL BLACKINTON

The trilliums at Thompson Wildlife Management Area are magnificent, blooming in late April or early May.

to your left, and then veer right when the trail splits again after about 200 yards. This trail will lead back past the lake to the parking lot.

Options

In summer, visit one of the pick-your-own farms that lie along the same road as the Thompson Wildlife Management Area. Known for their peaches, the farms also offer a variety of other produce. **Hollin Farms** (http://hollinfarms.com) is just a mile north of Thompson Wildlife Management Area.

Directions

Take I-495 to westbound I-66. Drive 45.9 miles, and then take exit 18 and turn right onto Route 688. The entrance to G. Richard Thompson Wildlife Management Area will be on your left after 3.9 miles.

Information and Contact

There is a fee of $4 per person 17 years and older for an access permit. The permit must be purchased in advance and can be purchased online. An annual pass, good at all Virginia Wildlife Management Areas, can be purchased for $23. Those with a Virginia hunting, fishing, or trapping license and those who have registered a boat with the state are exempt from the access permit fee. Dogs on leash are allowed. Maps can be downloaded from the Thompson Wildlife Management Area website. For more information, contact the Virginia Department of Game and Inland Fisheries, 4010 West Broad Street, P.O. Box 11104, Richmond, VA 23230, 804/367-1000, www.dgif.state.va.us/wmas/detail.asp?pid=31.

29 RAVEN ROCKS

Appalachian Trail

Level: Strenuous

Hiking Time: 2.5 hours

Total Distance: 4.8 miles round-trip

Elevation Gain: 1,530 feet

Summary: Travel from Virginia to a lookout just across the West Virginia border on a section of the Appalachian Trail.

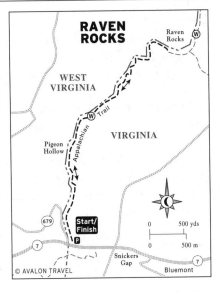

The Appalachian Trail traverses a wide range of landscapes as it weaves 2,175 miles from Georgia to Maine. The 2.4 miles of the trail that you'll hike to and from Raven Rocks is a well-maintained stretch of boulder-ridden path. It repeatedly rises and falls over rough terrain, providing a challenge to the casual day hiker as well as to the through-hiker shouldering a heavy backpack. A hike along this short section of the Appalachian Trail rewards with long views from a rocky precipice and also allows you to cross the border between Virginia and West Virginia on foot.

From the parking lot, begin your hike with the first of five ascents—the first being the easiest. Log steps lead uphill, disappearing as a mess of boulders takes over and the rugged, white-blazed trail begins to wind around the first ridge and through abundant mountain laurel. After making it over the ridge, the trail descends via rocky and steep switchbacks. About midway through the descent, at a turn in a switchback, a large boulder on your left offers partial views of the Winchester Valley. Continue making your way down from the ridge, reaching a draw after about 0.8 mile. The draw is divided into three sections, each of which can be crossed via boulders. In the summer, don't expect to find much water here.

Once across the draw, it's time for the second ascent. Again log stairs help you make your way uphill. Just past the end of the stairs, an unblazed trail intersects the Appalachian Trail, but you'll want to stay straight. The ascent eases beyond the intersection and remains rather gentle for most of the approach to the ridge. As the peak of the ridge comes into sight, however, the trail becomes steep, and you have to work to summit it. For the effort, you're rewarded with a lovely view of the Winchester Valley to your west. Proceed over the ridge, and then begin a sharp descent down to a hollow. On the return trip, this will prove the most difficult section of the hike.

About 1.2 miles after you crossed the draw, you'll arrive at the Raven Rocks Hollow spring. In wet seasons, you'll have to balance on the boulders to avoid getting wet, but in summer, you probably won't see much water, though you'll hear it running under the rocks. Beyond the springs, the final ascent to Raven Rocks awaits. Pass a blue-blazed spur

Fantastic valley views greet hikers at Raven Rocks.

trail on your left, and then make the 0.4-mile climb. Just as you approach the ridge, you'll pass a sign marking the Virginia–West Virginia border. From here, it's 17.4 miles of northbound hiking to Harpers Ferry or 41 miles of southbound hiking to Shenandoah National Park. You can also just continue a short distance to where the trail runs into the overlook that is Raven Rocks. Pick your perch, gaze out toward the Shenandoah Valley, and watch large birds of prey soar. To complete the hike, retrace your steps, this time making three descents and two ascents.

Options

Almost directly across the road from the trailhead is **Bears Den Trail Center** (18393 Blueridge Mountain Road, Bluemont, VA 20135, 540/554-8708, www.bearsdencenter.org), a lodge owned by the Appalachian Trail Conservancy. It provides a variety of services to Appalachian Trail hikers, and from the facilities, you can access more southern sections of the Appalachian Trail as well as explore shorter trails that meander through the center's property.

Directions

Take I-495 to exit 45A to merge onto westbound Route 267 (Dulles Toll Road). Drive 25.1 miles, and then take exit 1A to merge onto westbound Route 7. After 18.2 miles, turn right onto Pine Grove Road, and park in the small trailhead lot immediately on your right.

Information and Contact

There is no fee. Dogs on leash are allowed. Map 7 from the Potomac Appalachian Trail Club covers this region and can be purchased at www.patc.net. For more information, contact the Appalachian Trail Conservancy, P.O. Box 807, 799 Washington Street, Harpers Ferry, WV 25425-0807, 304/535-6331, www.appalachiantrail.org.

30 WILDCAT MOUNTAIN CIRCUIT

Wildcat Mountain Natural Area

Level: Moderate

Hiking Time: 2.5 hours

Total Distance: 5.2 miles round-trip

Elevation Gain: 1,510 feet

Summary: Managed by The Nature Conservancy, this parcel of publicly accessible land surrounded by private property serves as a quiet escape.

A tangle of trails—both narrow footpaths and broad fire roads—cuts across 655 wooded acres on the western slope of Wildcat Mountain. Fox, bobcats, deer, skunks, raccoons, and the occasional black bear tramp through the forest, though most often you'll find yourself walking only in the company of songbirds.

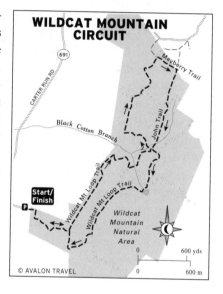

The hike begins about 100 yards up the gravel road from the parking area, past a chain gate. Yellow and green markers line this section of the trail, which is part of the Preferred Route, a 2.9-mile loop outlined on the official map. You get the hard part out of the way first, winding uphill for 0.4 mile.

Upon reaching the ridge, make a left onto the Wildcat Mountain Loop Trail. A low stone fence, which marks the boundary between the natural area and private property, will remain on your left side as you hike 0.6 mile, gradually losing elevation. Oaks and hickories dominate at canopy level, while beech, poplar, sassafras, and maple trees can be found in the midstory. Redwoods and dogwoods grow close to property boundaries as they were originally planted on neighboring farms.

The footpath ends as it makes a right turn and a steep decline, depositing you onto an old fire road, where you turn right. After 0.3 mile, make a left turn as the trail splits. Proceed downhill and over a stream. A short climb leads you to the next intersection. The trail markers point right, but to complete the 5.2-mile circuit, go left and hike 0.1 mile to a four-way intersection. A sign indicates that the path in front of you is John Trail. You'll return this way, but for now, go left.

This section of unnamed trail leads you west for 0.2 mile, then turns to the north and climbs uphill for an additional 0.2 mile, at which point you'll intersect with Enon Church Trail. Turn right here and walk a short 125 yards before taking the trail on your left.

A 0.2-mile climb will lead you to another stone fence and a split in the trail. Take the trail to the right of the fence, again heading uphill. The stone fence intersects the trail, and you can either go over it or around it via the loop to the left. Upon reaching the intersection with Mayberry Trail, marked by a sign on a tree, go right and hike another 0.2 mile to reach the intersection with John Trail, again turning right. Berry bushes, asters, and honeysuckle can be found along this downhill path, and butterflies dance from plant to plant.

Stay on John Trail for 0.5 mile, passing around a stone fence and hiking past an unnamed trail on your left and the signed Enon Church Trail on your right. At the four-way intersection that you encountered earlier in the hike, turn left and climb to another junction, where you will turn right. After about 0.3 mile, the trail splits. Stay to the right to reach the Smith House, a reminder that this area was farmland from the 18th century to the mid-20th century. If you'd like to visit the Spring House, take the trail that splits off to the right for a short detour, being mindful of the poison ivy that thrives near the path. Back at the Smith House, continue straight, passing a marsh on your left. The trail is once again marked, because you are now back on the main loop.

Follow the trail signs along the fire road, staying straight past a stone fence and fire road on your right. After 0.7 mile, the trail signs will lead you onto the footpath on your right. You'll hike downhill and then along a stone fence before arriving back at the beginning of the loop. Turn left and follow the trail 0.4 mile back to the gate.

Stone fences line sections of the trail.

Options

For a short hike, try the 2.9-mile route around the marked Wildcat Mountain Loop Trail, which is noted on the official map as the Preferred Route.

Directions

Take I-495 to westbound I-66. Drive 36.1 miles to exit 28. Turn left on southbound U.S. 17, drive 0.3 mile, and turn right on Carters Run Road. After 5.1 miles, turn left on England Mountain Road. Park in the marked area on the right, just beyond where the road becomes gravel.

Information and Contact

There is no fee. Dogs are not allowed. Trails are open from dawn to dusk daily. Maps are available at the information kiosk or can be downloaded from the website. For more information, contact The Nature Conservancy, 490 Westfield Road, Charlottesville, VA 22901, 434/295-6106, www.nature.org.

WESTERN MARYLAND

© THERESA DOWELL BLACKINTON

BEST HIKES

As you move from DC into western Maryland,

you'll notice striking changes in geography. This is not the swampy land-scape of the District. Instead the land becomes more rugged. Mountains interrupt your view, early morning fog cloaks deep valleys, and creeks become wider and wilder. The trails described in this chapter offer just about every feature a hiker could want. You can get a history lesson while you hike, check out the tallest waterfall in Maryland, bushwhack through paths trod by few visitors, perch on a high overlook, take a dip in a swimming hole, or spot wildflowers and wildlife.

Composing the easternmost ridge of the Blue Ridge Mountains, Catoctin Mountain stretches across Frederick County, Maryland, and features prominently in many of the hikes detailed here. At Catoctin Mountain Park, 25 miles of trail lead to scenic vista after scenic vista. Cunningham Falls State Park, which shares its northern boundary with Catoctin, offers you the opportunity to seek out more mountaintop viewpoints. You can also clamber over rocks to the park's namesake 78-foot waterfall. Climb another portion of Catoctin Mountain at Gambrill State Park and gaze through dogwood trees and mountain laurels toward the Monocacy Valley. From Greenbrier State Park, a hike along the Appalachian Trail leads you to one of the most beloved outcrops in Maryland. And so that you can say you've climbed a monadnock – a mountain that remains when the surrounding area erodes – you'll want to summit Sugarloaf Mountain, the closest peak to DC.

State-designated wildlands figure prominently in the parks in the westernmost reaches of Maryland, and it's in this area that you might see a black bear, bobcat, or fox. If you're looking to be challenged, the trails at Green Ridge State Forest beckon. Just see if you can make it across the 30-plus creek crossings on the Log Roll Trail without getting wet. High vistas provide 10-mile views into the surrounding states of Pennsylvania and West Virginia, while low stream valleys invite you to frolic in the water. Pitch a tent at one of the forest's many campsites to make the most of a visit. While you're so far west, you'll also want to explore the trail systems at nearby Rocky Gap and Cacapon State Parks and then enjoy the lakeside beaches at both spots. After a hard, hot hike, a little beach time is the perfect reward.

If history is what interests you, explore Maryland Heights and Loudoun Heights at Harpers Ferry, where some dramatic moments in our nation's history played out. The overviews to which the Harpers Ferry trails lead allow you a bird's-eye view of the town. At Antietam, the site of the bloodiest one-day battle of the Civil War, wildflowers bloom where soldiers once lay dying.

Speaking of wildflowers, they grow abundantly along the old lanes and narrow footpaths of Little Bennett Regional Park. If you're a birder, you must also have this park on your list, as there are even more bird species to be found here than wildflower species. The best part is that, like at the majority of the parks featured in this chapter, solitude abounds. Though the wild spaces of western Maryland offer some of the DC area's best trails, they remain off the radar of many hikers. Be sure they make it onto yours.

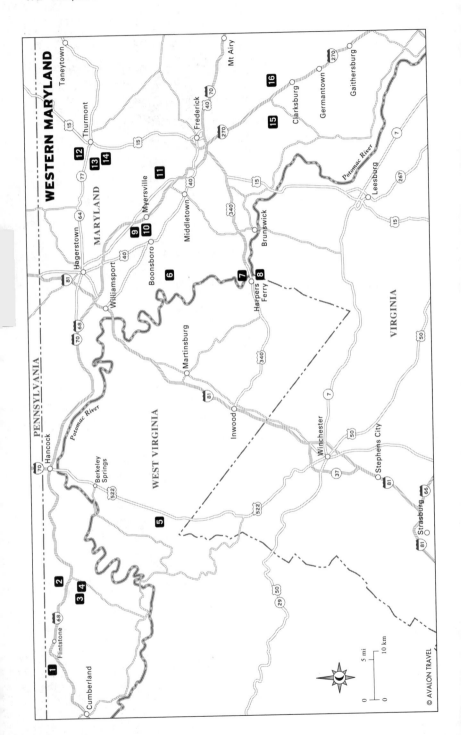

	TRAIL NAME	LEVEL	DISTANCE	TIME	ELEVATION	FEATURES	PAGE
1	Evitt's Mountain Homesite Trail	Moderate	6.5 mi rt	3.0 hr	1,220 ft		174
2	Twin Oaks–Pine Lick Circuit	Easy/Moderate	4.0 mi rt	1.75 hr	500 ft		177
3	Long Pond Trail	Moderate	9.0 mi rt	4.5 hr	900 ft		180
4	Log Roll Trail	Butt-Kicker	9.0–10.0 mi rt	4.75–5.75 hr	700 ft		183
5	Ziler Loop–Central Trail Circuit	Strenuous	5.5 mi rt	2.75 hr	1,450 ft		186
6	Snavely Ford Trail	Easy	1.8 mi rt	1 hr	150 ft		189
7	Maryland Heights Trail	Moderate	6.6 mi rt	3 hr	1,150 ft		192
8	Loudoun Heights Trail	Moderate	5.0 mi	2.5 hr	1,200 ft		195
9	Appalachian Trail to Annapolis Rock	Moderate	7.2 mi rt	3.5 hr	1,250 ft		198
10	Big Red Trail	Easy/Moderate	4.5 mi rt	2 hr	760 ft		201
11	Black Locust Trail	Moderate	3.3 mi rt	1.5 hr	660 ft		204
12	Chimney Rock–Wolf Rock Circuit	Strenuous	5.5 mi rt	2.75 hr	1,420 ft		207
13	Lower Trail–Cliff Trail Circuit	Easy	1.25 mi rt	0.75 hr	300 ft		210
14	Cat Rock–Bob's Hill Trail	Strenuous	8.0 mi rt	3.5 hr	1,340 ft		213
15	Northern Peaks–Mountain Loop Circuit	Moderate	7.5 mi rt	3.75 hr	1,800 ft		216
16	Little Bennett Circuit	Easy/Moderate	6.2 mi rt	2.75 hr	700 ft		219

1 EVITT'S MOUNTAIN HOMESITE TRAIL
Rocky Gap State Park

Level: Moderate

Hiking Time: 3.0 hours

Total Distance: 6.5 miles round-trip

Elevation Gain: 1,220 feet

Summary: Straddle the Maryland-Pennsylvania state line on this hike through wildlands to a mountain peak.

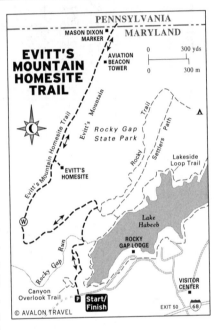

Don't let the developed lakefront at Rocky Gap State Park fool you into thinking that the term *hike* is being loosely applied to something more akin to a walk. The Evitt's Mountain Homesite Trail quickly leaves behind the bustle of the beaches and campgrounds to traverse state-designated wildlands that are home to white-tailed deer, black bears, foxes, and bobcats.

From the trailhead parking lot, walk 0.2 mile down the paved hike/bike road, passing the Canyon Overlook Trail on your left. The white-blazed Evitt's Mountain Homesite Trail will also be on your left, marked by a sign and a short section of fence. Your hike begins as you wind through hardwood forest along a moss-lined trail heavy with mountain laurel. After about 0.1 mile, you'll reach a fork, where you'll turn left and begin a 0.2-mile descent into a canyon. Large boulders require you to scramble down. The scenery becomes more lush as you lose elevation and approach the cascading Rocky Gap Run. Rhododendron thickets and tall ferns dominate the lower levels, while hemlocks tower above. As you cross the footbridge over the creek, look for warblers and ruffed grouse. You may also spot rock climbers exploring the layers of shale that compose the canyon.

Once across Rocky Gap Run, the trail proceeds upward, reaching an old farm road after 0.4 mile. Turn left onto this path, which will eventually lead past an old homesite, to a Mason-Dixon Line marker, and across the Pennsylvania border.

A hiker passes through clusters of blooming mountain laurel.

Though this part of the trail is entirely uphill, the grade is gentle, and the trail is broad and unencumbered by much in the way of rocks or roots. In the spring, anemones, spring beauties, and violets are common, while the bright purple flowers of spiderwort bring color to the trailside in summer. Mayapples are impossible to miss, growing so large here that you could use one as an umbrella should the day turn rainy.

Two miles from the trailhead, you'll reach Evitt's Homesite. Turn right onto a short trail marked with a sign to reach the clearing. According to local lore, a Mr. Evitt relocated to this patch of land in the early 1700s to live as a hermit after a failed relationship, thus becoming the first white settler in Allegheny County. The only remaining evidence of his life here is a stone well.

After exploring the homesite, turn right back onto the main trail and continue hiking. In 1.0 mile, you'll reach an aviation beacon tower. After an additional 0.25 mile, the trail ends in a gas pipeline clearing, from which you have broad views to the east and west. At this point, you'll have hiked all the way to Pennsylvania. Before you reach this final clearing, however, you'll pass a marker indicating the Mason-Dixon Line. It sits off the trail to your left. There's nothing on the trail itself to mark its presence, so keep a close eye out for a small footpath into the woods and follow it a few steps to the marker. After finding the marker and then enjoying the view at the clearing, retrace your steps to the trailhead.

Options

Just before you make it back to the trailhead, an unmarked trail turns off to the right. Follow this trail to connect to the 0.4-mile Canyon Overlook Trail, which provides stunning views of the gorge created by Rocky Gap Run.

Directions

Take I-270 north to westbound I-70. Proceed 52.7 miles to westbound I-68. Drive 29.4 miles, and then take exit 50 to Pleasant Valley Road. Turn right, entering Rocky Gap State Park. Follow the road left around Lake Habeeb to the trailhead parking lot.

Information and Contact

There is a fee of $4 per person on weekends and holidays, Memorial Day–Labor day; $2 per vehicle at all other times. Out-of-state visitors pay an additional $2. Maryland State Park passes are accepted. Dogs on leash are allowed. The park is open from sunrise to sunset daily. Maps are available for purchase from the Maryland Department of Natural Resources (410/260-8367, www.dnr.maryland. gov). For more information, contact Rocky Gap State Park, 12500 Pleasant Valley Road, Flintstone, MD 21530, 301/722-1480, www.dnr.maryland.gov/publiclands/western/rockygap.asp.

2 TWIN OAKS–PINE LICK CIRCUIT

Green Ridge State Forest

Level: Easy/Moderate

Hiking Time: 1.75 hours

Total Distance: 4.0 miles round-trip

Elevation Gain: 500 feet

Summary: Circle through diverse ecosystems on this hike, including a stream valley, mature oak forest, pine plantation, and wildlife clearings.

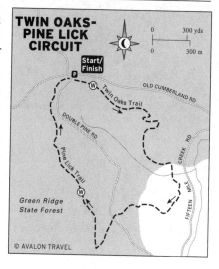

TWIN OAKS–PINE LICK CIRCUIT

Together the Twin Oaks and Pine Lick Trails provide one of the few circuit opportunities in Green Ridge Forest, so if you don't like the retracing required by out-and-back hikes, this is the option for you. From the parking lot near the old one-room schoolhouse from which Twin Oaks Trail takes its name, walk downhill on the fire road before quickly turning off onto a white-blazed dirt trail on your left. The oak forest is lush with ferns, and dogwoods blossom in early spring. You'll hike through a hollow and down to a small, easy-to-cross stream. From here, the trail ascends a ridge and passes through a wildlife clearing. Look for deer, turkeys, and the flittering of a red-spotted purple butterfly. At 0.7 mile, you'll reach a pine grove that carpets the forest floor with needles.

The trail through the pine grove is broad and shaded, but past the grove, the trail becomes a narrow footpath, which leads steeply downhill to a second stream. After crossing the stream and rising along a ridge, you'll encounter a post emblazoned with an image of a hiker, which indicates a sharp right turn. You'll again be on a broad path, though this one is almost completely exposed. It appears as if this area was wiped out by fire or clear-cut and is in the process of recovering. You don't want to do this hike in peak heat because there is little shade. Because of the lack of mature trees, blazes are infrequent, but just stay to the path. After about 0.4 mile, you'll encounter another hiker post, which will again indicate a right turn. You'll ascend for 0.25 mile through forest, cross Double Pine Road, and then emerge onto a wooded road. Turn left onto the road, and after a few yards turn left off it to descend via footpath to the junction with Pine Lick Trail.

© THERESA DOWELL BLACKINTON

A butterfly rests on a trailside branch.

Make a right turn onto white-blazed Pine Lick Trail, which runs along a stream. After 0.3 mile, you'll pass a log shelter on your right. It's a good place for a break, especially if you find yourself on this trail in the heat of the day. For another 0.4 mile, you'll be in the stream valley. You'll then cross the water for the third time before making a short, steep climb to a ridge. At an unsigned fork, stay left with the white blazes, arriving at the backside of campsite 5 about 0.55 mile after you left the valley. Less than 0.2 mile past the campsite, the trail splits. One section runs straight down to Old Cumberland Road, whereas the other section turns right. Follow the trail to the right to arrive back at Double Pine Road and the trailhead parking lot.

Options

Add 1.6 miles and a stop at a swimming hole with a rope swing to your hike by turning left when the Twin Oaks Trail hits the Pine Lick Trail. Then hike 0.8 mile to where the Pine Lick Trail meets Fifteen Mile Creek. Enjoy a swim before retracing your steps and then continuing on the Pine Lick section described in the main listing. You could also start your hike at Fifteen Mile Creek.

Directions

Take I-270 north to westbound I-70. Proceed 52.7 miles to westbound I-68. Drive 17.8 miles, and then take exit 62 to Fifteen Mile Creek Road. Turn right at the end of the ramp, and then make an immediate left onto National Pike. Drive 3.3

miles, and then turn right on Old Cumberland Road. After another 3.3 miles, pass the intersection with Double Pine Road, and park in the trailhead lot on the right.

To do the 5.6-mile hike starting at Fifteen Mile Creek, stay straight on Fifteen Mile Creek Road rather than turning onto National Pike. Drive 0.8 mile to the parking lot by the swimming hole on your right.

Information and Contact

There is no fee. Dogs on leash are allowed. The forest is open 24 hours daily. Maps are available for purchase from the Maryland Department of Natural Resources (410/260-8367, www.dnr.maryland.gov). For more information, contact Green Ridge State Forest, 28700 Headquarters Drive NE, Flintstone, MD 21530, 301/478-3124, www.dnr.maryland.gov/publiclands/western/greenridgeforest.asp.

3 LONG POND TRAIL

Green Ridge State Forest

BEST C

Level: Moderate

Total Distance: 9.0 miles round-trip

Hiking Time: 4.5 hours

Elevation Gain: 900 feet

Summary: Sample the best of Green Ridge State Forest on this hike that offers creek crossings, swimming holes, waterfalls, and outstanding views.

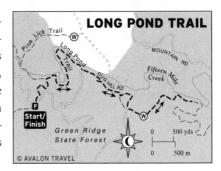

Encompassing 44,000 acres of oak-hickory forest, Green Ridge State Forest is one of the largest wilderness areas in Maryland. Steep ridges, low valleys, and wide streams create a landscape that begs to be explored. This section of trail along Fifteen Mile Creek combines the forest's highlights and offers what just might be its best scenery.

You'll begin with a 0.5-mile hike along Deep Run as it flows downstream to Fifteen Mile Creek. Large hemlocks spread their branches overhead, and enormous rock outcrops jut from the ridge, often sticking out over the creek. Whenever this happens, you'll have to hopscotch your way across the water via slippery rocks, picking up the white-blazed trail on the other side. In total, there will be four major crossings before you reach Fifteen Mile Creek. Unless you're an expert creek crosser, expect to get your feet wet at least once.

When you arrive at Fifteen Mile Creek, you'll see a sign with trail information. The trail on the left bank of Deep Run is Pine Lick Trail, and the trail on the right bank is Long Pond Trail. You'll want to go right on Long Pond Trail and keep a close eye on the blazes, which will lead you along the base of an embankment and then up a narrow, hill-hugging path. After leveling out, the trail will turn right, climb again, and then descend to a small stream. Just over the stream on the bank of Fifteen Mile Creek is a campsite with a stone picnic table and chairs. Check out this great backcountry site, and then follow the trail as it turns right and makes a rather steep climb to a ridge. In late spring, look for cancer root and wild ginger. The descent is much more gradual than the ascent, allowing you to take in the mountain views. In fall, the colors are terrific.

Back down at creek level, you'll reach a second campsite, this one ideally located at a swimming hole. It's definitely worth a dip if you have the time and inclination. Beyond the campsite, the trail again makes a steep climb on a very narrow ridge. Rocks and roots make the footing tricky, and the drop-off to your left is significant. This isn't a hike for those with a fear of heights. Your hard work is rewarded, however, with a trickling waterfall that acts as the perfect outdoor shower. Be careful of the slippery rocks, but go ahead and let the water wash over you.

Once refreshed, continue the climb, arriving at Dug Hill Road about 0.6 mile from the second campsite. Turn left onto Dug Hill Road, a gravel road with little traffic, and proceed about 1.0 mile to a gated fire road on your left marked by the white blazes. The fire road is often muddy, but it's wide and relatively flat. You'll pass through tall grasses and a wildlife clearing where you might see some of the animals common to Green Ridge State Forest—wild turkey, grouse, squirrel, fox, and deer. Beyond the clearing, the trail will begin to descend back to the water, turning right once it reaches Fifteen Mile Creek. After a short stretch, approximately 1.4 miles since you left Dug Hill Road, you'll spot an Adirondack log shelter on the hill to your right. Turn right onto the trail leading up to it and enjoy a snack and a break at this sylvan spot. If you have a backcountry permit, you can stay the night here. Otherwise enjoy it during the day, and then return the same way you came.

Options

From the shelter, continue along the trail for another 4.0 miles to reach the C&O Canal at Lock 58. If you have two cars, you can park one at each end and make it a shuttle hike. Otherwise consider taking advantage of the campsites along the trail and making the hike into a 17.0-mile backpacking trip.

Directions

Take I-270 north to westbound I-70. Proceed 52.7 miles to westbound I-68. Drive 17.8 miles, and then take exit 62 to Fifteen Mile Creek Road. Turn left at the end of the ramp, entering the state forest. The road becomes gravel. Stay to the left to remain on Fifteen Mile Creek Road as it intersects with Green Ridge Road 2.0 miles after you exited the interstate.

© THERESA DOWELL BLACKINTON

A hiker pauses to cool off under a natural outdoor shower.

After another 0.5 mile, cross Deep Run and park in the trailhead lot immediately on your left.

Information and Contact

There is no fee. Dogs on leash are allowed. The forest is open 24 hours daily. Maps are available for purchase from the Maryland Department of Natural Resources (410/260-8367, www.dnr.maryland.gov). For more information, contact Green Ridge State Forest, 28700 Headquarters Drive NE, Flintstone, MD 21530, 301/478-3124, www.dnr.maryland.gov/publiclands/western/greenridgeforest.asp.

4 LOG ROLL TRAIL   BEST ◖
Green Ridge State Forest

🏕 🌸 🐎

Level: Butt-Kicker   **Total Distance:** 9.0-10.0 miles round-trip

Hiking Time: 4.75-5.75 hours   **Elevation Gain:** 700 feet

Summary: Dozens of water crossings allow you to put your balance to the test . . . or provide an excuse for a splash in a cool creek.

On paper, the Log Roll Trail doesn't look like anything out of the ordinary—a 2.5-mile trek alongside a creek followed by a 2.5-mile hike through a hardwood forest to an overlook. What isn't revealed by that brief description, however, is the more than 30 creek crossings you're required to make in the first 2.5 miles. Massive rock outcrops interrupt the trail, making it impossible for you to hike along either bank of Big Run for any significant distance. Instead you must almost continuously cross back and forth, testing your balance on slippery rocks or tightrope-walking across fallen trees. It might be the lengthiest 2.5 miles you'll ever hike.

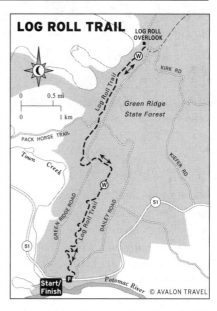

The trail begins across the road from the parking lot on a short boardwalk that descends to Big Run. White blazes mark the way, and when you can't figure out just how the trail continues, take a look across the water. Chances are you'll see the next blaze on the opposite bank. Soaring hemlocks dominate the first section of the hike, which takes place in a narrow, rocky gorge, but as the gorge widens into a valley, hardwoods take over. Look for clusters of cancer root at the base of trees. Heavy, knee-high undergrowth crowds the trail in many areas and requires bushwhacking, so you'll want to wear pants to avoid scratches and rashes.

At about the 1.25-mile mark, you'll spot one of the forest's log shelters on your left. The shelter and a transmission line a bit farther along are the only landmarks you'll pass before the trail turns left off Big Run at 2.5 miles. Once you make the turn, you'll hike uphill for 0.2 mile via an old fire road, which is often mucky.

© THERESA DOWELL BLACKINTON

Creek crossings are a regular occurrence on the Log Roll Trail.

The road will then turn back into a footpath and ascend steeply for another 0.3 mile before reaching and crossing Green Ridge Road. The next 0.75-mile stretch, which is also uphill but at less of a grade, alternates between easy-to-traverse mature forest and open areas that require bushwhacking. Spring beauties, bluets, and wild geraniums prosper in springtime.

After crossing Pack Horse Trail at about the 3.75-mile mark, you'll soon find yourself on a narrow ledge trail cut into the side of Green Ridge Mountain. About 1.25 miles after the intersection with Pack Horse Trail, you'll return to Green Ridge Road. Log Roll Overlook is to your left. Take a seat at the picnic table, and from your perch in Maryland look left to the mountains of West Virginia and right to the mountains of Pennsylvania.

With sufficient time and daylight, you can return the way you came, but don't underestimate how long the final 2.5-mile section will take. If you've had enough creek crossings for one day, make the 4.0-mile return trip via Green Ridge Road, a gravel forest road that receives little traffic. Turn left at the end of Green Ridge Road onto Route 51 and walk a short distance back to your car.

Options

Across the road from the overlook, Log Roll Trail connects to 7.0-mile Deep Run/Big Run Trail. Combining the two makes for an excellent daylong shuttle hike or a two-day, out-and-back hike. Deep Run/Big Run Trail involves additional creek crossings, though not nearly as many as Log Roll Trail, and it traverses a shale barren where you can see plants unusual for this area, such as the prickly pear cactus and the large blazing star.

Directions

Take I-270 north to westbound I-70. Proceed 52.3 miles to exit 1B and merge onto southbound U.S. 522. After 6.2 miles, turn right on Route 9 and drive 7.8 miles. Turn right on Detour Road, drive 10.9 miles, and then turn right back onto Route 9. After 2.0 miles, the road turns into Route 51, and after an additional 5.5 miles, you'll reach the parking lot on your left. The trailhead is across the road.

Information and Contact

There is no fee. Dogs on leash are allowed. The forest is open 24 hours daily. Maps are available for purchase from the Maryland Department of Natural Resources (410/260-8367, www.dnr.maryland.gov). For more information, contact Green Ridge State Forest, 28700 Headquarters Drive NE, Flintstone, MD 21530, 301/478-3124, www.dnr.maryland.gov/publiclands/western/greenridgeforest.asp.

5 ZILER LOOP-CENTRAL TRAIL CIRCUIT
Cacapon Resort State Park

Level: Strenuous

Hiking Time: 2.75 hours

Total Distance: 5.5 miles round-trip

Elevation Gain: 1,450 feet

Summary: Challenge yourself on a steep climb to a ridge on Cacapon Mountain.

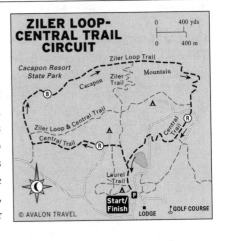

Maybe it's Cacapon's many amenities—a beach, golf course, clay shooting range, and tennis courts—that keep the majority of park visitors off the trails. Or maybe it's the fact that the main trail demands that you climb steeply for more than 1.5 miles without so much as a switchback to serve as an aid that has most visitors saying, "No, thank you." Though the park itself may seem a bit luxurious, its trails appeal to those who prefer things rugged.

From the entrance of the lodge parking lot, take a left toward the four-way stop and then proceed 0.15 mile to cabin 21, picking up green-blazed Laurel Trail just to the right of the cabin. You'll quickly pass both ends of Cabin Loop Trail on your left and then begin an ascent, which leads you past red-blazed Central Trail on your right at 0.3 mile. After another 0.1 mile, you'll reach another junction with the Central Trail. This time turn left onto it.

The red blazes will lead you downhill and over a park road. After you cross the road, you'll hop over Middle Fork Indian Run and pass a cluster of cabins on your right. Shortly after leaving the cabins behind, you'll climb a small ridge and then make your way through an immature forest. Notice the blueberry bushes, which usually ripen in July, crowding the trail, and in spring look for pink lady slippers.

At about the 1.25-mile mark, Central Trail will end at Ziler Loop Trail. Turn right onto the blue-blazed trail and begin the ascent, knowing that this climb doesn't end until you reach the 2,200-foot ridge of Cacapon Mountain. It doesn't seem that difficult as you hike the first 0.1 mile, passing the combined Ziler Loop & Central Trail on your right, and the ascent is relatively gentle for another 0.2 mile, at which point you cross a gulch and the grade increases dramatically. It's all you can do to keep putting one foot in front of the other. A short, flat section after one of the toughest parts of the ascent provides a good spot for a well-earned break. Enjoy it while you can, because the ascent resumes, and the trail provides little relief until you're up on the ridge. In winter, valley views are abundant, but leaves impede the view the rest of the year.

An easy walk along the ridge will lead you to a junction at about 2.75 miles with the Ziler Trail, which leads straight down the mountain, should you want an express route. If you want to finish the entire loop, however, first enjoy a rest on the bench at the junction, then continue hiking along the ridge on Ziler Loop Trail. Just as the trail begins to descend, mountain laurels appear, looking resplendent in June when they're in full bloom. A series of switchbacks eases the descent, but it's still a bit tricky because the trail is rocky and often covered in leaves.

Upon reaching an intersection with the other end of the combined Ziler Loop & Central Trail at about 4.0 miles, stay straight on red-blazed Central Trail. Cross a park road, descend again through immature forest, and then cross another park road. The trail will lead over North Fork Indian Run, reaching a reservoir at about 4.75 miles. As soon as you reach the reservoir, the trail will begin to climb a small ridge, reaching the top at about 4.9 miles and reconnecting with the Laurel Trail. Turn left and hike 0.3 mile back to the trailhead. Then retrace your path 0.15 mile to the lodge parking lot.

© THERESA DOWELL BLACKINTON

Indian Run crosses the trail.

Options

If you'd prefer not to climb all the way to the top, make a right turn onto the combined Ziler Loop & Central Trail shortly after you turn onto the Ziler Loop Trail. This will lead you across the mountain on an intermediate ridge, ending where the Ziler Loop Trail connects to the Central Trail. Turn right and follow the preceding directions.

Directions

Take I-270 north to westbound I-70. Proceed 52.3 miles, and then take exit 1B to southbound U.S. 522. Drive 15.8 miles, and then turn right onto Cacapon Lodge Drive. Follow the signs to the lodge parking lot.

Information and Contact

There is no fee. Dogs on leash are allowed. Trails are open from dawn to dusk daily. Maps are available from the lodge. For more information, contact Cacapon Resort State Park, 818 Cacapon Lodge Drive, Berkeley Springs, WV 25411, 304/258-1022, www.cacaponresort.com.

6 SNAVELY FORD TRAIL   BEST ☾

Antietam National Battlefield

Level: Easy

Total Distance: 1.8 miles round-trip

Hiking Time: 1 hour

Elevation Gain: 150 feet

Summary: A once-bloody battleground has been transformed into a serene site graced by wildflowers and songbirds.

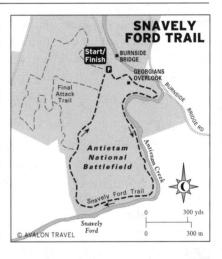

On September 17, 1862, in the quiet town of Sharpsburg, Maryland, the Union and Confederate armies clashed in what would be the bloodiest one-day battle of the Civil War. During the 12-hour battle, approximately 22,720 men were killed, wounded, or taken prisoner. At the end of the day, the battle lines were about the same as they had been that morning; however, the Union army claimed victory because they had successfully prevented the Confederates from gaining any ground in their attempt to march north. In fact, the next day Confederate General Robert E. Lee withdrew his troops into Virginia.

This hike takes place alongside Antietam Creek, just south of the highly contested Burnside Bridge. Only a few markers containing historical information give away the fact that this ground was once marked by the blood of dying and wounded soldiers. In fact, it is almost impossible to imagine the carnage that took place here as you walk through the brilliant wildflowers lining the banks of the swift creek while songbirds provide a melodious soundtrack.

From the parking lot, proceed down the stairs and follow the signs and the paved path to the Georgians Overlook, from where Confederate sharpshooters harassed Union troops. Continue along the trail as it turns into a dirt path and leads downhill to Antietam Creek, which you'll meander along for the majority of the hike. In spring, dame's rocket grows unabashedly along the bank, and other wildflowers also hold court. Some you can't miss while others you'll have to search for. Try to find red trillium, dwarf ginseng, wild geranium, bishop's cap, celandine, garlic mustard, rue anemone, and violet (white, yellow, and purple).

If you prefer birds to flowers, scan the dogwoods, redbuds, pawpaws, poplars, and other trees and bushes for some of the 77 species that have been found here. Bluebirds, cardinals, goldfinches, and tree swallows are common finds, while spotting indigo buntings and redheaded woodpeckers requires a bit of luck. Benches along the water allow you to enjoy the views and the nature.

A small island divides the creek, and as you come to the part of the path parallel to the end of the island, the trail turns right away from the water. Take a moment to read the sign about Snavely Ford, the spot where Union troops made their way across the creek, and then continue on your way. A connector to the Final Attack Trail will be on your left, but it is unmarked and easy to miss. It's better to connect to this trail from the parking lot, so continue straight until you reach a broad gravel road. Turn left here, passing between two fields where deer like to graze. Upon reaching the parking lot, head over to the Burnside Bridge and take in the various monuments and memorials.

Options

The Final Attack Trail lies to the west of the Snavely Ford Trail but begins from the same parking lot. You can take the connector trail, but that puts you in the very middle of the trail. Since this is an interpretive trail with a detailed map and signed posts explaining the battle, it's best to complete the Snavely Ford Trail, and then do the 1.7-mile Final Attack Trail from the beginning. Pick up an interpretive map at the visitors center.

© THERESA DOWELL BLACKINTON

Phlox is one of many wildflowers you'll find at Antietam.

Directions

Drive north on I-270 to westbound I-70. After 4.3 miles, take exit 49 to westbound U.S. 40-Alt. Follow U.S. 40-Alt. for 11.4 miles, then turn left on Route 34 and drive 5.8 miles. Turn left on Rodman Avenue, and after 0.5 mile, turn left on Branch Avenue. The road ends at the parking lot, and the trailhead is at the bottom of the stairs.

Information and Contact

There is a fee of $4 per person or $6 per family, which covers admission for three days. A $20 annual pass is available. America the Beautiful passes accepted.

Dogs on leash are allowed. Trails are open 8:30 A.M.–5 P.M. daily Labor Day–Memorial Day, 8:30 A.M.–6 P.M. daily Memorial Day–Labor Day. Maps are available at the visitors center (5831 Dunker Church Road, Sharpsburg, MD 21782). For more information, contact Antietam National Battlefield, P.O. Box 158, Sharpsburg, MD 21782, 301/432-5124, www.nps.gov/anti.

7 MARYLAND HEIGHTS TRAIL   BEST **◖**

Harpers Ferry National Historical Park

Level: Moderate   **Total Distance:** 6.6 miles round-trip

Hiking Time: 3 hours   **Elevation Gain:** 1,150 feet

Summary: Travel along old military roads for a bird's-eye look at the historic town of Harpers Ferry.

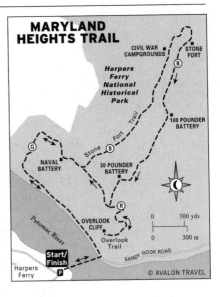

MARYLAND HEIGHTS TRAIL

To anyone who remembers the U.S. history learned in middle school, Harpers Ferry is synonymous with John Brown's ill-fated raid of 1859 in which he tried to arm an uprising of slaves. But that's not all history had in store for this town that sits surrounded by high cliffs at the meeting point of the Potomac and Shenandoah Rivers. The largest surrender of Union troops would take place here just a few years later, and in the post–Civil War years, some of the earliest integrated schools would open within the town's borders. You can learn all about the history of Harpers Ferry in the preserved buildings of this town, then make your way to the top of Maryland Heights to see it spread out before you.

The hike starts out innocuously as you cross the railroad bridge over the Potomac and turn left for a 0.7-mile stroll alongside the C&O Canal. Enjoy this effortless stretch, because as soon as you turn onto the green-blazed trail on your right, you'll begin an uphill haul that doesn't end until you've reached the first of the hike's two vistas. Fortunately, an old forest of chestnut oaks, tulip poplars, and red maples provides a thick canopy, so shade is abundant. The trail has its origins as a military road, so it's quite wide, though still rather rocky.

Marked points of interest line the trail. At the first trail split after turning right off the canal, take the path to the right to visit the third marked spot, a Union naval battery. Upon reconnecting with the main trail, turn right. You'll soon reach a junction. Blue-blazed Stone Fort Trail runs uphill to the left, whereas red-blazed Overlook Trail lies straight ahead. Turn left on Stone Fort Trail, which will lead you to the crest of Maryland Heights and then loop back down to the Overlook Trail.

You'll be gaining elevation for about another 1.7 miles, but five designated interest points provide convenient excuses for breaks. The most interesting sites are those closest to the ridge: the remains of a military camp, exterior fort, interior fort, and stone fort. Had these fortifications been available when the Confederates attacked in 1862, the Union may not have had to give up 12,500 men. They weren't, however, built until 1863, after the Union reclaimed the area.

After you investigate these sites, your hike becomes much easier, because you now head downhill. At the intersection with the Overlook Trail, turn left and proceed to a rocky shelf providing an extremely scenic view of the two converging rivers and the old town of Harpers Ferry. In the summer, you'll likely see hundreds of people floating down the rivers in inner tubes. Look up, and you may witness bald eagles, peregrine falcons, and red-tailed hawks soaring in the thermals. Snap some pictures, enjoy a snack, and then follow first the red blazes, then the green blazes, back to the C&O Canal, where you'll turn left and return to Harpers Ferry.

Options

If you want to get the view without the history lesson, do not turn off onto Stone Fort Trail, but instead continue along red-blazed Overlook Trail. This shortens the hike to 4.2 miles and eliminates a few hundred feet of elevation gain.

Directions

Drive north on I-270 to westbound I-70. After 1.3 miles, take exit 52 to merge

To begin the hike, first cross over the river via the railroad bridge.

onto U.S. 340. Stay on U.S. 340 for 22.0 miles, crossing the Potomac and Shenandoah Rivers. After crossing the second bridge, advance to the stoplight at the top of the hill. Turn left into Harpers Ferry and park in the visitors center lot. A shuttle will take you down to the old town, from where you can cross the bridge and begin the hike.

Public Transportation: MARC commuter trains (www.mtamaryland.com) and Amtrak trains (www.amtrak.com) run between Union Station and Harpers Ferry. You'll have to make the trip into a minivacation, however, because trains only depart from Washington DC in the evening and from Harpers Ferry in the morning.

Information and Contact

There is a fee of $10 per vehicle, which covers admission for three consecutive days. A $30 annual pass is available. America the Beautiful passes accepted. Dogs on leash are allowed. The park is open 8 A.M.–5 P.M. daily, except New Year's Day, Thanksgiving, and Christmas. A trail map is available at the visitors center. For more information, contact Harpers Ferry National Historical Park, P.O. Box 65, Harpers Ferry, WV 25425, 304/535-6029, www.nps.gov/hafe.

8 LOUDOUN HEIGHTS TRAIL

Harpers Ferry National Historical Park

Level: Moderate   **Total Distance:** 5.0 miles

Hiking Time: 2.5 hours   **Elevation Gain:** 1,200 feet

Summary: Summit Loudoun Heights via the Appalachian Trail, and then continue to an overlook with views across to Maryland Heights.

Loudoun Heights acts as the counterpoint to Maryland Heights, and together these two peaks nearly surround the town of Harpers Ferry. At this point in time, they seem to shelter the town, but during the Civil War, they were used to attack it. From the heights, artillery rained down upon Harpers Ferry. A few stone ruins along the way allude to this history.

To reach Loudoun Heights, you must first make your way across the Shenandoah River via the U.S. 340 bridge. You'll then begin climbing to the crest via the white-blazed Appalachian Trail. This is the most strenuous part of the hike as you gain the majority of the elevation here. After about 0.5 mile from the Shenandoah River, the trail crosses over Chestnut Hill Road; stay straight.

After another 0.2 mile, you'll reach an intersection. The Appalachian Trail continues to the right, whereas an orange-blazed trail goes off to the left. You'll come back via the Appalachian Trail, but for now, turn left onto the Orange Trail, walking along an intermediate ridge. This path was used in previous centuries for the transport of coal down to the town. Look past the power lines that mar the view to take in the town, Virginius Island, the Shenandoah and Potomac Rivers, and Maryland Heights.

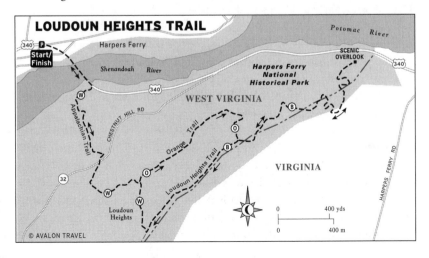

The Potomac River, which is popular for tubing, can be viewed from the trail.

The Orange Trail stretches for 0.7 mile before ending at blue-blazed Loudoun Heights Trail. Turn left onto this trail, which straddles the Virginia–West Virginia boundary. At times, you'll be walking with one foot in West Virginia and the other foot in Virginia. The trail descends gently until you reach the scenic overlook. Whereas the overlook on Maryland Heights looks directly over the town, this promontory provides a view of the rolling natural terrain around Harpers Ferry. It's a great spot for a picnic lunch.

On the return trip, bypass the turnoff to the Orange Trail, staying on Loudoun Heights Trail for about 1.5 miles. Along the way you'll pass some Civil War ruins, although they aren't easily distinguished by the untrained eye. What may appear to be a pile of rocks was very likely once a stone redoubt or rifle pit. Loudoun Heights Trail will end at the Appalachian Trail. Turn right onto it, passing the Orange Trail after 0.2 mile and reaching Chestnut Hill Road after another 0.2 mile. From this intersection, make the final 0.5 mile descent to the Shenandoah River and cross back over into town.

Options

The 0.9-mile Virginius Island Trail is certainly worth a visit if you're at Harpers Ferry. The trail leads through the ruins of an industrial town. The guide and map that are available in the visitors center highlight 16 points of interest. Completing the Virginius Island Trail along with both the Loudoun Heights Trail and the Maryland Heights Trail will provide you with a well-rounded view of this historical site.

Directions

Drive north on I-270 to westbound I-70. After 1.3 miles, take exit 52 to merge onto westbound U.S. 340. Stay on U.S. 340 for 18.7 miles. After crossing the Shenandoah River, turn right on Shenandoah Street and park in the lot immediately on your right.

Public Transportation: MARC commuter trains (www.mtamaryland.com) and Amtrak (www.amtrak.com) run between Union Station and Harpers Ferry. You'll have to make the trip into a minivacation, however, since trains only depart from Washington DC in the evening and from Harpers Ferry in the morning.

Information and Contact

There is a fee of $10 per vehicle, which covers admission for three consecutive days. A $30 annual pass is available. America the Beautiful passes accepted. Dogs on leash are allowed. The park is open 8 A.M.–5 P.M. daily, except New Year's Day, Thanksgiving, and Christmas. A trail map is available at the visitors center. For more information, contact Harpers Ferry National Historical Park, P.O. Box 65, Harpers Ferry, WV 25425, 304/535-6029, www.nps.gov/hafe.

9 APPALACHIAN TRAIL TO ANNAPOLIS ROCK

Greenbrier State Park

Level: Moderate

Total Distance: 7.2 miles round-trip

Hiking Time: 3.5 hours

Elevation Gain: 1,250 feet

Summary: Get a taste of the Appalachian Trail on a hike to a popular overlook.

Almost 40 miles of the 2,175-mile Appalachian Trail cut through Maryland, and on this hike, you can experience 3 of those miles. The highlight is the panoramic view from Annapolis Rock, the turn-around point of the hike. You might just be inspired to spend more time out on this classic trail, but don't be fooled into thinking you can make the famed through-hike—at least not without a lot of preparation and determination. The Maryland section of the Appalachian Trail is considered one of the easiest, especially because it involves little elevation change.

In fact, the most difficult part of this out-and-back hike is the 0.6-mile spur that connects Greenbrier State Park to the Appalachian Trail. You'll find the trailhead of the blue-blazed Bartman Hill Trail on the left side of the visitors center.

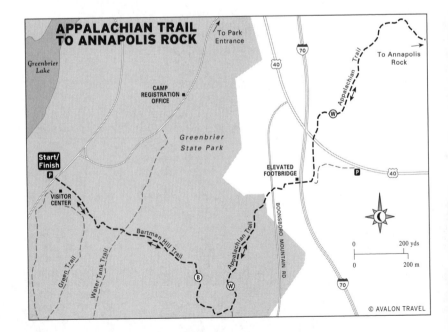

Water from a natural spring cascades down at Annapolis Rock.

This trail climbs 600 feet in 0.6 mile, and the ground is uneven and rocky. A small spring leaves an early portion of the trail sodden year-round, so muck your way through or around. After about 0.2 mile, you'll pass through an intersection with the Water Tank Trail, and after about another 0.2 mile, just past a signboard, the trail turns right. This connector trail ends at a mound of boulders, where you have the option of turning right and following the Appalachian Trail a little more than 1,000 miles to its southern end at Springer Mountain, Georgia, or turning left and following it a little more than 1,100 miles to its northern end at Mount Katahdin, Maine. Choose to head toward Maine, and go left onto the white-blazed trail, which is flat with a slight downhill grade at this point.

When you reach Boonsboro Mountain Road, cross and take the small timberlined path between the houses to the elevated footbridge over I-70. Once over the interstate, turn left. You'll parallel I-70 for a short stretch before the trail veers east. As you cover the remaining 2.2 miles to Annapolis Rock through hardwood forest with minimal undergrowth, you'll pass a few blue-blazed spurs. These lead to shelters for overnight hikers, so stay on the white-blazed trail and make the gradual ascent until you reach the posted turnoff to Annapolis Rock. Follow this trail 0.25 mile downhill.

Popular with hikers, campers, and rock climbers, Annapolis Rock came close to being loved to death. Now with camping more tightly regulated and a caretaker living on-site seasonally, the area is recovering, with vegetation even sneaking in among the rocks that make up the ledge. Look for Greenbrier Lake to your left, which will give you perspective on how far you've come. After enjoying the view, continue a short way on the trail through the designated camping spots to a natural spring. Water gushes up from multiple spots, forming small, clear pools and then cascading down.

Once you're refreshed, turn around and head back the way you came. About 0.8 mile after you cross the interstate, look for the turnoff to the Bartman Hill

Trail. If you're not paying attention, you could miss it and end up on your way to Georgia. Be careful descending the steep trail.

Options

Instead of turning left where Bartman Hill Trail ends at the Appalachian Trail, turn right and proceed 3.0 miles to Washington Monument State Park. The park is home to a 34-foot rugged stone tower built in 1827 to honor George Washington. The terrain is very similar to that leading to Annapolis Rock, and there is little change in elevation.

Directions

Drive north on I-270 to westbound I-70. After 11.5 miles, take exit 42 to merge onto northbound Route 17. Follow Route 17 as it turns right after 1.0 mile, then turn left onto westbound U.S. 40. The park entrance is on the left after 3.5 miles. Follow the entrance road to where it forks. Turn left and park in the lot across from the visitors center.

Information and Contact

There is a fee of $3 per person on weekdays Memorial Day–Labor Day and weekends in May and September; $5 per person on weekends and holidays Memorial Day–Labor Day; $3 per vehicle all other times. Out-of-state visitors pay an additional $2. Maryland State Park passes are accepted. Dogs on leash are allowed on the Appalachian Trail but not on the trails in Greenbrier State Park. The park is open 8 A.M.–sunset daily. Maps are available for purchase from the Maryland Department of Natural Resources (410/260-8367, www.dnr.maryland.gov). For more information, contact Greenbrier State Park, 21843 National Pike, Boonsboro, MD 21713, 301/791-4767, www.dnr.maryland.gov/publiclands/western/greenbrier.asp.

10 BIG RED TRAIL
Greenbrier State Park

Level: Easy/Moderate   **Total Distance:** 4.5 miles round-trip

Hiking Time: 2 hours   **Elevation Gain:** 760 feet

Summary: Escape a busy lake with a peaceful loop through a mature hardwood forest.

The majority of visitors to Greenbrier State Park come for the 42-acre lake, where you can bask on the beach, race model boats, swim, paddle, and fish. In summer, the lakefront can get rather crowded, but year-round you can slip onto the trails and have limited encounters with other people. You may, however, run into deer, frogs, snakes, turkeys, foxes, and raccoons.

To reach the trailhead, cut through the grass at the north end of Greenbrier Lake to the map signboard at the edge of the woods. Start the red-blazed trail here. Tall hardwood trees shade the path, providing minimal light to the forest floor. Mountain laurels survive in the midstory, but you'll see little in the way of understory, except for young trees fighting for the right to grow.

Copperhead Trail intersects with Big Red Trail after about 0.3 mile. Stay straight on Big Red Trail, and you'll shortly reach a junction where the trail in front of you is closed for habitat restoration, so you must turn left. Travel over the rocky ground, passing a marshy area on your left and weaving downhill before hitting an intersection with Rock Oak Fire Trail after less than 0.3 mile. You'll turn right, staying on the red-blazed trail as it becomes a broad gravel path. The 0.2 mile you'll cover as you return north to where the closed path would have led goes through forest that was very recently a field. Notice the open patches and the stand of tall, skinny poplars on your left.

When you reach the four-way intersection, go left. This stretch is very open overhead and is dense with sticker bushes. It can also be rather muddy, and you'll soon approach a creek that you must cross via stones. The trail will turn left shortly after this, continuing through more open terrain before intersecting with Snelling Fire Trail about 0.7 mile after the four-way intersection. Take the right branch and begin the trail's major ascent, once again through hardwood forest. The ascent is gradual at first but then becomes pronounced. In about 0.3 mile, you'll climb over 200 feet, then intersect with a connector trail on your left. Stay right, going uphill for another 0.25 mile, before turning left and proceeding about 0.8 mile on the ridge to the intersection with the other end of Snelling Fire Trail.

The trail varies from broad path to narrow single-track.

Remain on the red-blazed trail, passing Rock Oak Fire Trail on your left as the trail goes gradually uphill and makes a wide turn to the north. Nearly 0.5 mile after the previous intersection, you'll pass a connector trail to the camping area. Here the trail levels out, and large pines dominate. Pass the Camp Loop Trail on your right after 0.3 mile and begin the descent to the lake. It gets steep in the last stretch before you reach the lake, so watch your footing on the loose rock. The trail ends as you cross over the dam; make a few small ups and downs on the gravel path beside the lake, and you'll arrive back at the trailhead. If you're hot and sweaty at hike's end, head to the beach for a swim.

Options

To shorten the hike by about 0.8 mile, turn left at the first intersection with blue-blazed Rock Oak Fire Trail. Upon reconnecting with the red-blazed trail, turn left and continue the loop as previously described.

Directions

Drive north on I-270 to westbound I-70. After 11.5 miles, take exit 42 to merge onto northbound Route 17. Follow Route 17 as it turns right after 1.0 mile, then turn left onto westbound U.S. 40. The park entrance is on the left after 3.5 miles. Follow the entrance road to where it forks. Turn right and park in the boat launch lot.

Information and Contact

There is a fee of $3 per person on weekdays Memorial Day–Labor Day and week-ends in May and September; $5 per person on weekends and holidays Memorial Day–Labor Day; $3 per vehicle at all other times. Out-of-state visitors pay an additional $2. Maryland State Park passes are accepted. Dogs are not allowed. The park is open 8 A.M.–sunset daily. Maps are available for purchase from the Maryland Department of Natural Resources (410/260-8367, www.dnr.maryland. gov). For more information, contact Greenbrier State Park, c/o South Mountain Recreation Area, 21843 National Pike, Boonsboro, MD 21713, 301/791-4767, www.dnr.maryland.gov/publiclands/western/greenbrier.asp.

11 BLACK LOCUST TRAIL
Gambrill State Park

🧍 🦌 🐕

Level: Moderate

Hiking Time: 1.5 hours

Total Distance: 3.3 miles round-trip

Elevation Gain: 660 feet

Summary: Two overlooks make good rest stops on a trail that proves that short doesn't mean simple.

Statistics never tell the whole story. Though this hike doesn't cover a lot of distance and though the elevation gain seems minimal, it's not easy. When the trail changes elevation, it does so hard and fast, with both steep descents and ascents over uneven, rock-strewn trail. For your effort, the hike rewards with two overlooks from the 1,600-foot summit of High Knob on Catoctin Mountain—one with a view of the city of Frederick and one with a view of the more agrarian valley town of Middletown.

The trailhead of the black-blazed Black Locust Trail lies to the right of the signboard near the parking lot entrance, with the Red Maple and Cato-

ctin Trails sharing the path through mountain laurels that show off white flowers in early June. The red-blazed trail promptly veers off, and, staying on the black-blazed trail, you commence a descent of about 400 feet. It begins as a gradual decline, quickly becomes steep, and then flattens out for a few dozen yards. This process continues until the Green Ash Trail joins with the Black Locust Trail, at which point you'll turn right and cross a creek where ferns grow trailside. Then the uphill climb begins.

After about 0.4 mile of ascending you'll turn left—the Catoctin Trail continues on straight—and after a steep 0.1 mile, you'll reach Bootjack Spring. Here you get a quick moment of relief in the form of flat ground. Watch the blazes here, because the green-blazed trail continues straight, but the black-blazed trail, which you want to follow, turns off to the right. At this point, you'll be stepping up from

From the Middletown Overlook, you can gaze out over farmland and the eponymous town.

rock to rock, climbing toward the summit, weaving back and forth to temper the grade. Just as you approach North Frederick Overlook on Gambrill Park Road—the highest point of this hike at 1,600 feet—the yellow-blazed trail merges in.

Catch your breath while taking a long look at the city of Frederick below. Then cross Gambrill Park Road and continue straight through two intersections with the yellow-blazed trail. For this 0.6-mile stretch, you'll be hiking along a ridge at a pretty constant elevation, though the ground is still rocky and there are a couple of small ups and downs. You'll pass a spur trail on the left that leads to the visitors center, but you'll want to stay straight and then turn right with the black blazes when the yellow-blazed trail splits off.

At this point, you'll pass by the nature center and some picnic pavilions and reach Middletown Overlook. Take a peek at the rolling countryside below. From the overlook, you'll continue around the pavilion area and past the Tea Room, a lodge built by the Civilian Conservation Corps (CCC) that is now available for private events. This section isn't as forested, and the large rock formations to your left are striking. Upon reaching a junction with the green-blazed trail, make a right turn and begin the final descent. For the last 0.1 mile, the black-, green-, yellow-, and red-blazed trails converge, leading back to Gambrill Park Road. Cross the road to the parking lot where you began.

Options

For a longer, but perhaps easier, hike, explore 7.1-mile Yellow Poplar Trail. This loop, which leads up to the summit and then farther into the park along the ridge line, doesn't have the steep ascents and descents of Black Locust Trail, with most of the hike taking place between 1,500 and 1,600 feet. In the further reaches of the park covered by this trail, you have a better chance of seeing wildlife, but it's still not likely that you'll see one of the park's resident black bears or coyotes.

Directions
Drive north on I-270 to westbound U.S. 40. After 1.2 miles, take exit 13B to continue on U.S. 40. Drive 4.6 miles, and then turn right on Gambrill Park Road. Trailhead parking is in the lot on the right.

Information and Contact
There is a fee of $3 per vehicle. Out-of-state visitors pay an additional $2. Maryland State Park passes are accepted. Dogs on leash are allowed. Trails are open 8 A.M.–sunset daily Apr.–Oct., 10 A.M.–sunset daily Nov.–Mar. Maps are available for purchase from the Maryland Department of Natural Resources (410/260-8367, www.dnr.maryland.gov). For more information, contact Gambrill State Park, 8602 Gambrill Park Road, Frederick, MD 21702, 301/271-7574, www.dnr.maryland.gov/publiclands/western/gambrill.asp.

12 CHIMNEY ROCK-WOLF ROCK CIRCUIT

BEST (

Catoctin Mountain Park

Level: Strenuous

Total Distance: 5.5 miles round-trip

Hiking Time: 2.75 hours

Elevation Gain: 1,420 feet

Summary: A little-used trail passes a charming creek, then more beaten paths ascend to multiple vistas.

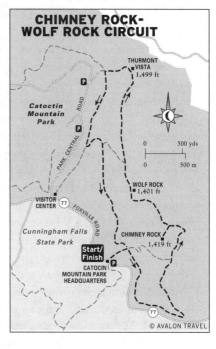

Somewhere on Catoctin's 5,000 acres is the presidential retreat Camp David, but it's not on the route for this hike. In fact, Camp David isn't even on the map, and unless you have connections in high places, you won't so much as catch a distant glimpse of it. What you will be privy to on this hike, however, is the splendor of a rushing creek, the grandeur of towering rock formations, and the luxury of 10-mile views.

A signpost along the road and to the left of the National Park Service Administration Office marks the trailhead. At the four-way intersection after less than 0.2 mile, turn right onto Crow's Nest Trail, a narrow path infrequently traveled. Sticker bushes crowd the path and ferns become dominant as you descend to Big Hunting Creek. Look closely at the bases of the oak and beech here, and you might find cancer root, a parasitic plant resembling a skinny, white pinecone.

The creekside walk is strikingly beautiful. Hemlocks grow dense along the trail, streams of sunlight make the water glisten, and clusters of rocks form cascades loud enough to drown out any traffic on the opposite bank. This isn't a place you want to hurry past. At about 0.8 mile, huge greenstone formations on your left add another element to the hike, and when you reach a trail junction at 1.0 mile, you'll be reluctant to make the left turn, but do so anyway.

For the next 0.6 mile, you'll be climbing through century-old hardwood forest toward Chimney Rock. The unblazed path seems to go straight up. (No trails in Catoctin are blazed, but important intersections are marked with signs.) Although easy to follow at first, the trail can at some points practically disappear under leaf cover that remains heavy even in summer. Just remember that you're headed for the ridge, so always take the option that leads up. You'll likely encounter deer on the way up—or at least hear them racing off through the leaves. Also, be alert for snakes, which can easily blend in among the ground cover.

Big Hunting Creek tumbles along beside the trail.

At 1.6 miles, a signpost points you straight, and after another 0.5 mile, you'll arrive at Chimney Rock, a quartzite formation that allows for fine views. Wolf Rock, located 0.4 mile farther along the trail, is also made of quartzite, but it's quite different from Chimney Rock. It's not an outcrop so much as a long, high mound marked with deep crevices. It's fun to scramble around, but be careful, especially since rattlesnakes like to hang out here.

Proceed from Wolf Rock for another mile along the mountain laurel–lined trail to reach Thurmont Vista at 3.5 miles. A strategically positioned bench provides a view through the trees. Beyond Thurmont Vista, the path is broad and made of gravel for the 0.4 mile it travels toward a parking lot. Before the lot, you'll hit an intersection with a dirt path, where you'll turn left. A signpost notes that the visitors center is to the left, and though you won't go so far as to reach it, you want to head that way. At 4.5 miles, you'll find yourself at another intersection. Again, go left, hiking uphill. As you pass a connector on your left, the trail flattens out and then descends for the remaining 0.9 mile. You'll see the administration building through the trees and then reach the final intersection. Turn right to return to the road and complete the hike.

Options

Extend your trip for another 3.1 miles by turning right at the intersection past Thurmont Vista. Pass by Blue Ridge Summit Overlook before turning south on Hog Rock Nature Trail. A left turn at Falls Nature Trail will take you to the visitors center. From there, take the trail north toward Wolf Rock, making a right at the first intersection you reach to complete the hike with the descent previously described.

Directions

Drive north on I-270 to northbound U.S. 15. After 16 miles, exit onto westbound Route 77. Drive 1.9 miles, and park in the lot on the right side of the road at the National Park Service Administration Office.

Information and Contact

There is no fee. Dogs on leash are allowed. The park is open from dawn to dusk daily. Maps are available from the visitors center (10 A.M.–4:30 P.M. Mon.–Thurs., 10 A.M.–5 P.M. Fri., 8:30 A.M.–5 P.M. Sat.–Sun.; closed Wed. Dec.–Mar.). For more information, contact Catoctin Mountain Park, 6602 Foxville Road, Thurmont, MD 21788, 301/663-9388, www.nps.gov/cato.

13 LOWER TRAIL-CLIFF TRAIL CIRCUIT

BEST ◖

Cunningham Falls State Park

Level: Easy

Total Distance: 1.25 miles round-trip

Hiking Time: 0.75 hour

Elevation Gain: 300 feet

Summary: Take a walk to the park's namesake waterfall, then scramble back to the start.

There's no doubt that the Lower Trail and Cliff Trail are the most hiked trails in 5,000-acre Cunningham Falls State Park. Nearly everyone who comes to the park—whether to hike, fish, swim, boat, or picnic—makes the trip to the park's eponymous waterfall. You shouldn't expect anything close to solitude, but the falls are scenic enough to overpower the crowds.

Of the two trails, the Lower Trail is the easier, as it's both shorter and much more of a groomed path. Marked with red arrows, the Lower Trail splits to the right from the parking lot and proceeds gently uphill on a wide gravel path. You'll pass through an oak-hickory forest, which a signboard explains is a second-growth forest that is around 100 years old. In centuries past, this land was clear-cut for farming, and much of the timber was made into charcoal used to power the Catoctin Iron Furnace, which operated in the area from 1777 to 1903. Iron from this furnace was turned into cannons and cannonballs during the Revolutionary War, and during the Civil War, it was used to plate battleships. If you're interested, you can visit the ruins of the furnace in the Manor Area of the park. In the century since the furnace shut down, the forest has gone through the various stages of succession and is again mature.

After 0.5 mile, the trail ends at a boardwalk leading out to the falls. At this 78-foot cascade—the highest in Maryland—the water rushes white over midnight black rock, creating an arresting view. If you come in the winter, you just might get a moment alone at the falls, when ice and snow only contribute to the area's beauty. When you're ready to return, take yellow-blazed Cliff Trail, which

LOWER TRAIL-CLIFF TRAIL CIRCUIT

Boardwalk Trail

77

FOXVILLE RD

Cunningham Falls

Lower Trail

R

Catoctin Trail

Cunningham Falls State Park

Cliff Trail

Y

Start/ Finish P

P

Catoctin Trail

WILLIAM HOUCK ROAD

Hunting Creek Lake

0   300 yds

0   300 m

© AVALON TRAVEL

Three different trails lead to Cunningham Falls, the highest waterfall in Maryland.

branches off to the right from the end of the Lower Trail. For the first 0.25 mile, you'll have to scramble through a boulder field. The trail then levels out for the next 0.4 mile, winding past massive greenstone rock formations. Greenstone, also known as metabasalt, is one of the main components of Catoctin Mountain, on which you're hiking. A part of the Blue Ridge Mountains, which are in turn part of the Appalachians, Catoctin belongs to the oldest mountain range above sea level on earth. The rocks here are hundreds of millions of years old. Take a minute to try to comprehend that kind of history, then complete the final section of the 0.75-mile Cliff Trail, a downhill slope back to the parking area.

Options

With small children, it's best to take the Lower Trail both to and from Cunningham Falls for a 1.0-mile hike. Older children, however, love the rock scramble, so you may want to take the Cliff Trail both ways for a 1.5-mile hike. A 0.25-mile boardwalk trail, with its trailhead on Route 77, provides a wheelchair-accessible route to Cunningham Falls.

Directions

Drive north on I-270 to northbound U.S. 15. After 16 miles, exit onto westbound Route 77. Drive 2.9 miles, and then turn left on Catoctin Hollow Road. Proceed 1.3 miles before turning right onto William Houck Drive. The trailhead parking lot will be on your left after about 0.5 mile.

Information and Contact

There is a fee of $3 per person on weekdays Memorial Day–Labor Day; $5 per person on weekends and holidays Memorial Day–Labor Day; $3 per vehicle at all other times. Out-of-state visitors pay an additional $2. Maryland State Park passes are accepted. Dogs are not allowed on Lower Trail Memorial Day–Labor Day; at other times and on other trails, dogs on leash are allowed. The park is open 8 A.M.–sunset daily Apr.–Oct., 10 A.M.–sunset daily Nov.–Mar. Maps are available for purchase from the Maryland Department of Natural Resources (410/260-8367, www.dnr.maryland.gov). For more information, contact Cunningham Falls State Park, 14039 Catoctin Hollow Road, Thurmont, MD 21788, 301/271-7574, www.dnr.maryland.gov/publiclands/western/cunningham.asp.

14 CAT ROCK-BOB'S HILL TRAIL   BEST ☾
Cunningham Falls State Park

Level: Strenuous

Hiking Time: 3.5 hours

Total Distance: 8.0 miles round-trip

Elevation Gain: 1,340 feet

Summary: Rolling views of Maryland's piedmont reward those who make the climb to two rocky overlooks.

There's no getting around it. If you want to enjoy the vistas from the two named overlooks in Cunningham Falls State Park, you have to start by going up. In the first 1.5 miles, you'll gain the bulk of the hike's elevation. That might explain why many visitors drive right past this trail without giving it a second thought. If you don't mind putting your legs, lungs, and heart to work, however, you'll be rewarded with boulder-top perches from which the view extends for miles.

From the Cat Rock trailhead on Route 77, ascend the wide, rock-strewn path, lined by bright moss. It's partic-

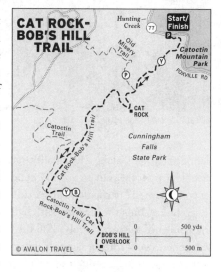

ularly spectacular after rain. Overhead the branches of mature oak, beech, and poplar create a canopy shading the trail. Yellow arrows mark the trail, and the few intersections along the way are clearly signposted. Though undergrowth in this stretch is minimal, you'll notice a profusion of ferns as you approach and cross Bear Branch. Shortly past this narrow creek you'll pass pink-blazed Old Misery Trail on your right. Continue through the power line clearing to where the trail splits at about 1.3 miles. A signpost points you straight ahead to Cat Rock, elevation 1,562 feet. Go ahead and clamber up the boulders, but be watchful of your footing and the deep crevices. Enjoy both the view and the beautiful quartzite rock. The foliose lichen covering the rocks is also worth a closer look.

To continue on the hike, return to the split and turn left. Though you still have elevation to gain on your way to 1,765-foot Bob's Hill, the gain is moderated by the 2.7 miles left to travel, so after a short span of distinctly uphill hiking past Cat Rock, the rest of the way seems almost flat. On this ridge of Catoctin Mountain, the canopy isn't as thick as it is below, and you'll notice abundant mountain

Hikers take a break atop Cat Rock.

laurel and azalea, along with smaller trees such as sassafras. In some sections, pine needles carpet the trail, so you might be surprised when you look up and see that evergreens aren't particularly dominant.

Upon reaching the junction with blue-blazed Catoctin Trail, turn left. For the remainder of the way to Bob's Hill the two trails share a path. At almost exactly 4.0 miles, you'll reach a signpost indicating North Bob's Hill Overlook to your left and South Bob's Hill Overlook to your right. The north overlook is just a few steps off the trail, and from a wall of boulders, you can peer through the trees at the piedmont and back to Cat Rock. The south overlook is not far from the trail but is a bit more removed than the north overlook. Sugarloaf Mountain stands out to the east. After comparing the view from both sides, complete the hike by returning the 4.0 miles to the parking lot.

Options

If you have two cars, you can make this a shuttle hike by parking the second car at the Manor Area parking lot off U.S. 15. Follow the hike as described, but instead of turning around at Bob's Hill, continue for another 1.5 miles for a one-way hike totaling 5.5 miles. This last section is almost entirely downhill, with the trail leading you from an elevation of 1,765 feet to just about 600 feet.

Directions

Drive north on I-270 to northbound U.S. 15. After 16 miles, exit onto westbound

Route 77. Drive 1.9 miles, then park in the trailhead lot on the left side of the road across from the National Park Service Administration Office.

Information and Contact

There is a fee of $3 per person on weekdays Memorial Day–Labor Day; $5 per person on weekends and holidays Memorial Day–Labor Day; $3 per vehicle at all other times. Out-of-state visitors pay an additional $2. Maryland State Park passes are accepted. Dogs on leash are allowed. The park is open 8 A.M.–sunset daily Apr.–Oct., 10 A.M.–sunset daily Nov.–Mar. Maps are available for purchase from the Maryland Department of Natural Resources (410/260-8367, www.dnr.maryland.gov). For more information, contact Cunningham Falls State Park, 14039 Catoctin Hollow Road, Thurmont, MD 21788, 301/271-7574, www.dnr.maryland.gov/publiclands/western/cunningham.asp.

15 NORTHERN PEAKS-MOUNTAIN LOOP CIRCUIT
Sugarloaf Mountain

🏛 🐎

Level: Moderate

Hiking Time: 3.75 hours

Total Distance: 7.5 miles round-trip

Elevation Gain: 1,800 feet

Summary: Take in the panoramic views from the peaks of the closest mountain to DC.

If you're looking for a mountain to hike but don't want to venture too far from the city, then Sugarloaf is where you want to go. You can get a workout roaming the peaks and valleys of this unique landscape. Not part of a mountain range, Sugarloaf instead stands alone, its 1,282-foot peak towering over quiet farmland. Technically speaking, Sugarloaf is a monadnock, a mountain that remains after erosion of the surrounding land. Here, the process took 14 million years, and it is only because Sugarloaf is primarily composed of rugged quartzite rather than the surrounding soft limestone that it remained.

You'll get a good look at the ragged rocks that compose this geologic feature as you begin your hike by taking the green-blazed A. M. Thomas Trail from the West View parking lot. This 0.25-mile trail follows a series of stone steps up through a field of boulders to the summit. Rock climbers love this area, and on any nice day, you'll find them here in droves. From the top, the vista is broad, encompassing miles of rolling fields dotted with cows and weathered red barns.

After enjoying the view, follow red-blazed Monadnock Trail downhill to Bill Lambert Overlook for a slightly different perspective. Then turn left on blue-blazed

NORTHERN PEAKS-MOUNTAIN LOOP CIRCUIT

Some stretches of the trail are dense with mountain laurel.

Northern Peaks Trail and proceed back to the parking lot along a path lined with hearty mountain laurels. Once back at your point of origination, cross the driving circle to reconnect with the Northern Peaks Trail.

Proceed past the picnic tables, then turn right and continue on the trail that has both white and blue blazes. This shared path lasts for about 0.5 mile before the blue-blazed trail, which you will follow, branches off to the left. You'll descend gradually through hardwood forest, passing a small creek where skunk cabbage thrives. When you reach Mount Ephraim Road, you'll turn right onto it and follow it as it veers left, picking up the trail on your right after crossing a stream. Here you'll begin the first of four ascents to peaks ranging from about 900 feet to nearly 1,100 feet. Thanks to the fact that you descend between each peak, you'll rack up significant elevation as you complete the Northern Peaks Trail section of this hike.

Before you reach the apex of the first peak, you'll have an opportunity for a break at White Rocks, an outcrop with a view. Take it; your legs will thank you later. As you rove up and down, notice the way the elevation changes create multiple microclimates. Mountain laurel grows in abundance, then vanishes. Pine clusters in select areas. You'll even cross two spots where the deciduous forest, dominated by oak, is replaced by a meadow of wheat-colored grass.

Shortly after the fourth peak, the Northern Peaks Trail meets the Mountain Loop Trail. Turn left and follow the white blazes as you wind your way down to the base of the mountain. Turn right on the road, and then right again on the service road, before picking up the natural-surface trail again. Just in case your legs aren't yet tired, the hike ends by gaining 400 feet on the way back to the parking lot.

Options

If you want a long hike but aren't keen on the elevation changes, park in the lot at the entrance to the mountain and follow the yellow-blazed Saddleback Horse Trail for a 7.0-mile trip around the base. For a short hike with prime views, join the majority of Sugarloaf visitors and opt simply to do the summit hike from the West View parking lot, creating a loop with the A. M. Thomas, Monadnock, and Northern Peaks Trails.

Directions

Drive north on I-270 to exit 22 to merge onto southbound Route 109. Proceed 2.9 miles, then turn right on Comus Road, which leads to the mountain entrance. Follow the signs to the West View parking lot.

Information and Contact

There is no fee. Dogs on leash are allowed. Trails are open 8 A.M. to one hour before sunset daily. Maps are available at the trailhead or on the park's website. For more information, contact Stronghold Inc., 7901 Comus Road, Dickerson, MD 20842, 301/869-7846, www.sugarloafmd.com.

16 LITTLE BENNETT CIRCUIT   BEST ◖
Little Bennett Regional Park

Level: Easy/Moderate   **Total Distance:** 6.2 miles round-trip

Hiking Time: 2.75 hours   **Elevation Gain:** 700 feet

Summary: Riotous wildflowers and a bounty of birds make this quiet park a refuge for nature lovers.

Little Bennett Regional Park is Montgomery County's largest park and the only one with a campground. Given these facts, you'd think it would be busy, but it's rare that you have to share the trails. The only people you're likely to encounter are bird-watchers searching for warblers, tanagers, vireos, Baltimore orioles, indigo buntings, eastern phoebes, northern parulas, and the scores of other birds—both common and rare—that nest here.

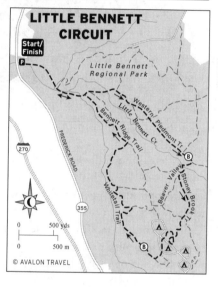

This hike begins on the Western Piedmont Trail on the eastern side of the creek, where bikes and horses are also allowed. This trail isn't blazed, but it's the only one that Hyattstown Mill Road connects directly to, and for most of its length, it's a broad gravel path that was once open to automobiles. It has the feel of an old country road, the type your grandparents would have sought out for a Sunday drive. Mayapple, jack-in-the-pulpit, spring beauty, wild ginger, and aster line the sun-sprinkled road.

After about 0.3 mile, the trail turns right and a concrete bridge leads over a wide section of Little Bennett Creek. Numerous trails branch off to both the left and right on this hike, but you'll want to stay straight on the main path. At 1.0 mile, you'll have to ford Little Bennett Creek. If the water is low, you can use the stones to get across. Otherwise your best bet is the downed tree stretching across the water. Though mainly hardwood forest lines the path, evergreen trees pop up in spots. Honeysuckle crowds the road, and butterflies flitter between the bushes. Birders often have luck in Wims Meadow, which you will pass on your right. At about 2.1 miles from the beginning of the trail, look for the Beaver Valley Trail on your right and turn onto it.

In addition to flowers and birds, sharp-eyed hikers at Little Bennett could also spot creatures such as this toad.

Stay left through the grass, over the creek, and at the split to transfer to the Stoney Brook Trail. This and all other trails west of the creek are foot traffic only and are marked with blue blazes. Trail intersections are also signposted. Follow wildflower-laden Stoney Brook Trail to the Acorn Hollow Trail to the Big Oak Trail, which leads to Hawk's Reach Activity Center. Cross the road in front of the activity center, pick up the trail, take the fork left, and then cross another road. This section isn't well marked, but signs recur across the road, where you'll take the Nature Trail to the Whitetail Trail. About 0.75 mile after you crossed the road, you'll intersect with the Antler Ridge Trail. Stay left, continuing about 0.25 mile to the Woodcock Hollow Trail, which will lead you along a ridge before descending into meadows painted yellow by buttercups. In the middle of a meadow, after about 0.5 mile on this trail, a signpost will direct you left to the Bennett Ridge Trail. Take a moment to marvel at the huge anthills you'll see along Bennett Ridge Trail. These multifoot-high structures built by Allegheny mound-building ants are not your everyday anthills.

After about 0.3 mile on the Bennett Ridge Trail, pass the fork to Owl Ridge on your right. Stay straight for another 0.3 mile on an often muddy trail. Once back at the Western Piedmont Trail, a left turn and about 0.75 mile of hiking will have you back at the trailhead.

Options

Any number of circuits can be made using the park's many connecting trails.

For a shorter version of this hike, turn right off the Beaver Valley Trail onto the Mound Builder Trail. When this trail ends, turn right onto Bennett Ridge Trail and follow the preceding directions. The total distance will be about 4.2 miles.

Directions

Drive north on I-270 to exit 22 to merge onto northbound Route 109. Turn left at Old Hundred Road, drive 0.4 mile, and then turn right onto Route 355. Drive less than 400 feet, and then turn left onto Hyattstown Mill Road. Park in the playground lot across from the fire station. The trailhead is at the end of Hyattstown Mill Road.

Information and Contact

There is no fee. Dogs on leash are allowed. Trails are open from sunrise to sunset daily. Maps are available on the park's website. For more information, contact Little Bennett Regional Park, 23701 Frederick Road, Clarksburg, MD 20871, 301/972-6581, www.montgomeryparks.org/facilities/regional_parks/little_bennett.

EASTERN MARYLAND

© THERESA DOWELL BLACKINTON

BEST HIKES

Water. It's the key ingredient to almost all of

the hikes featured in this region. Travel east to where the Chesapeake Bay cuts into Maryland, and you'll find beaches and bayside bluffs. Come a bit inland, and you'll find myriad rivers – including the Susquehanna, Patuxent, Patapsco, and Gunpowder – carving their way through forests; creating freshwater swamps, tidal marshes, and estuaries; and eventually flowing into the bay.

Where land meets water, unique ecosystems evolve. They are at once fragile, threatened constantly by erosion, and resilient, producing bountiful wildflowers each spring. It's vital that you tread lightly but at the same time observe closely. Watch the mayapple pop open like an umbrella. Count the leaves, petals, and flowers of the trillium, noting that each comes in threes. Admire the delicate blooms of the spring beauty, the hidden flower of the jack-in-the-pulpit, and the brilliant color of the Virginia bluebell. Marvel at your luck when you spot a rare find, such as the purple fringeless orchid, the pink lady's slipper, or the northern pitcher plant.

You won't be the only creature enjoying the features of this area. Birds, in particular, find much to love here. The Atlantic Flyway crosses eastern Maryland, and many of the parks play a vital role as sanctuaries for hundreds of species of migrating birds. At Merkle Wildlife Sanctuary, Canada geese nest in the thousands. Elsewhere you might spot an osprey diving for fish, raptors feeding in an open field, or a heron standing regally on the edge of a marsh. And don't forget the other field and forest birds –

vireos, hummingbirds, finches, bluebirds, warblers, thrushes, chickadees, and an entire chorus of songbirds.

While exploring these trails you might also see a beaver gnawing at a tree, a red fox scurrying through the undergrowth, a white-tailed deer watching you carefully, or a bullfrog bellowing a message. When you come across a squirrel, don't just dismiss it as an everyday sight; you might actually be gazing on an endangered species – the Delmarva squirrel, a native of the Eastern Shore.

Though these trails have many features in common, they each offer their own highlights. On the western side of the bay, Calvert Cliffs State Park boasts more than 600 species of fossils. As you hike along the beach, keep your eyes open for shark's teeth, which you're free to take home. At Elk Neck State Park, you can hike to the highest lighthouse on the Chesapeake, enjoying a sweeping view of the bay. It's unlikely you've seen a holly tree as big as the centuries-old one on Wye Island, and the enormous beech tree at Susquehanna State Park will leave you in awe. Soldiers Delight Natural Environment Area and Cedarville State Forest each shelter unusual ecosystems – the first, a savanna; the second, the headwaters of Maryland's largest freshwater swamp. And at Rocks State Park you can sit in the same seat that Native American royalty once occupied, taking in broad views of this enchanting area. Whatever your interest, the manifold trails of eastern Maryland invite you to explore. You'd be remiss not to accept.

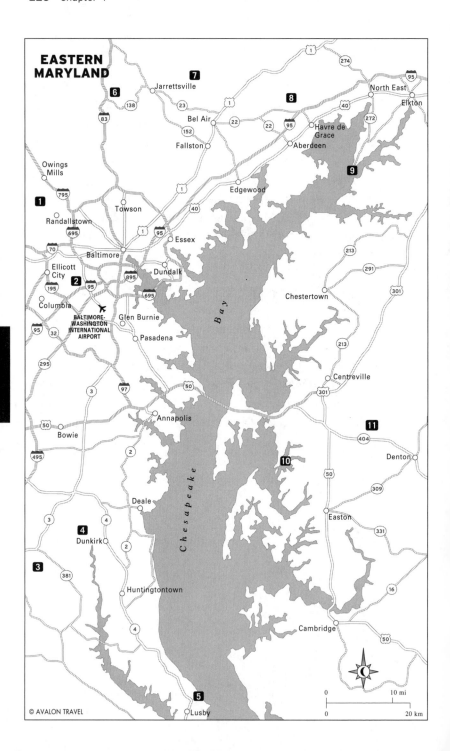

EASTERN
MARYLAND

© AVALON TRAVEL

TRAIL NAME	LEVEL	DISTANCE	TIME	ELEVATION	FEATURES	PAGE
1 Serpentine Circuit	Easy/Moderate	5.3 mi rt	2.25 hr	350 ft		228
2 Cascade Falls Circuit	Moderate	5.7 mi rt	2.5 hr	1,170 ft		231
3 Cedarville Blue Trail	Easy	4.0 mi	2 hr	175 ft		234
4 Paw Paw, Poplar Springs, and Mounds Loop	Easy	4.5 mi rt	2 hr	250 ft		237
5 Calvert Cliffs Beach Trail	Easy	3.6 mi	1.5 hr	130 ft		240
6 Gunpowder North–South Circuit	Moderate	4.9–9.2 mi rt	2.5–4.5 hr	500–820 ft		243
7 King and Queen's Seat Loop	Moderate	3.2 mi rt	1.5 hr	900 ft		246
8 Susquehanna Ridge Circuit	Easy/Moderate	4.7 mi rt	2.25 hr	940 ft		249
9 Turkey Point Lighthouse Trail	Easy	2.0 mi rt	0.75 hr	100 ft		252
10 Ferry Landing Trail	Easy	1.6 mi rt	0.75 hr	0 ft		255
11 Tuckahoe Valley Circuit	Easy/Moderate	8.1 mi rt	3.5 hr	400 ft		258

1 SERPENTINE CIRCUIT

Soldiers Delight Natural Environment Area

Level: Easy/Moderate

Total Distance: 5.3 miles round-trip

Hiking Time: 2.25 hours

Elevation Gain: 350 feet

Summary: Tramp (but gently!) across a serpentine barren, home to rare grassland species and valuable bedrock.

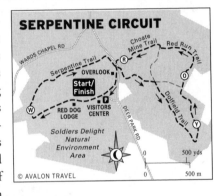

The majority of the ecosystem at Soldiers Delight is vastly different from what you'll encounter in other parts of Maryland. Though you will pass through hardwood forest and along a creek, the bulk of the hike is across a serpentine grassland and oak savanna—or at least what remains of this historic geologic site. A bedrock valued for building projects and as a source of chromium ore, serpentine is poor in nutrients needed by plants. Thus Soldiers Delight is not a particularly lush area, but it is home to 39 rare, threatened, or endangered plant species.

In centuries past, the ecosystem was maintained by fires caused by lightning or started by Native Americans as a means of hunting deer, but since human settlement ended these fires, invasive species such as Virginia pine and red cedar have begun to take over. Current restoration efforts include controlled burns, and you'll pass the charred remains of many pines.

Begin your hike on white-blazed Serpentine Trail, which runs along the right side of the Soldiers Delight Visitors Center. You'll pass by a picnic area and the Red Dog Lodge, and then under a set of power lines. Notice the sharp gray, green, and brown rock underfoot. This is serpentine. Geologists believe that serpentine, which is very rare in the eastern region of the United States, was part of the earth's mantle and was pushed to the surface during cataclysmic geologic events. Rich in magnesium, chromium, nickel, iron, and other metals, it has many uses. A trailside signboard just beyond the Red Dog Lodge provides more information on its formation and uses.

About halfway around the 2.5-mile Serpentine Trail, you'll follow the path as it turns right, then twice crosses Chimney Run. Look for fringed gentian along the creek bank in autumn; it's the only place in Maryland you can find this bright purple flower. Beyond the creek, the rock-studded trail makes a gradual climb

The trail passes Red Dog Lodge.

uphill. Bunches of serpentine chickweed, a white wildflower, poke up through the rocks, and hawks circle in the thermals overhead. After again passing under the power lines, you'll enter a forest stretch. Here red clay dominates the serpentine, allowing oaks and other hardwoods to grow. Upon exiting the woods, you'll reach an overlook on Deer Park Road.

Cross the road, picking up red-blazed Choate Mine Trail on your right. In this 0.3-mile section, you'll pass an old chromite mine that operated during the 1800s, which helped make Maryland the world center of chrome production at that time. Upon reaching a four-way intersection, turn right onto yellow-blazed Dolfield Trail. The southern section of this trail is rocky, brambly, and not very visually appealing. After you turn north, however, you'll enter a forest of tall hardwoods and midstory dogwoods. The difference is striking, especially because the two sides of the trail are never more than 0.15 mile apart.

Dolfield Trail runs into orange-blazed Red Run Trail, and you'll proceed straight onto it into a typical Maryland deciduous forest. Mountain laurel prospers, and skunk cabbage thrives on the banks of Red Run, which you'll walk along after the trail turns east. After about 0.25 mile, the trail veers left off the creek and enters a rocky area of cleared trees. Red Run Trail then connects with another section of red-blazed Choate Mine Trail, which you'll turn right onto and follow back to Deer Park Road. Turn left and cross the road to again reach the overlook. Take a moment to peer out at the sea of Indian grass and little bluestem, then pick up the Serpentine Trail on your left and follow it back to the visitors center.

Options

This hike can be divided into two distinct loops. The Serpentine Trail creates a 2.5-mile loop, and the Choate Mine–Red Run–Dolfield Trails create a 2.8-mile loop. This second loop can also be broken down into smaller sections, such as a 1.7-mile loop around the Choate Mine and Red Run Trails.

Directions

Drive north on I-95 to northbound I-695. After 11.2 miles, take exit 18B to merge onto westbound Route 26, and drive 5.2 miles before turning right on Deer Park Road. The entrance to the visitors center will be on your left after about 1.8 miles.

Information and Contact

There is no fee. Dogs on leash are allowed. Trails are open from sunrise to sunset daily. A map can be purchased from the visitors center (11 A.M.–3 P.M. Sat.) or the Maryland Department of Natural Resources (410/260-8367, www.dnr.maryland. gov). A free laminated map is available for use at the trailhead, but you must return it before leaving. For more information, contact Soldiers Delight Natural Environment Area, 5100 Deer Park Road, Owings Mill, MD 21117, 410/461-5005, www.dnr.maryland.gov/publiclands/central/soldiersdelight.asp.

2 CASCADE FALLS CIRCUIT

BEST (

Patapsco Valley State Park, Orange Grove Area

Level: Moderate

Total Distance: 5.7 miles round-trip

Hiking Time: 2.5 hours

Elevation Gain: 1,170 feet

Summary: A tranquil waterfall awaits hikers near the end of this loop through deciduous forest.

Covering nearly 32 miles along the Patapsco River, Patapsco Valley State Park is divided into five recreational areas, with opportunities for hikers, mountain bikers, horseback riders, campers, anglers, and boaters. This hike traverses forest and field and ends with a visit to a waterfall.

From the parking lot, climb the stairs to blue-blazed Cascade Falls Trail, taking the split to the right uphill through a forest of beech, maple, and tulip poplar trees. At 0.3 mile, you'll reach an intersection with a connector trail that is also blazed blue. Continue straight. The trail will approach a creek, turning east (left) to parallel it through a lush forest. At an intersection at 0.9 mile, turn right, crossing over the creek, and proceed for another 0.2 mile to the next intersection. Veer left here to connect to yellow-blazed Morning Choice Trail.

Over the next 0.4 mile, you'll cover a stretch of forest with very little understory and pass over Norris Lane, remaining on the yellow-blazed trail until you junction with red-blazed Old Track Loop. Turn left, and follow this loop for 0.3

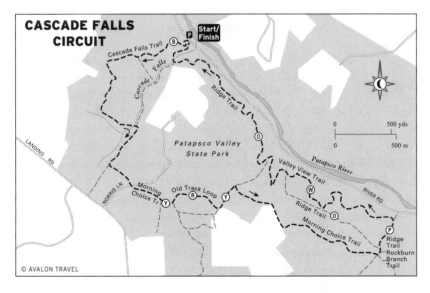

Patapsco Valley State Park has many intersecting trails, so you'll want to pay close attention to the blazes.

mile until it reconnects with yellow-blazed Morning Choice Trail. Turn left, hike 0.2 mile to the next intersection, and turn right, emerging into a field lined with sweet-smelling bushes. The buildings uphill belong to the Belmont Research Conference Center. When you reenter the woods, you'll encounter the ruins of two houses. You might see a turkey vulture pop out of a collapsing roof, but don't venture into or near the houses because they are unstable. After passing a spur trail on your left, you'll exit into another field. Deer congregate here, and it's common to see more deer than you can count.

Upon returning to the forest, notice the pawpaw trees, which appear almost tropical thanks to their long, skinny leaves. The Morning Choice Trail ends at purple-blazed Rockburn Branch Trail, which you'll turn left onto for a very short stretch. Stay straight when it connects to orange-blazed Ridge Trail, following Ridge Trail downhill, and then veering left over the creek immediately before you reach River Road. Pass a shelter, and then pick up 0.9-mile-long, white-blazed Valley View Trail. This is a foot-traffic-only trail, so there's no need to look out for the mountain bikers prevalent on other trails, but you should watch your footing on the steep, narrow sections.

The Valley View Trail ends at an intersection with orange-blazed Ridge Trail. Turn right and follow Ridge Trail as it weaves down to creeks and then up to the ridge. The trail passes shelters ideal for breaks as well as the ruins of stone structures that may have once housed workers from the old flour mill on the opposite side of Patapsco River. A couple of spurs on your right lead down to the road, but stay straight until the trail ends at blue-blazed Cascade Falls Trail. Turn right to reach Cascade Falls. Enjoy the waterfall and dip your feet in the cool pool before finishing the hike by following Cascade Falls Trail 0.1 mile back to the parking lot.

Options

From the parking lot, cross the Patapsco River via the swinging bridge and then explore the wheelchair-accessible Grist Mill Trail. Go left for 0.8 mile to reach Bloedes Dam or turn right and travel 1.3 miles along the river to Lost Lake, a fishing hole reserved for youth, senior citizens, and those with disabilities.

Directions

Drive north on I-95 to eastbound I-195. After 1.2 miles, take exit 3 to U.S. 1 toward Elkridge. Take a right at the end of the ramp, and then make an immediate right onto South Street. The entrance to the park is on your left. Follow the park entrance road to where it ends at Gun Road. Turn left to cross the Patapsco River, and then turn right. Proceed 1.7 miles to the Orange Grove Area, and park in the lot across from the swinging bridge.

Information and Contact

There is a fee of $2 per vehicle weekdays Apr.–Oct. and daily Nov.–Mar.; $3 per person weekends and holidays Apr.–Oct. Out-of-state visitors pay an additional $2. Maryland State Park passes are accepted. Dogs on leash are allowed. Trails are open 9 A.M.–sunset daily. Maps are available for purchase from the Patapsco Valley State Park Headquarters (8 A.M.–4:30 P.M. weekdays) or the Maryland Department of Natural Resources (410/260-8367, www.dnr.maryland.gov). For more information, contact Patapsco Valley State Park, 8020 Baltimore National Pike, Ellicott City, MD 21043, 410/461-5005, www.dnr.maryland.gov/publiclands/central/patapsco.asp.

3 CEDARVILLE BLUE TRAIL
Cedarville State Forest

Level: Easy

Hiking Time: 2 hours

Total Distance: 4.0 miles

Elevation Gain: 175 feet

Summary: Pass along and over creeks that feed Maryland's largest freshwater swamp on this looping forest hike.

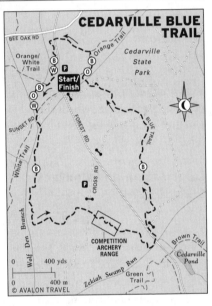

CEDARVILLE BLUE TRAIL

Established as a recreation area in the 1930s, Cedarville State Forest has 19 miles of trail that were carved out by a mostly African American unit of the Civilian Conservation Corps (CCC) and have been maintained since. This hike covers a 4.0-mile loop over terrain that is primarily flat or gently rolling thanks to the forest's location at the headwaters of Zekiah Swamp, the largest freshwater swamp in Maryland. This location provides the forest with unique features, including the presence of insect-eating plants such as the northern pitcher plant, but it also means the trails quickly get muddy during wet periods.

From the trailhead signboard, start down the combined Blue and White Trails, then turn left at the first split. The trail heads gently downhill on a sandy path through oak, birch, and maple trees. The Orange Trail will enter from the right and share the path with the Blue and White Trails for a bit; stay straight. The trail then approaches Wolf Den Branch, and the area becomes boggy, rich with ferns, tall grasses, and, in the spring, wildflowers. Look for beavers, which have left their marks on the trees, and listen for frogs. You might also see deer drinking from the creek.

At 0.25 mile, you'll reach Sunset Road, where the three trails will split. Turn right to follow the Blue Trail, which is well marked with blue blazes and with posts every 0.25 mile. While on Sunset Road, you'll cross over a creek; turn left immediately after the creek, following the trail into a sea of ferns and then crossing the creek again via footbridge. From here, the trail winds uphill through forest to a ridge, reaching a more recently cleared area of young pine trees at about 1.25 miles. When the trail intersects with Cross Road, cross and continue straight, reaching the forest's Competition Archery Range at about 1.5 miles. Just past mile 1.75, you'll approach Zekiah Swamp Run, which the trail parallels for a short stretch to Forest Road.

The Blue Trail picks up across the road, and at mile 2.0, you'll reach an intersection with a service road. Stay straight as the trail continues through the forest. About 0.75 mile later, the trail

The landscape is marshy along Wolf Den Branch.

© THERESA DOWELL BLACKINTON

again intersects Cross Road; proceed straight across. Around mile 3.0, you'll come across an interesting feature in the middle of the woods—an old outhouse labeled "#6." It's not clear where the other five outhouses might be. Just beyond the outhouse, you'll cross Mistletoe Road, after which the landscape changes from forest to ferns. You're again approaching Wolf Den Branch, which you'll traverse by footbridge.

Once over the creek, the Blue Trail reconnects with the Orange Trail. Turn right and proceed on the shared trail to a T intersection, where you'll turn left and split from the Orange Trail. From here, cross another bridge, pass the forest amphitheater and water tower at mile 3.5, and then cross Forest Road. As you complete the loop, you'll pass by a picnic area and the backside of the charcoal kiln before turning left at loop's end to return to the parking lot.

Options

The forest's five loop trails easily connect to one another, allowing for longer hikes. Branch off the shared path onto the 7.0-mile Orange Trail for a better chance at spotting marsh plants, or switch to the White Trail for an additional 3.5 miles through forest. To reach the 2.5-mile Brown Trail, which passes along a four-acre pond, or the 2.0-mile Green Trail, which covers the swamp headwaters, turn right when you reach Forest Road at Zekiah Swamp Run. You'll reach the trailheads for both in less than 0.1 mile.

Directions

From I-495, take exit 7A and merge onto southbound Route 5. Drive 12.1 miles, then turn left on Cedarville Road. Drive 2.3 miles on Cedarville Road, then turn right on Bee Oak Road, which leads into the park. At the fork with Hidden Springs Road, stay left on Bee Oak Road. Then turn right onto Forest Road and proceed to the parking lot on your right at the Charcoal Kiln.

Information and Contact

There is a fee of $3 per vehicle. Out-of-state visitors pay an additional $2. Maryland State Park passes are accepted. Dogs on leash are allowed. Trails are open from sunrise to sunset daily. Maps are available for purchase from the park office (9 A.M.–5 P.M. daily except holidays) or the Maryland Department of Natural Resources (410/260-8367, www.dnr.maryland.gov). For more information, contact Cedarville State Forest, 10201 Bee Oak Road, Brandywine, MD 20613, 301/888-1410, www.dnr.maryland.gov/publiclands/southern/cedarville.asp.

4 PAW PAW, POPLAR SPRINGS, AND MOUNDS LOOP

Merkle Wildlife Sanctuary

Level: Easy

Hiking Time: 2 hours

Total Distance: 4.5 miles round-trip

Elevation Gain: 250 feet

Summary: Bird lovers can spot their favorite species while hiking through open fields and hardwood forests and past wetlands.

If you have an affection for Canada geese, Merkle Wildlife Sanctuary is the place for you, since up to 5,000 geese can be found on the refuge's 1,670 acres at the peak of winter. If you aren't so keen on geese, wait until spring when most of the population takes flight and the diversity of wildlife increases. Other winged inhabitants of the sanctuary's fields, forests, and ponds include herons, ospreys, hummingbirds, finches, purple martins, bluebirds, and the occasional eagle.

This hike begins at the signboard next to Merkle House and proceeds along the edge of the field on yellow-blazed Paw Paw Trail. Go past the first post and

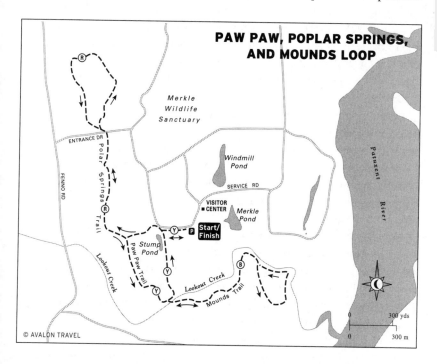

then, just past it, follow the path into the woods on your left. This is a bright stretch of forest filled with the twittering of birds. The trail will lead you back out to the field, which you'll edge around until you reach the red-blazed Poplar Springs Trail at about 0.3 mile.

Turn right onto this broad trail and enjoy the flowers—abundant daffodils in early spring, azaleas a bit later. After passing a meadow where grasshoppers hum, the trail narrows, and when you make a left-hand turn less than 0.1 mile later (straight ahead is a field), the forest becomes denser. Ferns grow underfoot, and mayapples crowd the path. Look for the white flowers that blossom

One of many mayapples along the trail blooms.

© THERESA DOWELL BLACKINTON

underneath the umbrella-like leaves of the mayapple. In summer, you'll find fruit on the mature plants. Though every other part of the mayapple plant is toxic (and thus should not be consumed), the ripe fruit is not. Shortly after you cross the entrance drive at about the 0.8-mile mark, you'll reach a split where the trail makes a loop. Take the right branch and pass spring beauties and jack-in-the-pulpits as you proceed slightly downhill toward Mattaponi Creek, at which point you begin the return loop. Follow the trail back to where it reconnects with the Paw Paw Trail at about 2.25 miles.

Keep to the mown path to the right, walking along the field for 0.25 mile, before turning right into a section of woods where deer are abundant. You'll certainly hear them as they crash through the undergrowth, and you might catch a glimpse of their white tails. When you intersect with blue-blazed Mounds Trail, turn right. You'll repeatedly go up and down slopes—some gentle, some a bit steep. Lookout Creek will be to your left, and farmland can be seen through the trees to your right.

Upon reaching the loop section of this trail, go right, leaving the best part for last. The return section brings you past the wetlands created by the creek before it flows into the Patuxent River. You might spot beavers, frogs, ducks, and herons. After finishing the loop, head back the way you came, reconnecting with Paw Paw Trail at about 4.25 miles. Turn right, and after a short span in the woods, you'll exit back into the fields, passing between Stump Pond and a red barn. At the road, turn right and return to your starting point.

Options

The 4.0-mile Chesapeake Bay Critical Area Driving Tour (www.pgparks.com/Things_To_Do/Nature/Chesapeake_Bay_Critical_Area_Tour.htm) explores the ecosystem of the Patuxent River, with one end at Merkle and the other at Patuxent River Park. It's actually only open to cars 10 A.M.–3 P.M. on Sunday. Other days, it's reserved for hikers, bikers, and horseback riders.

Directions

Take I-495 to exit 11A to merge onto southbound Route 4. Drive 6.0 miles to Old Crain Highway, turn right, and then make a left on Croom Station Road in 0.1 mile. After 2.5 miles, turn left on Croom Road, drive another 2.6 miles, and turn left on St. Thomas Church Road, which turns into Fenno Road. Follow Fenno Road to the sanctuary entrance and park in the visitors center lot. To get to the trailhead, turn left out of the lot and walk past Merkle House to the bulletin board.

Information and Contact

There is no fee. Dogs are not allowed. The sanctuary is open from sunrise to sunset daily. Maps are available at the visitors center (10 A.M.–4 P.M. weekends), at the trailhead, or on the sanctuary's website. For more information, contact Merkle Wildlife Sanctuary, 11704 Fenno Road, Upper Marlboro, MD 20772, 301/888-1410, www.dnr.maryland.gov/publiclands/southern/merkle.asp.

5 CALVERT CLIFFS BEACH TRAIL   BEST ◖

Calvert Cliffs State Park

Level: Easy   **Total Distance:** 3.6 miles

Hiking Time: 1.5 hours   **Elevation Gain:** 130 feet

Summary: Search for shark's teeth on a cliffside beach that you reach by following a creek as it expands into a marsh and then joins the Chesapeake Bay.

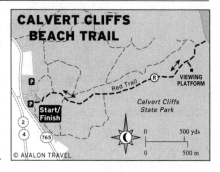

More than 15 million years ago, the area that is now Calvert Cliffs State Park was covered by a shallow sea. When it receded, hundreds of types of fossils were left behind along with towering Miocene-era cliffs. The cliffs run 30 miles down the coast of Maryland, but most of the land is privately owned, making the state park one of the few places where the public can enjoy these ancient wonders. Unfortunately, erosion has been eating away at the 100-foot cliffs to the tune of 3 feet per year. Visitors are thus no longer allowed to climb on the cliffs but can still enjoy the striking shoreline view.

The red-blazed trail, which begins just to the right of the pond, offers the most direct route to the beach, so begin by following the boardwalk over the pond's edge while keeping an eye out for otters. Most of the trail is a mix of sand and dirt, although boardwalk takes over in places where the ground is especially marshy. Markers indicate every 0.1 mile, and whenever the trail intersects with another, posts with colored triangles point you in the right direction.

Although you shouldn't have any trouble following the trail, you can ensure that you're headed the right way by keeping Gray's Creek on your right side as you hike toward the beach. The creek starts out small—an adult could easily step over it—with tiny ripples and falls providing a lilting melody. It quickly grows, however, and by the time you reach the 1.1-mile marker, an entire marshland exists to the right. Green ash snags jut from the water, providing perches for large birds such as ospreys, hawks, and herons, while smaller birds flitter around the marsh plants, which include spatterdock, arrow arum, and broad-leaved arrowhead. An observation deck, from which you might spot beavers or bullfrogs, leads out into the marsh at mile marker 1.3.

The trail begins beside a creek, which expands into a marsh before you reach the beach.

About 0.5 mile later the trail ends at the shore of the Chesapeake Bay. The cliffs loom to the left, while tall, golden grasses sway in the bay breezes to your right. If you can, plan to come at low tide, because the beach is rather narrow, although even at high tide, there's enough room to explore the 100 yards of accessible shore. More than 600 species of fossils have been identified here. Shells, many containing fossils, are abundant, and you'll want to scour the sand for shark's teeth, the most common find. If you're lucky, you might find the monstrous three-inch tooth of a great white, but you're more likely to come across a tiny quarter-inch tooth. You're welcome to take your finds home with you.

As you head back along the same path, observe the forest opposite the marsh. Chestnut oaks, tulip poplars, hollies, sweet gums, American beeches, red maples, and Virginia pines rise along a slight embankment. If you walk quietly and look carefully, you might spot a fox cutting through the undergrowth of mountain laurel and blueberry.

Options

To turn the hike into a loop, follow the service road as it turns right off the red-blazed trail on your return trip, then make another right onto the orange-blazed trail. This 2.4-mile trail will lead you through forested wilderness. The trail will end at the service road, at which point you will turn right to return to the parking area by the pond.

Directions

From I-495, take exit 11A to merge onto southbound Route 4. Drive 21.5 miles, and then turn left on Route 765. The park entrance will be on your left after 1.5 miles.

Information and Contact

There is a fee of $5 per vehicle. Out-of-state visitors pay an additional $2. Maryland State Park passes are accepted. Dogs are not allowed in the park. The park is open from sunrise to sunset daily. A trail guide can be purchased from the Maryland Department of Natural Resources (410/260-8367, www.dnr.maryland.gov). For more information, contact Calvert Cliffs State Park, c/o Smallwood State Park, 2750 Sweden Point Road, Marbury, MD 20658, 301/743-7613, www.dnr.maryland.gov/publiclands/southern/calvertcliffs.asp.

6 GUNPOWDER NORTH-SOUTH CIRCUIT

BEST 🌙

Gunpowder Falls State Park, Hereford Area

Level: Moderate

Total Distance: 4.9-9.2 miles round-trip

Hiking Time: 2.5-4.5 hours

Elevation Gain: 500-820 feet

Summary: There's hardly a more scenic river walk to be found in the DC area than this hike along the Gunpowder.

Protecting the waters and valleys of the Big and Little Gunpowder Falls and the Gunpowder River, Gunpowder Falls State Park offers nearly 18,000 acres and more than 100 miles of trails to explore. This specific hike concentrates on the northernmost section along Big Gunpowder Falls, which is renowned for its trout fishing. The "falls" moniker is a bit misleading since there are no waterfalls. The name derives from the fact that the river lies on the fall line, the geologic drop from piedmont plateau to coastal plain. The "gunpowder" part of the name comes from the mills that once lined the river.

To reach the trailhead from the parking area on the west side of York Road, cross York Road, turn left and follow the road over the creek, and then scramble down a run of loose white rocks at an opening in the guardrail. Beginning rough and hilly, blue-blazed Gunpowder North Trail eases down to a flat, narrow path along the water. In spring, violets and spring beauties mix with Dutchman's breeches, wild columbines, trout lilies, and trailing arbutus. You may even spot the rare purple fringeless orchid or pink lady's slipper under the cover of hickory, oak, and mountain laurel.

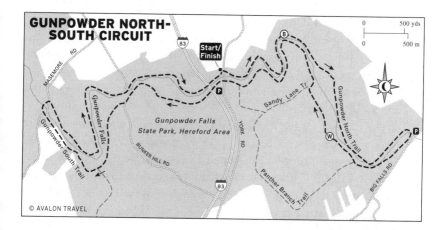

After about 1.0 mile, you'll cross a stream and reach Raven Rock Falls, which is more a downhill stream of water than a waterfall. As you continue, you'll pass towering schist formations, and then, turning away from the river, you must literally part a sea of skunk cabbage. Once you are riverside again, follow the Gunpowder's bend to a gravel road, and turn right to reach the Big Falls Bridge 2.4 miles from your starting point.

Cross the bridge and follow white-blazed Gunpowder South Trail upstream. In April, look for morels, a prized mushroom, growing on the trail's edge. In the first 0.5 mile, you'll cross two streams, reaching the Panther Branch

A footbridge provides transport across one of the trail's many streams.

Trail turnoff immediately after the second. Stay straight. The next 0.7-mile section leads uphill to a ridge, then brings you back down, though to a marsh and not the river. Peer across the marshland, and you might spot a rusted old-time car hidden within the stand of pines to your right. At the Sandy Lane Trail junction, stay straight. For the majority of the remaining 1.2 miles, you'll be at the water's edge, though you'll make one last ascent to a piney ridge before passing the other end of Panther Branch Trail and reaching York Road.

At this point, you can end your hike, or you can pick up the trail across the road. If you choose to continue, you'll travel on a ridge above the river for about 0.9 mile, descending just before Bunker Hill Road and the Camp Wood picnic area. Watch carefully for the blazes as you leave this area. The trail again goes up on the ridge, though there appears to be a path on the water. This path, however, is overgrown and leads through some treacherous rock stretches, although there is fantastic evergreen scenery. Pass the Mingo Forks Trail on your left at 0.6 mile, and then return to the water's edge for the last 0.6 mile to Masemore Road.

Traverse the river via the wrought-iron bridge. Once you reach the opposite bank, note the cypress knees that spring from the ground and look like tiny gnome dwellings. Then head back on blue-blazed Gunpowder North Trail, where riverside trees bear signs of beaver activity. On this side, the trail hugs the river for almost the entire 2.2 miles, straying only when you have to make a creek crossing. The trail ends as you cross under I-83 and scramble back up to York Road.

Options

North of Masemore Road, both the Gunpowder South and North Trails continue for another 0.7 mile to Falls Road. Beyond that, the South Trail extends an additional 1.5 miles to the dam at the Prettyboy Reservoir. Go ahead and hike those extra miles, thus covering every bit of these two trails.

Directions

Take I-95 north to northbound I-695. Drive 17.1 miles, then take exit 24 to merge onto northbound I-83. After 12.8 miles, take exit 27 to merge onto eastbound Route 137 and drive 0.4 mile. Turn left on York Road and proceed 1.3 miles to the parking area on the left side of the road just south of Big Gunpowder Falls.

Information and Contact

There is no fee. Dogs on leash are allowed. The park is open from sunrise to sunset daily. Maps are available for purchase from the Maryland Department of Natural Resources (410/260-8367, www.dnr.maryland.gov). For more information, contact Gunpowder Falls State Park, 2813 Jerusalem Road, P.O. Box 480, Kingsville, MD 21087, 410/592-2897, www.dnr.maryland.gov/publiclands/central/gunpowder.asp.

7 KING AND QUEEN'S SEAT LOOP   BEST **C**
Rocks State Park

Level: Moderate

Hiking Time: 1.5 hours

Total Distance: 3.2 miles round-trip

Elevation Gain: 900 feet

Summary: Discover why the Susquehanna Indians held these grounds sacred on a loop hike with a view.

Though Rocks State Park might not be the most original park name, it's certainly fitting. More sections of the trail than not are covered by rocks—small ones that jut out of the ground, large ones that act as stepping stones, and giant ones that literally pave the path. And then there is the huge rock outcropping that is the hike's prime attraction, the King and Queen's Seat. This isn't a long hike, but it still gets your heart beating.

KING AND QUEEN'S SEAT LOOP

Hop onto the white-blazed trail at the end of the parking lot, passing a second parking area before entering onto the 2.2-mile main loop. You'll be moving uphill, following the signs toward the Rock Ridge picnic area. At the turnoff for the orange-blazed trail, proceed straight, enjoying an unusually level section of trail. Continue straight again through the intersection with the red-blazed trail, which leads to Rock Ridge, beginning a downhill walk through maples and mountain laurels. The trail gets rockier in this section and switches back and forth to ease the descent.

Upon reaching an intersection with the blue-blazed trail, turn left for an out-and-back with an attached loop totaling about 1.0 mile. You'll continue to descend, stepping from large stone to large stone. Notice the proliferation of ferns growing under the tall oaks. As the trail levels out, you reach the loop, which circles over a branch of Deer Creek. Turn right, crossing the bridge over the creek and entering a picnic area. Pick up a copy of the nature trail brochure available here. The brochure, created by Girl Scouts, contains information that corresponds to numbered green metal posts and points out skunk cabbage, poison ivy, and other natural features. (The numbered wooden posts can be ignored. They correspond to an old brochure no longer available.)

The path isn't particularly obvious here, but you're making a counterclockwise loop, so head left, and you'll catch sight of the blazes and enter a wooded area. After a second crossing of the creek, you'll come to the end of the loop, at which point you must make the uphill climb back to the white-blazed trail. Just over 0.1 mile later, the trail branches into two blue-blazed paths. You can take either, although the upper branch is a bit shorter and not as steep as the lower branch. Regardless, you'll end up back on the white-blazed trail, which will lead you past the Collier Pit, where charcoal was manufactured from 1785 to 1886. Here the trail is composed almost entirely of very large, but primarily flat, boulders.

After passing over a road that leads up to the picnic area, you'll be treated to views of Deer Creek, a popular fishing and tubing spot. A short green-blazed trail leads to the water, but stay on the white-blazed trail to head toward the prized view near the end of the hike. Pass the steep purple-blazed trail on your left, proceeding instead to the King and Queen's Seat, a 190-foot rock promontory used by the Susquehanna Indians for ceremonial gatherings. You may have also seen it in the movie *Tuck Everlasting.* Go ahead and join the clambering crowds. The views of the creek valley and the rolling farmland are breathtaking, and it's immediately obvious why the Native Americans found this site to be so special. From the King and Queen's Seat, it's just a short downhill hike on the white-blazed trail back to the parking lot, so enjoy the view for as long as you'd like.

Options

Though only 19 feet tall, nearby Kilgore Falls is the second-highest natural vertical waterfall in Maryland. You can do a 1.0-mile round-trip hike to and from the falls. To get there, follow Route 24 north through the park, turning left onto Saint Mary's Road, and then turning right on Falling Branch Road. Park in the lot marked Rocks Falling Branch Area.

Directions

Drive north on I-95 to exit 77B to merge onto northbound Route 24. Remain on Route 24 for 15.3 miles, then turn left on Rocks Chrome Hill Road. The park

© THERESA DOWELL BLACKINTON

With dramatic rock structures all along the trail, it's easy to see how the park got its name.

office will be on your right after 0.2 mile. The trailhead is at the end of the parking lot.

Information and Contact

There is a fee of $2 per vehicle, weekdays; $3 per person, weekends and holidays. Out-of-state visitors pay an additional $2. Dogs on leash are allowed. Trails are open 9 A.M.–sunset daily Mar.–Oct., 10 A.M.–sunset daily Nov.–Feb. Maps are available from the mailbox outside the Rocks State Park Office (7 A.M.–3 P.M. weekdays year-round; 8 A.M.–4:30 P.M. weekends May–Sept.). For more information, contact Rocks State Park, 3318 Rocks Chrome Hill Road, Jarrettsville, MD 21084, 410/557-7994, www.dnr.maryland.gov/publiclands/central/rocks.asp.

8 SUSQUEHANNA RIDGE CIRCUIT   BEST **(**

Susquehanna State Park

Level: Easy/Moderate   **Total Distance:** 4.7 miles round-trip

Hiking Time: 2.25 hours   **Elevation Gain:** 940 feet

Summary: A wildflower lover's dream, this trail reveals just how beautiful nature can be.

This hike is composed of five trails that crisscross the forested and fielded area on the west bank of the Susquehanna River. Three trails make up the bulk of it, with the first two acting as transits. From the parking lot, follow the white blazes of the Land of Promise Trail to yellow-blazed Rock Run "Y" Trail, which you'll travel on for less than 0.2 mile before turning right immediately at a low stone wall and crossing Rock Run to join blue-blazed Farm Road Trail. Already in this short span, the variety of wildflowers is staggering. In spring, you'll see trilliums, violets, mayapples, and jack-in-the-pulpits at a minimum.

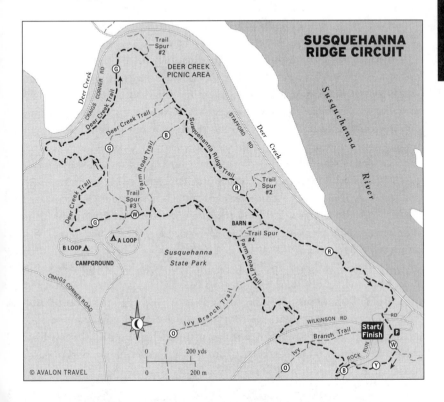

The trail goes left along the creek, then hits Rock Run Road. Pick up the trail across the road, heading uphill via log steps. After about 0.25 mile, you'll cross orange-blazed Ivy Branch Trail. A creek and road crossing follow, and you'll then find yourself in a tangled and overgrown forest. In early spring, daffodils brighten the path, and later honeysuckle perfumes the air. About a mile after turning onto the blue-blazed trail, you'll edge around a field on a single dirt track, passing the other end of the orange-blazed trail on your left and Trail Spur #4 on your right. Once back in the woods, you'll hike a short distance downhill, and then at about

Jack-in-the-pulpits are one of the many types of wildflowers you'll find at Susquehanna.

1.8 miles leave Farm Road Trail to cross the creek on your left via Trail Spur #3, marked with a white blaze. Proceed straight through two four-way intersections to connect to green-blazed Deer Creek Trail.

Eastern redbuds color the understory in spring, and pileated woodpeckers hammer away overhead. Mature oak and beech make up much of the forest through which you are winding up and down, and some of the specimens are downright magnificent, particularly a sprawling beech you'll encounter after about 0.6 mile on the green-blazed trail. Shortly beyond the massive beech, you'll pass a spur leading down to Deer Creek. Stay on the ridge, enjoying the views as well as the zebra swallowtail butterflies flittering around you. As you turn to head southeast parallel to the Susquehanna River, you'll pass Trail Spur #2 on your left. When you reach the Deer Creek Picnic Area at about 3.5 miles, you'll join red-blazed Susquehanna Ridge Trail and then intersect with the blue-blazed trail. They share the path for a brief moment, but then you'll break off on the red-blazed trail with a turn to the left.

The spring wildflower display as you head back to Rock Run is nothing short of phenomenal. Phlox and Virginia bluebells carpet the ground, their purple-blue flowers the dominant sight as far as you can see. After passing Trail Spur #4 on your right, the trail begins descending until you are once again at Rock Run, just a bit downstream from where you first crossed. At the road, turn left, and then turn right into the Archer House parking area to return to your car.

Options

If you'd like a closer look at the Susquehanna River, take a hike on the Lower Susquehanna Heritage Greenways Trail, which runs 2.7 miles one-way from Deer Creek to Conowingo Dam. From the hike described here, you can access the Greenway Trail via Trail Spur #2 off the Deer Creek Trail. Along the river, you can watch anglers cast for shad, herring, bass, and other freshwater fish; search the skies for kingfishers, gulls, ospreys, herons, and bald eagles; and enjoy more of the area's wildflowers.

Directions

Drive north on I-95 to exit 89 to merge onto westbound Route 155. Proceed 2.9 miles, then turn right on Route 161. After 0.4 mile, turn right on Rock Run Road and continue 2.8 miles to the driveway of Archer House on your right. Park in the back lot. The trailhead is at the end of the parking area.

Information and Contact

There is no fee. Dogs on leash are allowed. The park is open 9 A.M.–sunset daily. Maps are available for purchase from the Maryland Department of Natural Resources (410/260-8367, www.dnr.maryland.gov). For more information, contact Susquehanna State Park, 4122 Wilkinson Road, Havre de Grace, MD 21078, 410/557-7994, www.dnr.maryland.gov/publiclands/central/susquehanna.asp.

9 TURKEY POINT LIGHTHOUSE TRAIL
Elk Neck State Park

Level: Easy

Hiking Time: 0.75 hour

Total Distance: 2.0 miles round-trip

Elevation Gain: 100 feet

Summary: Take a pleasant stroll past fields where hawks feed to a historic lighthouse overlooking the Chesapeake Bay.

This easy and enjoyable walk leads you to the narrow tip of the Elk Neck peninsula, which stretches out into the Chesapeake Bay. The park is popular with campers, and in addition to hiking trails, Elk Neck State Park offers opportunities for boating, fishing, and swimming. Though the elevation gain on this hike is minimal, this small peninsula rises above sea level, with high bluffs making most of the beach area inaccessible. There are, however, a few spots where you can sink your toes into the sand.

From the parking lot, begin walking down the broad blue-blazed gravel road lined by fields that are backed by forest. In spring, enjoy the upside-down maroon flowers on the pawpaw trees along the road. In late summer, the pawpaw fruit ripens. This green-skinned, yellow-fleshed, tropical-tasting fruit is the largest edible fruit native to the United States.

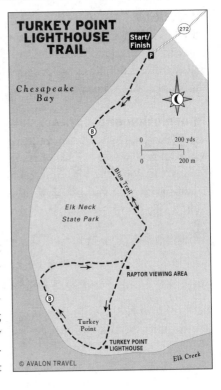

After about 0.75 mile, you'll reach a large open field that attracts raptors. The best time to view them is early in the morning after a cold front has moved through. You may spot a variety of vultures, buteos, falcons, eagles, accipiters, kites, and ospreys. A "hawk watch" bulletin board in the field provides information on the various hawks, as well as pictures, so even amateur birders can identify what they see. Data posted on the board reveal that more than 3,000 birds are seen in a typical year.

Once you're done bird watching, continue straight down the trail to the Turkey Point Lighthouse. This 35-foot structure was built in 1833 and is the highest

© THERESA DOWELL BLACKINTON

The trail loops around the bluff upon which Turkey Point Lighthouse stands.

lighthouse on the Chesapeake Bay thanks to the 100-foot bluff on which it stands. From April through November, the lighthouse is open 10 A.M.–4 P.M. on weekends. It's worth a peek inside. Make a careful arc along the cliff edge to drink in the views before continuing on the loop section of this trail by entering into the woods at the concrete post painted with the blue blazes that mark the lighthouse trail. You'll travel downhill until you're just above water level. A few spurs lead out to a seawall; from there you can watch the boats sailing and motoring around the bay.

Turning east, the trail passes over a creek and widens back into a gravel path before meeting up with the main trail at the raptor viewing area. Veer left—unless you want to take another moment to scout for birds—and then continue back to the parking lot.

Options

Four other short trails are located within Elk Neck State Park. If you'd like to learn to better identify trees, take a loop around the 0.75-mile white-blazed trail, where an interpretive brochure provides information on numbered tree species. The 4.0-mile orange-blazed trail is the longest of the park's offerings and leads you through a mature forest and around a marsh with an observation deck for examining a beaver lodge.

Directions

Drive north on I-95 to exit 100 to merge onto southbound Route 272. Follow

Route 272 for about 14 miles, until it ends in the trail parking lot at the end of the peninsula.

Information and Contact

There is no fee for access to the lighthouse. For other areas of the park, there is a fee of $3 per vehicle, weekdays; $3 per person, weekends and holidays. Out-of-state visitors pay an additional $2. Maryland State Park passes are accepted. Dogs on leash are allowed. Trails are open 9 A.M.–sunset daily. Maps are available for purchase from the Elk Neck State Park Office (8 A.M.–3 P.M. weekdays) or the Maryland Department of Natural Resources (410/260-8367, www.dnr.maryland.gov). For more information, contact Elk Neck State Park, 4395 Turkey Point Road, North East, MD 21901, 410/287-5333, www.dnr.maryland.gov/publiclands/central/elkneck.asp.

10 FERRY LANDING TRAIL

Wye Island

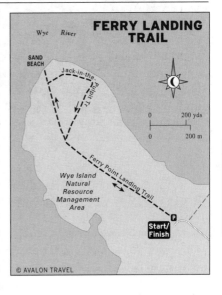

Level: Easy

Total Distance: 1.6 miles round-trip

Hiking Time: 0.75 hour

Elevation Gain: 0 feet

Summary: Pass under a canopy of Osage orange trees on your way to a small beach that once served as a ferry landing.

Surrounded by tidal rivers that empty into the Chesapeake Bay, Wye Island consists of 2,800 fielded and forested acres and 30 miles of shoreline awaiting exploration. An important migratory stop for waterfowl, Wye Island hosts Canada geese and a variety of ducks on its shores. Inland, songbirds such as the vireo nest. Turkey vultures are also commonly spotted scavenging in the island's open fields. Additionally, Wye Island is home to an endangered species, although it's not the most exciting one you can think of. In fact, it's a squirrel. The Delmarva fox squirrel, which you can distinguish from a gray squirrel by its larger size and more silver coat, has been dramatically affected by habitat loss and can now only be found in four counties.

Numerous short trails are scattered around the island and introduce visitors to the range of habitats on this small parcel of land. The hike outlined here is a great one for children because it is short, flat, and offers a fun diversion of a beach at the midpoint. It also features a tree species not found very frequently in this region—the Osage orange tree. Originally a hedgerow tree found in Texas and Oklahoma and named for the Osage Indians native to that area, the tree's dense, thorny branches grow low over the trail here, forming a canopy. As you begin your hike on the Ferry Point Landing Trail by walking down the broad, grassy path that was once an access road, you'll pass right under the trees. They are rather striking and have a slightly spooky look to them, as if they belong outside a haunted house.

© THERESA DOWELL BLACKINTON

The branches of Osage orange trees reach across the trail.

This section of the hike is a straight shot to the water, so just stay on the path and enjoy the pleasant walk. Keep an eye out for the fruit of the Osage, which is green, wrinkled, and nearly the size of a softball. It's not too often you find one intact, however, since squirrels love to munch on them. After about 0.6 mile, you'll approach the shore. Notice the second turnoff to the Jack-in-the-Pulpit Trail on your right, but continue on to the water. A hand-drawn ferry once ran from here to Bennett's Point across the river, providing the only means of accessing the island. Now it's a tiny beach where you can get your feet wet or let your dog splash around. A picnic table and a tire swing make this an ideal spot for lingering or a lunch break.

After you've had your fill of water time, head back toward the Jack-in-the-Pulpit Trail and follow it as it loops around for 0.5 mile. Look for the perennial from which the trail takes its name. Before the green and purple–striped hooded flower appears, the plant closely resembles poison ivy, so be careful not to mix them up. When the trail ends at the Ferry Point Landing Trail, make a left turn and proceed back to the parking lot to complete this short hike.

Options

Visit a 275-year-old holly tree—it's bigger than any holly you've ever seen—on the 1.5-mile Holly Tree Trail, which circles the edge of a field. Then connect to the Schoolhouse Woods Natural Trail, which leads you through an old-growth forest and a swampy area on your way to Grapevine Cove, a great spot for swimming.

Directions

Travel east on U.S. 50, continuing for 12.5 miles after you cross the Bay Bridge. Then turn right onto Carmichael Road and proceed for 4.4 miles, crossing onto the island via Wye Island Bridge. Follow Wye Island Road until it ends at the parking lot at the Ferry Landing Trail.

Information and Contact

There is no fee. Dogs on leash are allowed. Trails are open from sunrise to sunset daily. Maps are available for purchase from Wye Island Headquarters (8 A.M.–4:30 P.M. daily) or the Maryland Department of Natural Resources (410/260-8367, www.dnr.maryland.gov). For more information, contact Wye Island Natural Resources Management Area, 632 Wye Island Road, Queenstown, MD 21658, 410/827-7577, www.dnr.maryland.gov/publiclands/eastern/wyeisland.asp.

11 TUCKAHOE VALLEY CIRCUIT
Tuckahoe State Park

Level: Easy/Moderate

Hiking Time: 3.5 hours

Total Distance: 8.1 miles round-trip

Elevation Gain: 400 feet

Summary: A hike along a creek valley and across a small arboretum on the Eastern Shore.

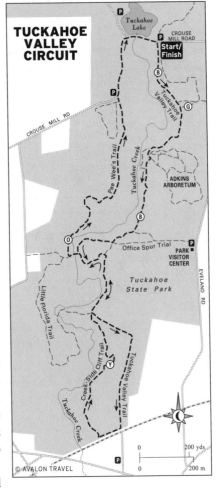

Most of what surrounds Tuckahoe State Park is flat, open farmland. This stretch of the Eastern Shore is rural in nature, so the park isn't so much an escape from development, as many parks are, but rather a break from agrarian scenery. Here you can trade fields for forests while exploring the park's 3,800 acres.

The three trails that make up this loop follow the north–south run of Tuckahoe Creek. Begin on blue-blazed Tuckahoe Valley Trail, which stays close to the creek for its first 3.5 miles before veering east and finishing with a stretch surrounded by tall pines. In the first section of this trail, only a narrow stand of trees separates you from open field; you quickly move into deeper forest, though it's never particularly dense. Plenty of sunlight reaches through the canopy, and you'll be treated to multiple wildflowers in the spring. The spring beauties—five white petals marked with bright pink lines—really stand out, and violets also grow with gusto.

Around 0.5 mile into the hike, you'll pass two turnoffs to the short Piney Branch Loop Trail, and 0.1 mile later, you'll cross two bridges over Piney Branch. Upon stepping off the bridge, you'll be on

Spring beauties are commonly found trailside.

the grounds of Adkins Arboretum. At all three trail intersections in the arboretum, you'll turn right to stay on the Valley Trail. Use the plant markers the arboretum provides to identify the beeches, birches, oaks, and sassafras surrounding you, and watch for tiny wood frogs. At 1.65 miles, you'll cross a small creek, thus exiting the arboretum.

Stay straight through the intersection with the Arboretum Spur Trail, arriving at a four-way intersection at about 2.2 miles. It's not immediately clear which way to proceed, but if you look closely, you'll see that the trails straight and to your left have blue triangle blazes. Follow instead the blue rectangle blazes to your right. Notice the bridge over the creek at 2.65 miles. You'll cross it on the return trip, but for now stay straight. At the intersection at 3.5 miles, stay left, hiking down a pined path until you reach the edge of the woods a mile later.

At this point, turn right and follow the railroad tracks for a short stretch before turning right onto yellow-blazed Creek-Side Cliff Trail. This 1.25-mile trail is elevated, thus providing a view of the valley below. The trail ends at an intersection with the Tuckahoe Valley and Turkey Hill Trails. Though you might be tempted to turn left onto the Turkey Hill Trail, resist. This trail ends at a high-water section of the creek. Instead return to the Valley Trail for about 0.75 mile, at which point you'll reach the bridge you passed earlier. Turn left, cross the creek, and then turn right onto orange-blazed Pee Wee's Trail. This 1.6-mile trail cuts through fields that are slowly becoming forested. Toward the end of the trail, you'll pass the Tuckahoe Equestrian Center on your left; you'll then parallel the southern branch of Crouse Mill Road. When the trail hits the road just across from Tuckahoe Lake, turn right to return to your car.

Options

There are 4.0 miles of paths to explore in **Adkins Arboretum** (12610 Eveland Road, P.O. Box 100, Ridgely, MD 21660, 410/634-2847, www.adkinsarboretum. org, 10 A.M.–4 P.M. daily, $5 adults, $2 youth 6–18, free children 5 and under). An audio tour can be borrowed from the visitors center.

Directions

Take eastbound U.S. 50 across the Bay Bridge. Continue north for an additional 18 miles on U.S. 301. Turn right on Ruthsburg Road. After 4.2 miles, turn right on Damsontown Road, proceed 2.1 miles, and then turn left on Crouse Mill Road. Park in the gravel lot on the right side of the road, directly across from the lake. The trailhead is just past the lot on the same side of the road.

Information and Contact

There is no fee. Dogs on leash are allowed. Trails are open from sunrise to sunset daily. Maps are available for purchase from the Maryland Department of Natural Resources (410/260-8367, www.dnr.maryland.gov). For more information, contact Tuckahoe State Park, 13070 Crouse Mill Road, Queen Anne, MD 21657, 410/820-1668, www.dnr.maryland.gov/publiclands/eastern/tuckahoe.asp.

VIRGINIA'S PIEDMONT AND COASTAL PLAINS

© THERESA DOWELL BLACKINTON

BEST HIKES

As the DC population continues on a path of seemingly endless growth, the suburbs expand ever farther outward. Consider that Richmond, only two hours south of DC down I-95, is also growing in girth, and you'll appreciate how precious the green space in this commuter's corridor is. But don't blame the dearth of public land entirely on modern life. As far back as the 17th and 18th centuries, royal land grants moved tracts of green space into private hands. Even so, this area still has a fine share of forests, parks, refuges, and former battlefields awaiting exploration.

In this strip of Virginia, the piedmont, an area characterized by low, rolling hills that range 200-1,000 feet above sea level, meets the coastal plain, an area adjacent to the sea marked by flat, low-lying lands. At this juncture, you'll find the region's fall line, a geomorphic feature that played a determining role in the settlement of the United States. Where a river crosses over a fall line, rapids and waterfalls occur, which naturally prevents boats from traveling any farther inland. Thus cities — such as Richmond and DC — were situated at the site of the fall line; later, interstate highways such as I-95 were built along them.

Today, while making a loop around Belle Isle, just a few blocks from downtown Richmond, you'll hike alongside the fall line rapids. As you watch kayakers try to surf this urban white water, you'll understand the difficulty early settlers faced in traveling these waterways, and as you pass the ruins of old factories, you'll see how the power generated by the rapids served as a boon to industry. At Prince William Forest Park, an enclave of nature among suburban sprawl, you can literally walk across the fall line, noticing the way the terrain changes as you move away from it – in one section the trail is flat and sandy, in another it is undulating and dirt packed.

Though many of the parks within this region are closely surrounded by human development, they host a remarkable array of wildlife. In fact, for a chance to spot the majestic bald eagle, this area of Virginia is hard to beat. Caledon State Park, Mason Neck State Park, and Mason Neck National Wildlife Refuge – all located on the banks of the Potomac River – host large numbers of eagles, acting as breeding grounds, fledgling nurseries, and even year-round nesting sites.

With the mountains of the Blue Ridge rising to the west and the shore beckoning to the east, this area sandwiched in between is often overlooked. For hikers, that's not a terrible thing. Even at some of the more popular parks – such as the award-winning Virginia state parks with lakes, beaches, and large campgrounds – the trails remain relatively untraversed. Additionally, the gentle terrain that marks the piedmont and coastal plains means that the region offers hikes for all abilities, ranging from short but scenic loops perfect for family outings to the magnificent 18 miles of the Bull Run-Occoquan Trail that will satisfy those who usually prefer the challenges of the mountains. So get out and blaze your way through the piedmont and riparian forests native to the region, enjoy a picnic lunch on a river bluff overlooking the Potomac, dip your toes into a secluded stream while taking a rest, or walk in contemplative silence across important Civil War sites.

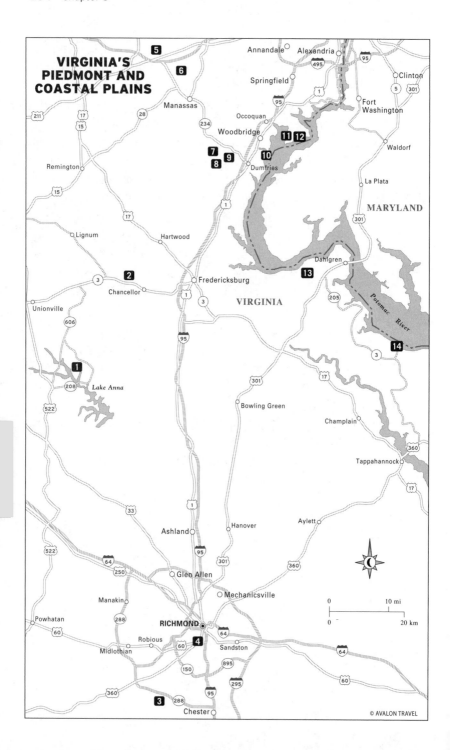

VIRGINIA'S
PIEDMONT AND
COASTAL PLAINS

© AVALON TRAVEL

TRAIL NAME	LEVEL	DISTANCE	TIME	ELEVATION	FEATURES	PAGE
1 Gold Hill Circuit	Moderate	7.0 mi rt	3.5 hr	600 ft		266
2 Chancellorsville History Trail	Easy	4.0 mi rt	2 hr	175 ft		269
3 Beaver Lake Trail	Easy	2.6 mi rt	1.25 hr	175 ft		272
4 Belle Isle	Easy	1.5 mi rt	0.75 hr	75 ft		275
5 First Manassas Trail	Easy/Moderate	5.4 mi rt	2.5 hr	350 ft		278
6 Bull Run–Occoquan Trail	Butt-Kicker	17.75 mi one-way	8.75 hr	1,600 ft		281
7 Farms to Forest Trail	Easy	2.7 mi rt	1.25 hr	250 ft		284
8 South Valley Circuit	Moderate	9.0 mi rt	4 hr	1,000 ft		287
9 North Valley Circuit	Moderate	6.8 mi rt	3 hr	1,000 ft		290
10 Lee's Woods Trail	Easy	2.0 mi rt	1 hr	200 ft		293
11 Woodmarsh Trail	Easy	3.0 mi rt	1.5 hr	100 ft		296
12 Belmont Bay	Easy	3.3 mi rt	1.5 hr	150 ft		299
13 Caledon Loop	Easy	4.0 mi rt	2 hr	530 ft		302
14 Turkey Neck Trail	Easy	2.5 mi rt	1.25 hr	600 ft		305

1 GOLD HILL CIRCUIT
Lake Anna State Park

Level: Moderate

Total Distance: 7.0 miles round-trip

Hiking Time: 3.5 hours

Elevation Gain: 600 feet

Summary: Explore the overlooked trails running through the piedmont forests that surround a popular lake.

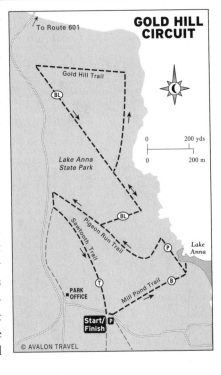

Built in 1971 to serve as a water coolant for the nearby Dominion Power nuclear plant, Lake Anna has been converted by the state of Virginia into a popular park. Though the lake can get rather crowded with swimmers, boaters, and anglers on a summer day, the trails are usually quiet, shared only by a handful of hikers, horseback riders, and bikers.

Blue-blazed Mill Pond Trail begins opposite the parking area. A mix of dirt and sand, the trail leads through hardwood and Virginia pine. Holly thrives in the sandy soil, and sassafras joins it in the midstory. Mostly flat with a few short uphills, Mill Pond Trail reaches an intersection in a power line clearing after 0.7 mile. Continue straight through it for 0.2 mile to reach a cove on Lake Anna where a water-powered gristmill once stood.

Retrace your steps back to the clearing, and then turn right onto purple-blazed Pigeon Run Trail. For 0.3 mile, you'll edge along the power line clearing, up and down steeply graded hills covered in loose gravel. Queen Anne's lace, ferns, and blackberries thrive here, while redbuds and dogwoods line the forest's edge. A finger of the lake reaches up, and you may see turtles sunbathing on logs. Named for the passenger pigeons that lived in the area before becoming extinct, this trail now welcomes warblers, cardinals, finches, blue jays, and other songbirds.

Just beyond the third uphill, follow the trail as it turns left, entering the woods. About 0.7 mile after entering the woods, you'll reach a junction on

© THERESA DOWELL BLACKINTON

Turtles sun themselves on a log in Lake Anna.

your right with black-blazed Gold Hill Trail. Turn here, and continue 0.3 mile through the woods before again entering into the clearing containing power lines and turning left. Trek up and down the hills for 0.3 mile, then turn right into another section of woods. In the 1800s, this area was referred to as Gold Hill because the Goodwin Gold Mine was located here, but now little evidence of shaft mining remains.

After 0.9 mile, you'll reach a junction; here you'll turn left onto a broad path and hike 0.4 mile back to the clearing. Turn left again, enjoying the blackberries, which bloom in July, as you hike 1.2 miles back to the point where Gold Hill Trail turns into the woods on your right. You'll reconnect with Pigeon Run Trail after an additional 0.3 mile. Turn right and continue 0.4 mile until Pigeon Run Trail ends at tan-blazed Sawtooth Trail. Turn left, walking beside the park road for a short stretch before the trail ducks back into the woods. After 0.9 mile, Sawtooth Trail crosses the road on which you are parked. Turn left on the road and return to your car after 0.2 mile.

Options

Turn this into an 11.7-mile hike (and cover nearly all the trail mileage in the park) by continuing straight on Sawtooth Trail as it extends about 1.2 miles to green-blazed Glenora Trail. Follow Glenora Trail for about 1.1 miles through mixed forest to the remains of Pigeon Plantation, then backtrack to the junction with silver-blazed Big Woods Trail and turn right. This 1.2-mile trail skirts the lake in sections and then connects to yellow-blazed Turkey Run Trail. Turn left onto it and hike 1.2 miles back to the parking lot.

Directions

Take southbound I-95 to exit 118 for westbound Route 606. Turn right at Mudd Tavern Road, which becomes Morris Road. After 5.0 miles stay straight as the road becomes Route 208. Drive an additional 11 miles, and then turn right on Lawyers Road. The entrance to Lake Anna State Park is on your left after 3.3 miles. Follow State Park Road to the park office, and then turn left on the road just past it. Trailhead parking will be on your right.

Information and Contact

There is a fee of $4 per vehicle on weekdays, $5 on weekends and holidays. Virginia State Park passes are accepted. Dogs on leash are allowed. The park is open from sunrise to sunset daily. Maps are available at the entrance station. For more information, contact Lake Anna State Park, 6800 Lawyers Road, Spotsylvania, VA 22551, 540/854-5503, www.dcr.virginia.gov/state_parks/lak.shtml.

2 CHANCELLORSVILLE HISTORY TRAIL

BEST ☾

Fredericksburg and Spotsylvania National Military Park

Level: Easy

Total Distance: 4.0 miles round-trip

Hiking Time: 2 hours

Elevation Gain: 175 feet

Summary: Traverse the heavily forested grounds upon which the bloody Battle of Chancellorsville, an important Confederate victory, occurred.

Within the boundaries of Fredericksburg and Spotsylvania National Military Park, four Civil War battles took place. The first, the Battle of Fredericksburg, occurred in December 1862. The last two, the Battle of the Wilderness and the Battle of Spotsylvania Court House, took place in May 1864. In between, the Battle of Chancellorsville played out in the forests of a quiet crossroads town. It was at Chancellorsville that General Robert

E. Lee won his greatest victory, forcing an army twice the size of his own to retreat, and it was also here that the legendary General Stonewall Jackson was accidentally shot by his own men, resulting in an injury that would lead to his death. On this hike, you'll cover the ground over which the troops fought on the decisive day of May 3, 1863.

The hike begins with a short 0.4-mile loop that isn't connected with the rest of the trail. Walk straight across Bullock Road from the battle painting outside the visitors center to the narrow dirt path, where a sign indicates the trail begins. In less than 0.1 mile, the trail splits. Follow the loop to the left, where you'll encounter the first of 11 signs that contain historical information about the battle along with quotes from the men who fought and survived. This sign directs you to look at the earthworks, or trenches, that served as fortified positions for the armies. Once you know what to look for, you'll find yourself noticing the trenches all along the hike.

After completing this short loop, walk 50 yards down the parking lot to where the trail picks up on the left side. You'll proceed for about 0.25 mile before once again reaching a split that creates a loop. This time go right, following the dark blue blazes that lead you through the hardwood forest thick with underbrush. As you read the descriptions of breakthroughs, counterattacks, and burning forest, take the time to look around and imagine what it must have been like 150 years ago. Though the area is quiet and peaceful now (except for the faint, but always present, sound of cars on Route 3), during the battle, the woods here were extremely dangerous. Spotting an enemy was difficult, as was maintaining a line, because the heavy forest growth severely limited sight lines.

Signs provide historical information that brings the battle to life.

When you reach the seventh trail sign, you'll emerge into a clearing with Route 3 directly in front of you. Hug the tree line until you reach Ely's Ford Road, then observe the ruins of the Chancellorsville Inn, which was burned during battle. In this area, Confederate troops attacked Union troops for five hours, during which time 17,500 men were killed, wounded, or captured. That's one man every second. Across Ely's Ford Road, there are two options for continuing on. Take the near path through the woods rather than the far path, which involves walking along a road. The two converge before you reach stop eight.

As you continue the loop, note the large stand of pines, the fern ground cover, and the increased amount of tangled undergrowth. There is no doubt that this was a difficult landscape to maneuver across. After reaching stop 11, you'll reconnect with the spur that leads back to the parking lot. If you didn't stop in the visitors center before your hike, you may want to check out the displays before you leave.

Options

Two shorter trails, McLaws Trail and Hazel Grove Fairview, take in additional sites related to the Battle of Chancellorsville. You can get interpretive maps and directions from the visitors center.

Directions

Drive south on I-95 to exit 130B to merge onto westbound Route 3. After about

8.5 miles, turn right at the entrance to Chancellorsville Battlefield. Park in the visitors center lot.

Information and Contact

There is no fee. Dogs on leash are allowed. The park grounds are open from dawn to dusk daily. Trail maps are available at the visitors center (8 A.M.–6 P.M. daily June–Aug., 9 A.M.–5 P.M. daily Sept.–May, except New Year's Day, Thanksgiving, and Christmas). For more information, contact Fredericksburg and Spotsylvania National Military Park, 120 Chatham Lane, Fredericksburg, VA 22405, 540/786-2880, www.nps.gov/frsp.

3 BEAVER LAKE TRAIL
Pocahontas State Park

Level: Easy

Hiking Time: 1.25 hours

Total Distance: 2.6 miles round-trip

Elevation Gain: 175 feet

Summary: Loop around a lake that is in the process of becoming a freshwater marsh.

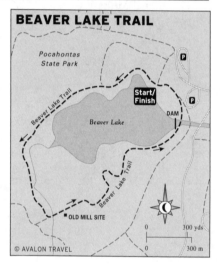

Constructed by the Civilian Conservation Corps (CCC) during the Great Depression, Pocahontas State Park was originally named the Swift Creek Recreational Demonstration Area. Built near urban centers, recreational demonstration areas were multipurpose: They took land that was less than ideal for farming and turned it into usable land, and they provided outdoor recreation options for those without the money or time to travel to national parks. Turned over to the state of Virginia in 1946 and renamed after the famed Powhatan Indian said to have saved John Smith's life, Pocahontas State Park, at more than 7,600 acres, is Virginia's largest state park.

To begin this hike, which circles around Beaver Lake, take the trail on the right side of the Civilian Conservation Corps Museum, and then turn left to travel a short distance along Old Mill Bicycle Trail. Directly behind the museum, you'll see a sign indicating that Beaver Lake Trail turns off to the right. Follow this sandy path downhill through a forest of tall hardwoods and pines.

After 0.13 mile, you'll reach the lake's edge, where you will turn right. But first venture out onto a small dock, taking in the fact that Beaver Lake is a bit of a misnomer. Due to inadequate erosion control, the lake is slowly transforming into a freshwater marsh. Only a few feet deep in most places, the lake's surface is consumed by water lilies, leaving only small patches of open water. After blooming, these lilies die and sink to the bottom, where they, along with leaves from the surrounding trees, build up.

For the first part of the hike, the trail, which is well marked with wooden

A great blue heron wades among the water lilies.

signposts, edges the lake, and you have multiple opportunities to enjoy the view from the bank or small piers. Admire the water lilies, and the herons that frequent the lake, and search for the frogs whose calls you'll certainly hear.

At the end of the lake, the trail continues along Third Branch, passing over wetlands via a boardwalk. In spring, jack-in-the-pulpits and spring beauties bloom underneath a canopy of sycamores, pawpaws, and ironwoods. After 1.3 miles, you'll reach an intersection with Third Branch Trail. Stay on Beaver Lake Trail, crossing over tiny Third Branch and passing the site of an old mill.

Continue back down the other side of the lake. At first, the trail will be some distance from the water, but then it returns to the bank and approaches the dam. Cross over the spillway, which will put you on the paved Spillway Trail for a short bit. Turn left to return to the water's edge. This is the last section of lake to be encroached upon, and you may spot an angler hoping to reel in a channel catfish, crappie, sunfish, or largemouth bass. From here, Beaver Lake Trail will lead back to the connector trail that returns you to the Civilian Conservation Corps Museum parking lot.

Options

Before or after your hike, spend some time in the small Civilian Conservation Corps Museum, which contains artifacts and information about the Depression-era organization responsible for the creation of many of our national and state parks. You'll come away with a greater appreciation of President Franklin D. Roosevelt's vision as well as the hard work of the three million men who, over the course of nine years, played a vital role in conserving America's natural resources.

Directions

Take southbound I-95 to exit 62 to merge onto northbound Route 288. After 6.3 miles, exit onto eastbound Route 10. Drive 1.8 miles, and then turn right onto Beach Road. Turn right onto State Park Road after 4.1 miles and proceed to the entrance station. Then follow the signs to the Civilian Conservation Corps Museum and park in the lot there.

Information and Contact

There is a fee of $4 per vehicle on weekdays, $5 on weekends and holidays. Virginia State Park passes are accepted. Dogs on leash are allowed. Trails are open from sunrise to sunset daily. Maps are available at the entrance station. For more information, contact Pocahontas State Park, 10301 State Park Road, Chesterfield, VA 23832, 804/796-4255, www.dcr.virginia.gov/state_parks/poc.shtml.

4 BELLE ISLE
James River Park

Level: Easy

Total Distance: 1.5 miles round-trip

Hiking Time: 0.75 hour

Elevation Gain: 75 feet

Summary: Though short, this hike packs in the history and geology lessons, and provides plenty of opportunities for water play.

Situated in the James River, in the heart of Richmond, Belle Isle is a haven for those who like to enjoy the outdoors without losing sight of the city. But it hasn't always been a place for fun. During its storied history, it has served as the site of an infamous Civil War prison and hosted a slew

of industrial enterprises. You'll witness evidence of this backstory on a tour around the isle.

From the parking lot, take the suspension footbridge that runs underneath the Robert E. Lee Bridge. This undulating path will deposit you at the end of the isle, in front of an open field where the Civil War prison once stood. Though numbers are disputed, estimates indicate that nearly 8,000 Union soldiers were once held here, with about 1,000 of them dying from starvation and disease.

Pass the prison site, and then stay to the right as the trail branches just before a mound of boulders. A mix of trees, vines, shrubs, and wildflowers surrounds you. In spring, you may spot aster, mayapple, spiderwort, wild rose, spring beauty, and buttercup. Virginia creeper covers the ground, and in summer the orange flowers of the trumpet vine bloom, as do wild hydrangea, rose mallow, and ivy-leaved morning glory. The fernlike leaves and feathery pink flowers of the mimosa tree add variety to the forest of sycamore, river birch, box elder, pawpaw, red maple, and green ash, but unfortunately the mimosa is an invasive species.

To your left, a hill makes up the interior of the island, and mountain bikers love to explore the small spur trails leading up it. To your right, the James River runs shallow and is littered with huge boulders that create Hollywood Rapids. These fall-line rapids, named for the cemetery across the river, create one of the best urban white-water paddling sites in the United States.

Just past the ramp leading down to the main beach area (crowded on any

The trail is dotted with ruins from manufacturing activity that took place on Belle Isle before it became a recreational spot.

summer day), you'll reach a quarry pond on your left. Where granite blocks were once carved, you can now cast a line for sunfish, catfish, and bass, or try to spot turtles, frogs, toads, snakes, skinks, and salamanders.

Beyond the quarry pond, the trail turns to the left, proceeding across the top of the island and then back down the other side. In this stretch, you'll pass the ruins of a hydroelectric plant, which created electricity used by the Richmond trolley system from 1903 to 1964, as well as the facade of the 19th-century Belle Isle Rolling, Milling, and Silting Manufactory, which produced nails, wire, and horseshoes.

At an intersection just beyond the remaining wall of the manufactory, you have a decision to make. You can either turn left, continuing on the broad, gravel path straight back to the bridge, or you can turn right, proceed a short distance to the south-end bridge, and then make a left just before the bridge onto a footpath. If you choose the footpath, you'll meander through a wooded area near the shore, perhaps spotting a great blue heron. You'll then pass behind the ruins of the Old Dominion Iron and Steel Company, touch the very end of the isle, and finally return to the footbridge.

Options

While you are in the area, enjoy the other parts of James River Park. Pony Pasture is a popular swimming spot, and the Wetlands offers good bird-watching opportunities. Visit the park's website for more information, directions, and maps.

Directions

Take southbound I-95 to exit 76B toward U.S. 1. Turn left on West Leigh Street, and then make an immediate right onto southbound U.S. 1. After 0.6 mile, turn left on West Cary Street. Drive 0.6 mile, and then turn right onto South 5th Street. After 0.3 mile, turn right on Tredegar Street and proceed about 0.2 mile to the parking lot under the overpass.

Information and Contact

There is no fee. Dogs on leash are allowed. The park is open from sunrise to sunset daily. A rough map of the island is available on the park website. For more information, contact Friends of the James River Park, P.O. Box 4453, Richmond, VA 23220, 804/646-8911, www.jamesriverpark.org.

5 FIRST MANASSAS TRAIL

Manassas National Battlefield Park

Level: Easy/Moderate

Total Distance: 5.4 miles round-trip

Hiking Time: 2.5 hours

Elevation Gain: 350 feet

Summary: Walk the forests and fields where Union and Confederate troops met for the first time in the Civil War.

On July 21, 1861, Union and Confederate troops, each certain of quick victory, met for the first time in the Civil War on the grounds of Manassas (also known as Bull Run). What resulted was 10 hours of intense fighting, 900 men dead, and the realization that the war would be long and bloody. On this hike, you'll visit the bridge where the battle's first shots were fired and traverse the land where the fighting raged.

Begin your hike at the First Manassas Trail sign at the end of the parking lot.

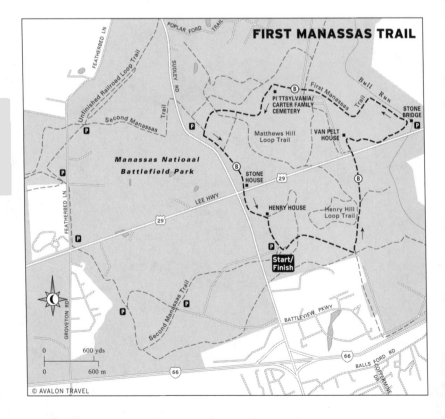

© THERESA DOWELL BLACKINTON

The Stone House is one of only two Civil War-era buildings still remaining at the battlefield.

Head out into the field, walking toward a line of cannons and passing a statue of Stonewall Jackson on your left. Just beyond the artillery, a sign points you onward through the tree line on a wide trail. The trail quickly splits; stay to the right, following the blue blazes, which will mark the entire route. Additional signposts mark critical junctions.

At the 0.5-mile mark, you'll reach an intersection in a clearing. Turn left and follow the trail, which straddles the line between the young forest on one side and meadows on the other. A bridle trail also proceeds this way; stay on the wider of the two trails. After about 0.3 mile, you'll notice the blazes veer off to the left; this is a small detour leading to a bridge over a creek. Take the detour, though in all but the wettest months, you could continue straight ahead and simply step over the creek. The two trails come together just after the creek. Beyond the creek, continue 0.3 mile through open meadow to U.S. 29.

After carefully crossing U.S. 29, continue straight along the field edge, then follow the trail around a curve to the spot where the Van Pelt House once stood. A signboard provides historical information. From the house site, turn right and proceed toward the Stone Bridge, 0.5 mile away. You'll go through an open field and then across a boardwalk, which reaches nearly all the way back to U.S. 29. The trail then becomes gravel and turns left, paralleling the road and taking you to the Stone Bridge. You can cross it if you wish, though you'll have to cross back to continue the trail, which follows Bull Run. Wildflowers are particularly pretty here in the spring.

When you reach a small footbridge after about 0.3 mile, don't cross it, but turn left and proceed uphill to an intersection with a sign pointing left toward Carter Cemetery. Take the left turn and then an immediate right turn at the next intersection, continuing through a field. After crossing a gravel path, you'll enter a young forest. You'll quickly reach the Carter Cemetery and the ruins of a home, Pittsylvania. Continue along the blue-blazed trail, keeping an eye out for deer. About 0.5 mile after the cemetery, the trail will exit into a field.

Charge straight up Matthews Hill to the line of cannons, then turn left to follow the trampled grass path as it parallels Sudley Road. At the intersection of Sudley Road and U.S. 29, stop at the Stone House, which was mentioned in multiple Civil War diaries and used as a field hospital.

To complete the hike, cross the street at the light, head uphill to the Henry Hill House, and then proceed to the visitors center.

Options

A second battle was fought at Manassas in August 1862, and a 6.2-mile trail covers the grounds on which it occurred. You can hike it on its own or connect the two trails into one large loop by turning right instead of left at the top of Matthews Hill and following the red blazes.

Directions

Take westbound I-66 to exit 43B, then merge right onto northbound U.S. 29. Drive 1.9 miles to the entrance to Manassas National Battleground Park, which will be on your right.

Information and Contact

There is a fee of $3 per person, which covers admission for three days; youth under 16 are free. A $20 annual pass is available. America the Beautiful passes are accepted. Dogs on leash are allowed. The park is open from dawn to dusk daily. Maps are available at the visitors center (8:30 A.M.–5 P.M. daily, except Thanksgiving and Christmas). For more information, contact Manassas National Battlefield Park, 12521 Lee Highway, Manassas, VA 20109, 703/361-1339, www.nps.gov/mana.

6 BULL RUN-OCCOQUAN TRAIL BEST ◐
Bull Run Regional Park/Fountainhead Regional Park

🏃 🏹 🚴 🌲 🏊 🦌

Level: Butt-Kicker

Hiking Time: 8.75 hours

Total Distance: 17.75 miles one-way

Elevation Gain: 1,600 feet

Summary: Find unexpected solitude among the splendid forest and waterway scenery of this long trail.

Running nearly 18 miles along the banks of Bull Run and the Occoquan Reservoir in Fairfax County, the Bull Run–Occoquan Trail is a gem, with scenery that rivals the best in the region. Its length, if traversed in one outing, will challenge serious hikers, but the option to break it up into sections makes it broadly accessible.

Begin at the northwest trailhead in Bull Run Regional Park, which is known for its springtime bluebell displays. From the parking lot, turn left and walk about 150 yards. A signboard on the right side of the road marks the trailhead, and the blue-blazed trail starts over a footbridge. Raised wooden trail carries you over marshy areas to Cub Run, where you might spot an otter at play. Upon reaching Cub Run, turn right, and hike along Cub Run to its mouth at Bull Run, about 1.0 mile into the hike. Keep an eye out for deer and other wildlife in this stretch and all along the trail. At the trail junction, turn left, cross over Cub Run, and continue downstream along Bull Run.

© THERESA DOWELL BLACKINTON

The trail stays close to the water for most of its length.

In this section, the trail becomes hillier. After crossing under a railroad bridge (after already passing under two road bridges), it also becomes rockier. It feels quite wild and solitary, not at all like you're in Virginia's most populous county. At this point, you reach the mouth of Popes Head Creek, which is crossed via concrete stepping stones. You're now in Hemlock Overlook Regional Park. Mountain laurel is particularly noticeable here. A yellow-blazed spur trail leads right to the parking area, but there are no other facilities at this park, so continue straight along Bull Run.

Early on in this next section, you'll pass a clearing and the ruins of a hydroelectric plant. For about another mile, you'll stay close to Bull Run. Then the trail turns left and proceeds uphill into the woods for another mile before returning to open field. At milepost 10.8, you'll cross a creek and then find yourself facing playing fields. Spot the post to your right and walk toward it, then continue to follow the posts until the trail turns right and goes back into the forest. You'll make a sharp turn to your left and then proceed uphill. Notice the hemlocks growing here. The trail soon takes you back to Bull Run, and you'll reach the Bull Run Marina.

To begin the last section, you must follow the marina entrance road to Old Yates Road, which you must cross before picking up the trail on the opposite side. Proceed downhill and then left to continue along Bull Run, which has

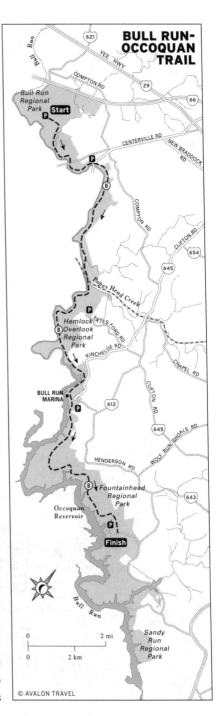

now met up with the Occoquan Reservoir. For a short stretch of about 0.5 mile, you'll remain along the water. The trail then turns into the woods, where it stays for the last 6.0 miles, leading up and down hills, crossing creeks, and offering occasional views of the reservoir. Finally, after 17.75 miles of hiking, you'll emerge in the parking area at Fountainhead Regional Park, exhausted but amazed at the beauty and tranquility hidden among the suburbs.

Options
This trail can be broken up into three main sections: a 6.64-mile section from Bull Run Regional Park to Hemlock Overlook Regional Park; a 4.66-mile section from Hemlock Overlook Regional Park to Bull Run Marina; and a 6.45-mile section from Bull Run Marina to Fountainhead Regional Park. Each can be done as a one-way shuttle hike or as a long out-and-back.

Directions
Because this is a one-way hike, you'll need to park cars at both ends or have someone pick you up. To reach Bull Run Regional Park, take westbound I-66 to exit 52. Turn right onto U.S. 29, and drive 2.1 miles to Bull Run Post Office Road. Turn left, drive 1.1 miles, continue straight onto Bull Run Drive, and proceed to the parking lot at the water park. To reach Fountainhead Regional Park, take southbound I-95 to exit 163. Turn right onto Lorton Road and drive 1.3 miles, then continue onto Furnace Road and drive 0.9 mile. Turn right onto Ox Road, drive 1.3 miles, and then turn left on Hampton Road. Drive 3.2 miles to the park entrance on your left.

Information and Contact
There is no fee. Dogs on leash are allowed. The trail is open from dawn to dusk daily. Maps are available from the camp store (8 A.M.–8 P.M. daily) at Bull Run Regional Park. For more information, contact Northern Virginia Regional Park Authority, 5400 Ox Road, Fairfax Station, VA 22039, 703/352-5900, www.nvrpa.org.

⑦ FARMS TO FOREST TRAIL   BEST ◖

Prince William Forest Park

🦌 🛬 ✋ 🐕 👨‍👩‍👧

Level: Easy   **Total Distance:** 2.7 miles round-trip

Hiking Time: 1.25 hours   **Elevation Gain:** 250 feet

Summary: A short hike that's long on interesting plant and animal life.

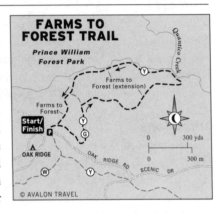

In 1933, when the Civilian Conservation Corps (CCC) created the Chopawamsic Recreational Demonstration Area—now Prince William Forest Park—forested area was in short supply. Small family farms that produced just enough for the subsistence of those who worked them dotted the land. The communities of Hickory Ridge and Batestown housed local laborers, most of whom toiled in the Cabin Branch Pyrite Mine; smaller numbers found employment on neighboring Quantico Marine Corps Base. The CCC worked hard to begin the process of returning the region to its natural state, and today, even though development encroaches, the park provides a welcome escape from the suburbs.

From the Farms to Forest trailhead, which is opposite the parking lot, follow the green and yellow blazes as they lead through a mixed forest of beech, black tupelo, oak, maple, and Virginia pine. In the midstory, holly trees dominate, and a mess of shrubs and blueberry bushes remind you that the forest here is not old. Where the trail splits after 0.1 mile, turn right and continue for 0.6 mile to where the extension trail branches off the main loop. Stay to the right, following the yellow blazes.

You're now heading toward Quantico Creek, and you can't help but notice how wet this area is. Fungi are abundant. Look for tall white mushrooms, tiny bright orange mushrooms, and mushrooms in just about every color and size in between. Bracket fungi grow from the trees, with the turkey tail fungus—perfectly described by its name—particularly prominent. As you approach the creek, after about 0.8 mile on the extension trail, New York ferns take over. The creek runs to your right, but if you look closely, you'll realize it's barely flowing. Continue your hike, and you'll soon realize why.

Signs of extensive beaver activity are everywhere, and the dams of these animals,

New York ferns grow dense along the trail.

which you may spot early in the morning or late at night, have stopped up the creek, creating a marsh. You have a good chance of sighting wildlife in this area. Salamanders scamper down fallen trees, great blue herons stand regally in the water, and snakes coil up in the shade during the heat of the day. You'll also hear the hammering of the pileated woodpecker, the call of the blue jay, and the mimicry of the brown thrasher. If you're interested in identifying plant and animal species you might see on this hike, stop in the visitors center before you hit the trail and take advantage of the multiple informative brochures with pictures that they offer.

For nearly a mile, you'll walk alongside Quantico Creek. You'll then reach an intersection with the first loop, marked by both yellow and green blazes. Continue straight onto this loop, keeping an eye out in spring for some of the park's wildflowers—wild geraniums, bluets, trilliums, and bloodroots, among others. At the end of the loop, turn right and return to the trailhead 0.3 mile after leaving the extension trail.

Options

If you're looking for a very short hike, you can just do the 1.0-mile inner loop of this hike. You'll miss the section along the creek, but you'll still be treated to a variety of tree species, fungi, wildflowers, and wildlife.

Directions

Take southbound I-95 to exit 150B to merge onto westbound Route 619. Drive

0.4 mile, and then turn right on Park Entrance Road. Follow Scenic Drive as it loops around the park toward the campground. Turn right on Oak Ridge Road, and park in the lot just outside Oak Ridge Campground.

Information and Contact

There is a fee of $5 per vehicle, which covers admission for seven consecutive days. A $20 annual pass is available. America the Beautiful passes are accepted. Dogs on leash are allowed. Trails are open from sunrise to sunset daily. Maps are available at the entrance station and visitors center (9 A.M.–5 P.M. daily, except New Year's Day, Thanksgiving, and Christmas). For more information, contact Prince William Forest Park, 18100 Park Headquarters Road, Triangle, VA 22172, 703/221-7181, www.nps.gov/prwi.

8 SOUTH VALLEY CIRCUIT   BEST ☾

Prince William Forest Park

Level: Moderate   **Total Distance:** 9.0 miles round-trip

Hiking Time: 4 hours   **Elevation Gain:** 1,000 feet

Summary: Circle through eastern piedmont forest on a long looping hike.

The trails that make up this circuit through the Prince William Forest run along the western section of Virginia's piedmont as it approaches the coastal plain. Of all the units in the national park system, Prince William protects the most acres of eastern piedmont forest. Made of rolling hills forested with mixed hardwoods, the eastern piedmont stretches from the coastal plain to the Appalachian Mountains, from New York to Alabama, but much of its forests have been lost to development. Here, however, you can explore the varied plant and animal life that make up such a forest.

Begin by following the white blazes of South Valley Trail, the park's longest path at 8.7 miles. Stay to the right as you pass Oak Ridge Trail (your return route) after

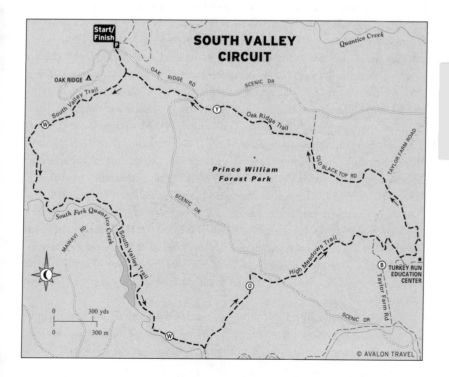

0.2 mile. In this region, you'll notice a proliferation of blackberry and blueberry bushes, lots of shrubs and vines, very little canopy, and blackened stumps—the result of a 318-acre forest fire in 2006. The fire damage peters out as South Valley Trail first leads to the south fork of Quantico Creek, then travels alongside the water. A buildup of silt and the structures built by beavers, whose work is highly evident, have resulted in a very marshy creek with many pools and little water flow. You'll likely spot salamanders, frogs, and turtles, as well as many dragonflies and damselflies.

South Valley Trail runs along the south fork of Quantico Creek.

Upon reaching an intersection with Mawavi Road, continue straight across the road and down the stairs on the opposite side. Mountain laurel grows thick, blooming in early June, and the trail becomes rockier. About 0.3 mile after crossing the road, you'll reach the top of a lake. You're allowed to swim here, so if you're feeling adventurous, leave your shoes on the shore and go for a dip. Though you can't see them, two cabin camps built by the Civilian Conservation Corps (CCC) lie across the lake. With 153 CCC structures located in the forest, Prince William Park preserves more CCC constructions than any other national park system site.

The trail will lead past a dam and a footbridge connecting to the cabins, and then intersect with High Meadows Trail about 1.7 miles from Mawavi Road. Turn left here and follow the orange blazes as the trail climbs up to a ridge and then traverses it. After 0.8 mile, you'll cross Scenic Drive, continuing straight. As you approach Taylor Farm Road, 0.9 mile beyond the last road crossing, you'll see signs of the farm that once stood here, as well as a family cemetery. Continue along the ridge, staying left and over the bridge at the intersection with Little Run Loop, reaching Old Black Top Road 0.4 mile past Taylor Farm Road. Turn left onto this broad gravel fire road. You may spot deer in this area. Surprisingly, they seem completely nonplussed by the sounds of artillery fire, which can frequently be heard thanks to the park's location near the Quantico Marine Corps Base.

Stay on Old Black Top Road until you reach Oak Ridge Trail, which will be on your left. This yellow-blazed trail runs 1.6 miles before ending at South Valley Trail. Ground cedar covers the forest floor, and as you get closer to South Valley

Trail, you'll again see signs of the 2006 forest fire. At the junction, turn right, returning to the parking lot in 0.2 mile.

Options
Stay overnight in the park in one of the historic CCC camp cabins. The cabins are open May–mid-October and can sleep 4, 6, or 10 people, with prices ranging $40–60 per night. More information can be found on the park's website.

Directions
Take southbound I-95 to exit 150B to merge onto westbound Route 619. Drive 0.4 mile, and then turn right on Park Entrance Road. Follow Scenic Drive as it loops around the park toward the campground. Turn right on Oak Ridge Road, and park in the lot just outside Oak Ridge Campground. The trailhead is in the corner of the lot.

Information and Contact
There is a fee of $5 per vehicle, which covers admission for seven consecutive days. A $20 annual pass is available. America the Beautiful passes are accepted. Dogs on leash are allowed. Trails are open from sunrise to sunset daily. Maps are available at the entrance station and visitors center (9 A.M.–5 P.M. daily, except New Year's Day, Thanksgiving, and Christmas). For more information, contact Prince William Forest Park, 18100 Park Headquarters Road, Triangle, VA 22172, 703/221-7181, www.nps.gov/prwi.

🟊 NORTH VALLEY CIRCUIT

Prince William Forest Park

🦌 🚲 🐎

Level: Moderate

Hiking Time: 3 hours

Total Distance: 6.8 miles round-trip

Elevation Gain: 1,000 feet

Summary: Traverse the fall line, transferring from coastal plain to eastern piedmont, on this circuit hike.

Geology features prominently on this circuit hike around the eastern part of Prince William Forest Park. As you pass from the coastal plain to the piedmont, you'll literally step across the fall line, visibly noting its location on Quantico Creek. You'll also visit the remains of the Cabin Branch Pyrite Mine and learn about the extraction process as well as the damaging effects mining had on the environment. Thanks to a scattering of signboards along the way, you'll gain a wealth of information about the region's geology.

Begin on yellow-blazed Laurel Trail Loop, which is misleadingly named since it features very little mountain laurel. Instead you'll walk downhill through a forest of pawpaws, beeches, redbuds, dogwoods, and other hardwoods. Continue straight as you pass Birch Bluff Trail on your right at 0.2 mile. For a short distance, the trail is both yellow and red blazed, but the red blazes end as you pass another section of Birch Bluff Trail. Upon reaching the bank of the creek, turn left at a T junction and follow the sandy trail along the creek's edge. Turn right when you reach an unmarked junction a bit past a footbridge, and then turn right again to cross the creek via a suspension bridge, about 1.0 mile after beginning the hike.

Once over the bridge, turn right onto a creekside path. Though listed on the park map as part of the North Valley Trail, it is blazed with the white marks of the South Valley Trail. Regardless of which trail it actually is, you'll follow it along Quantico Creek for 0.9 mile until it meets Pyrite Mine Road. Turn left onto this broad, blue-blazed gravel road, hiking 0.6 mile to Cabin Branch Mine Trail, which will be on your right. Turn right onto this orange-blazed trail. It will change from gravel to grass, at which point the blazes will lead you off to the left on a narrower path to the pyrite mine, 0.5 mile after leaving the road.

From 1880 to 1919, pyrite, also known as fool's gold, was extracted from three main shafts and then processed to create sulfuric acid, used in the manufacture of many household items as well as for the

A suspension bridge connects Laurel Trail Loop with the rest of the hike.

cleaning and refining of gunpowder. Though critical to World War I, the pyrite mine was also extremely damaging to the environment, leaking sulfuric acid into Quantico Creek even after the mine closed. Decades of reclamation work have helped return the area to a state that the Environmental Protection Agency considers healthy. The presence of wildlife, such as great blue herons, fish, turtles, frogs, and salamanders, gives credence to this claim.

Continue past the mine to the intersection with blue-blazed North Valley Trail. Turn left here and walk along the bank of Quantico Creek. As you continue along the creek, passing signs noting geologic features, you'll observe that small boulders begin to appear in the water. You're approaching the fall line, which marks the transition from the flat shelf of the coastal plain to the rolling hills of the piedmont.

At the intersection with yellow-blazed Quantico Falls Trail, about 1.2 miles from where you connected to North Valley Trail, turn left and walk across the fall line, which is noticeable thanks to the cascade in the creek. Stay on Quantico Falls Trail as it passes back over North Valley Trail before reaching Lake One Road. Turn left onto the road, then turn right onto red-blazed Mary Bird Branch Trail. Pass through a picnic area and cross Scenic Drive, continuing to follow the red blazes. After 0.5 mile, turn left onto Old Black Top Road, which leads past Turkey Run Education Center and Group Campground before reaching a junction with blue-blazed Turkey Run Ridge Trail on your left.

Turn here and begin the process of traversing a series of ridges. Cross Scenic Drive after 0.7 mile, and after another 0.7 mile, reach the trail's end at a junction with white-blazed South Valley Trail. Turn left and proceed alongside the creek to North Orenda Road, onto which you will turn right. About 0.9 mile after you turned onto South Valley Trail, you'll reach the suspension bridge you crossed earlier. Retreat over it, turning right to complete Laurel Trail Loop in 0.4 mile.

Options
The Pine Grove Forest Trail, which leaves from the same parking area, is a 0.4-mile loop that's a great leg-stretcher for kids or a good warm-up for this hike.

Directions
Take southbound I-95 to exit 150B to merge onto westbound Route 619. Drive 0.4 mile, and then turn right on Park Entrance Road. Follow signs to the Pine Grove Picnic Area and park in the lot that is straight ahead. The trailhead can be found at the back of the picnic area, behind the restrooms.

Information and Contact
There is a fee of $5 per vehicle, which covers admission for seven consecutive days. A $20 annual pass is available. America the Beautiful passes are accepted. Dogs on leash are allowed. Trails are open from sunrise to sunset daily. Maps are available at the entrance station and visitors center (9 A.M.–5 P.M. daily, except New Year's Day, Thanksgiving, and Christmas). For more information, contact Prince William Forest Park, 18100 Park Headquarters Road, Triangle, VA 22172, 703/221-7181, www.nps.gov/prwi.

10 LEE'S WOODS TRAIL   BEST ◖

Leesylvania State Park

Level: Easy

Hiking Time: 1 hour

Total Distance: 2.0 miles round-trip

Elevation Gain: 200 feet

Summary: Learn about the history of the lauded Lee family on a loop through their former estate.

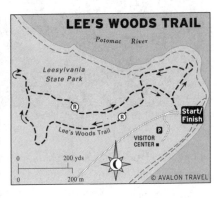

Though only a Virginia state park since 1992, Leesylvania has a long and storied history with important ties to our country's evolution. Before the United States was a nation, Algonquin Indians populated this area on the bank of the Potomac. Later the land became home to the Lee family. Henry Lee III (also known as Lighthorse Harry) was born here, growing up to be a Revolutionary War hero, governor of Virginia, and, perhaps most famously, father of Confederate general Robert E. Lee. Although General Lee never actually lived on this land, he was certainly familiar with the area and established a river battery here during the Civil War.

On the Lee's Woods Trail, this history comes to life thanks to interpretive sites outlined in a brochure available at the information board near the trailhead. Begin the hike by walking up the stairs toward the amphitheater. The trail is marked with red blazes. Proceed past stop one, which simply marks the beginning of the interpretive trail, and turn right. Notice the profusion of holly trees as you make a slight uphill climb to a clearing where three cannons mark the site where Lee established a battery in August 1861 in order to blockade the Potomac. A bench allows you to enjoy views toward the river and search for eagles, ospreys, herons, and cormorants in the shade of pawpaw, sassafras, and walnut trees.

Continue along the trail, passing stop three, where you can learn about the Niobsco village of the Doeg tribes of Algonquin Indians, and stop four, where you can gaze out upon Occoquan Bay, where trade thrived. Upon reaching a four-way intersection, turn right. You'll soon encounter a sign of early settlement—the chimney of the Fairfax House, along with the foundation of their barn. The Fairfax family, of which John Fairfax served as a colonel in the Confederate Army,

A doe and her two fawns graze at Leesylvania.

bought this land from the Lee family. Just past the house, near the old well, is a large white oak designated as the Prince William Bicentennial Tree.

As you continue down the broad, gravel path, notice the dense undergrowth and proliferation of raspberry bushes. In the late 18th century, Henry Lee II ran a tobacco plantation on this land. The Lee Home Site is the next stop on your hike, though nothing of the house remains. You will, however, find daffodils and daylilies growing in the clearing. These cultivated plants indicate human presence. From the clearing, the trail goes off to the left, and you'll soon pass "escaped" gardens on your right. Take a detour through here, noting the signs that reveal how the plants would have been used by early settlers.

Continue up a short hill to reach the Lee-Fairfax Cemetery, stop 9 on the interpretive trail, and then detour along the trail to the left to reach stop 10, which marks the location of a Richmond-to-DC railroad line that was in operation from 1872 to 1925. Backtrack to the cemetery, and then continue along the trail, which leads 0.5 mile back to the intersection near the Fairfax House. Turn left and proceed straight through oak, walnut, elm, and ash trees to return to the trailhead and complete your hike through history.

Options

When you arrive back at the trailhead, turn left and connect to the Potomac Trail. This yellow-blazed trail stretches for 0.5 mile along the river and provides access to a natural sand beach.

Directions

Take southbound I-95 to exit 156 to merge onto eastbound Route 784. Drive 1.9 miles, and then turn right on U.S. 1. After 1.1 miles, turn left on Neabsco Road and proceed 1.5 miles to Daniel K. Ludwig Drive. Turn right to enter the park. Follow the park road to where it ends, with a parking area on the right.

Information and Contact

There is a fee of $4 per vehicle on weekdays, $5 on weekends and holidays. Virginia State Park passes are accepted. Dogs on leash are allowed. The park is open from dawn to dusk daily. Maps are available at the entrance station. For more information, contact Leesylvania State Park, 2001 Daniel K. Ludwig Drive, Woodbridge, VA 22191, 703/730-8205, www.dcr.virginia.gov/state_parks/lee.shtml.

11 WOODMARSH TRAIL
Mason Neck National Wildlife Refuge

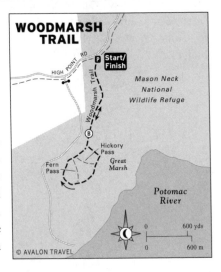

Level: Easy

Hiking Time: 1.5 hours

Total Distance: 3.0 miles round-trip

Elevation Gain: 100 feet

Summary: Hike to Eagle Point for an excellent chance at spotting graceful bald eagles soaring over the Potomac.

On February 1, 1969, Mason Neck National Wildlife Refuge was established, becoming the first national refuge with the specific task of protecting bald eagles. Today, the 2,277-acre reserve, along with Mason Neck State Park, with which it shares a border, stands as testament to the importance of conserving land. In the past, development and associated factors, such as the widespread use of DDT, decimated eagle populations along the Potomac, but now as many as 50 eagles spend the entire year here, and even more join them to nest in winter.

Begin your search for our national bird by crossing over a multiuse trail and proceeding to the trailhead of blue-blazed Woodmarsh Trail, which is on your right. Running cedar carpets parts of the oak-hickory forest floor, and in spring, wildflowers bloom trailside. Plenty of benches allow you to rest or search for birds. Wood thrushes, which make flutelike sounds, are often easy to pick out, and warblers, vireos, and ovenbirds have particularly distinct calls that you can learn to recognize with some patience. You may also hear the tapping of a pileated woodpecker or the screech of a blue jay.

Upon reaching the intersection with the loop part of the trail after about 1.0 mile, follow the signs to the left. Shortly down the moss-covered trail, you'll reach an intersection with another sign, which points you to the right. Bypass this turn to continue on to Eagle Point, where the trail will dead-end. Peer out into the marsh—at 250 acres, it's the largest freshwater marsh in Virginia—to look for herons, beavers, and muskrats as well as a variety of waterfowl. Then search the trees above you, particularly the large oaks and pines, for eagles. You may even

© THERESA DOWELL BLACKINTON

The broad trail is flat and easy except for the occasional scamper required by downed trees.

see one in flight; their 6- to 8-foot wingspans are bound to impress. Remember that bald eagles don't develop the white plumage from which they get their name until they are of breeding age, so the brown-headed birds you see may just be juveniles. If you own binoculars, consider bringing them with you to improve your chances of spotting and identifying an eagle.

When you're done eagle watching, return to the intersection you originally passed, and now turn left onto it. At the next intersection, turn left again; turning right will put you on Hickory Pass, a connector trail that is closed December–June for the protection of nesting eagles. Continue to follow the blue blazes, with the marsh to your left. Beyond the marsh, the Potomac River flows, and you're likely to see boat traffic floating by. Stay straight when you see Fern Pass on your right. Not long after you pass this connector trail, you'll begin to turn right, away from the water.

As you continue on the approximately 1.0-mile loop, you'll pass a display shelter with information on invasive species, bald eagles, and wildlife common to the area. It's all worth a read. Beyond the display, you'll proceed past the other ends of both Fern Pass and Hickory Pass, and then reach the end of the loop. Turn left and hike back to the parking lot the way you came.

Options

Directly north of the wildlife refuge is **Gunston Hall Plantation,** the home of George Mason, a notable figure in early U.S. history. You can tour the house, outbuildings, and grounds (10709 Gunston Road, Mason Neck, VA 22079, 703/550-9220, www.gunstonhall.org, 9:30 A.M.–5 P.M. daily, except New Year's Day, Thanksgiving, and Christmas, $10 for adults, $8 for senior citizens, $5 for youth 6–18, and free for children under 6).

Directions
Take southbound I-95 to exit 166A to merge onto southbound Route 7100. After 1.0 mile, turn right onto southbound Route 611. Drive 3.4 miles, and then turn left on Gunston Road. After about 3.5 miles, you'll reach a parking lot on your left.

Information and Contact
There is no fee. Dogs on leash are allowed. The refuge is open 7 A.M.–5 P.M. daily Oct.–Mar., 7 A.M.–7 P.M. daily Apr.–Sept. Maps can be downloaded from the website. For more information, contact Mason Neck Wildlife Refuge, 12638 Darby Brooke Court, Woodbridge, VA 22192, 703/490-4979, www.fws.gov/masonneck.

12 BELMONT BAY
Mason Neck State Park

Level: Easy

Hiking Time: 1.5 hours

Total Distance: 3.3 miles round-trip

Elevation Gain: 150 feet

Summary: Pass from forest to marsh to bay on this hike through bald eagle territory.

On this peninsula, named for George Mason IV, the author of the Virginia Declaration of Rights, development has not taken over as it has throughout most of Fairfax County. Instead, conservation efforts have defeated consumer interests, and nearly all of the peninsula is dedicated to the protection of natural spaces and the species that inhabit them. The hardwood forests, marshland, and Potomac waterfront enclosed within Mason Neck State Park harbor typical Eastern deciduous forest and house many bird species, including herons, egrets, and most notably, bald eagles.

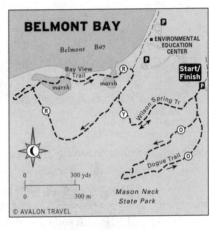

Start your exploration on yellow-blazed Wilson Spring Trail, which crosses over a paved multiuse trail and then reaches a split with Dogue Trail. Stay to the right, winding through mature second-growth forest and crossing over two footbridges. Holly, oak, hickory, and sweet gum trees are particularly prevalent. After 0.75 mile, Wilson Spring Trail ends at red-blazed Bay View Trail.

Turn left onto this trail, continuing through the forest. You may notice a difference in undergrowth here, with a preponderance of blueberries and huckleberries as well as mountain laurel. This is the result of a 1986 cool burn, a fire that destroyed the undergrowth but was contained before it could damage any trees.

Upon reaching a split in Bay View Trail, stay right to approach a viewpoint over the marsh. Continuing on, you'll pass a shelter from which you can see cattails, wild rice, and spatterdock growing in the marsh and hear the calls of ducks and geese. At a four-way intersection with blue blazes in all directions, continue straight down a set of stairs and onto a wooden walkway over the marsh. Look for beavers,

A system of boardwalks leads over the marsh and along the river.

muskrats, and birds, especially the great blue heron, which uses Mason Neck as a rookery. In winter, the eagle population soars as pairs nest along the Potomac.

Beyond the marsh, the trail parallels Belmont Bay. You can access the beach in multiple locations, but no swimming is allowed. You can, however, fish for crappie, bass, and bluegill as long as you have the proper license. Shortly after crossing over a second section of marsh, the trail will lead into a picnic and playground area. Stay right, hugging the trees, and then quickly reenter the forest. You'll pass a tall poplar with an opening in the trunk tall enough for a child to easily walk through and then reach a boardwalk. Just beyond the boardwalk, the 1.0-mile-long trail reconnects with Wilson Spring Trail. Turn left onto it and hike back toward the parking lot.

Just before you cross over the multiuse trail, turn right onto orange-blazed Dogue Trail. At the split, stay right to make a loop on a gravel path passing through mature forest. You may spot a snake slithering in the leaves or a salamander scurrying down a tree trunk, and you're certain to be treated to the songs of many birds. Relax on one of the benches if you'd like before completing the 0.8-mile loop, and then taking a right to return to the parking lot.

Options
If you'd like to explore more of the park, cross the road and pick up blue-blazed Kane's Creek Trail. This is a 1.0-mile forest loop. From it, you can connect to silver-blazed Eagle Spur Trail, which leads 1.25 miles to an overlook above the creek. Doing both the loop and out-and-back will add 3.5 miles to your hike.

Directions

Take southbound I-95 to exit 166A to merge onto southbound Route 7100. After 1.0 mile, turn right onto southbound Route 611. Drive 3.4 miles, and then turn left on Gunston Road. Make a slight right after 3.7 miles to turn onto High Point Road. Follow this road through the entrance station to the marked Wilson Spring Trail parking lot on your left.

Information and Contact

There is a fee of $3 per vehicle on weekdays, $4 on weekends and holidays. Virginia State Park passes are accepted. Dogs on leash are allowed. The park is open from dawn to dusk daily. Maps are available at the entrance station. For more information, contact Mason Neck State Park, 7301 High Point Road, Lorton, VA 22079, 703/339-2380, www.dcr.virginia.gov/state_parks/mas.shtml.

13 CALEDON LOOP
Caledon State Park

Level: Easy

Total Distance: 4.0 miles round-trip

Hiking Time: 2 hours

Elevation Gain: 530 feet

Summary: A series of interconnected loop trails leads through riparian forests and floodplains near where eagles nest.

With as many as 60 bald eagles occupying the Potomac River bluffs of Caledon State Park, this National Natural Landmark protects one of the largest eagle concentrations on the East Coast. As such, large swaths of the park are closed to the public each year between April and October to allow fledgling eagles to learn to fish, hunt, and survive in their natural habitat with the fewest possible disturbances. Fortunately, however, most of the trail system lies outside the closed area, meaning Caledon is open for hiking year-round.

From the parking area, follow the signposted path on the left through thick brambles of raspberry bushes that burst with fruit in midsummer. At the fork, turn right onto red-blazed Fern Hollow Trail, which descends gently through

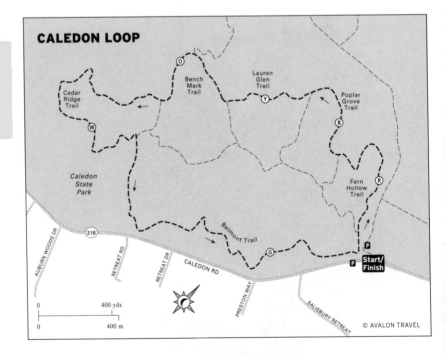

© THERESA DOWELL BLACKINTON

A footbridge keeps your feet dry on this creek crossing.

oaks and ferns, and then makes a short climb before again descending to a bridge over a small stream.

Once over the bridge, you reach your first junction. Turn right onto blue-blazed Poplar Grove Trail. As you travel along this dirt trail broken by many exposed roots, look for the remains of chestnut trees that fell victim to blight in the middle of the 20th century. You will also see more recently uprooted trees; these were toppled by Hurricane Isabel in 2003. After crossing the second bridge on the Poplar Grove Trail, you'll arrive at a junction with yellow-blazed Laurel Glen Trail. Turn right here, continuing through mature forest to a junction with orange-blazed Benchmark Trail, where you will again turn right.

The Benchmark Trail runs parallel to a creek through a marsh environment. Just before you reach a boardwalk, green-blazed Belmont Trail joins in from the right and shares the path for a time. As you pass over the boardwalk, look for signs of animals, such as the footprints of deer, raccoons, and opossums on the muddy banks of the creek.

Upon reaching white-blazed Cedar Ridge Trail, turn right. This trail almost constantly ascends and then descends, leading you up onto ridges, then down into ravines. You'll begin to loop back toward the visitors center on this trail, but rather than connecting back to the lower sections of the other four trails you've already traveled, you will, instead, turn right onto green-blazed Belmont Trail. This trail was built with the assistance of AmeriCorps members and opened in 2007.

Shortly after you begin down the Belmont Trail, you'll pass a small fenced-in cemetery on your right, evidence of Caledon's previous existence as a farm. Beyond this, the trail cuts through an area with many berry bushes. Here the land is slowly returning to forest. The trail nears Route 218, and you'll hear the rush of passing cars, but don't let that deter you from continuing on this path, because you'll soon encounter one of the hike's highlights—massive old-growth tulip poplars and oaks, some more than 60 inches in diameter. Admire these forest giants as you make your way back, the trail emerging from the woods near old farm buildings. From there, turn right onto the gravel road and follow it back to the parking lot.

Options

From October through March, explore the favored habitat of bald eagles on the Boyd's Hole Trail, the Rookery Spur Trail, and the Potomac Overlook Trail. From mid-June to Labor Day, guided tours of eagle nesting areas are offered on Saturday and Sunday. Reservations are required, and there is a per-person fee of $6.

Directions

Take southbound I-95 to exit 133A to merge onto southbound U.S. 17 Business. Drive 1.8 miles, and then continue on Route 218. After 20.2 miles, turn left at the park entrance, and proceed to the parking area near the visitors center.

Information and Contact

There is a fee of $2 per vehicle on weekdays, $3 on weekends and holidays. Virginia State Park passes are accepted. Dogs on leash are allowed. The park is open from dawn to dusk daily. Maps are available at the visitors center (10 A.M.–5 P.M. Wed.–Sun., Memorial Day–Labor Day). When the visitors center is closed, an electronic kiosk in front prints maps. For more information, contact Caledon State Park, 11617 Caledon Road, King George, VA 22485, 540/663-3861, www.dcr.virginia.gov/state_parks/cal.shtml.

14 TURKEY NECK TRAIL
Westmoreland State Park

Level: Easy

Hiking Time: 1.25 hours

Total Distance: 2.5 miles round-trip

Elevation Gain: 600 feet

Summary: Explore a marshy meadow, then visit a beach where you might discover Miocene-era fossils.

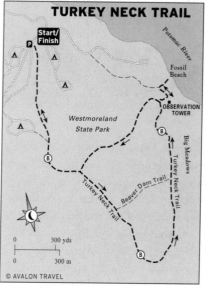

Located on Virginia's Northern Neck along a 1.5-mile stretch of the Potomac River, Westmoreland is one of the six original members of the Virginia state park system. The park was constructed by the CCC and opened in 1936. Since then, it has drawn visitors interested in exploring its coastal plain environment.

From the Turkey Neck trailhead, turn right, following the blue blazes as the path parallels the entrance road before turning left into the woods. Raspberries grow thick along the trail, maturing in early to mid-July. The seedpods of sweet gum trees litter the path, and holly trees fill in the midstory. To your left, the land drops down into a ravine, which the trail skirts for most of the hike.

After 0.5 mile, you'll reach a junction. Campground C lies to your right, but you'll turn left, continuing along a sandy trail under mature oak forest to the fork where the loop part of this trail begins. Stay straight, reaching a junction with Beaver Dam Trail about 0.3 mile from the first junction. Remain on Turkey Neck Trail, which will continue up above the ravine before turning to the left and beginning a downhill stretch. A set of stairs will lead you down to the level of Big Meadows, which would be more accurately named if it were called Big Marsh.

A symphony of frogs serenades you as you turn left at the bottom of the stairs and proceed along a narrow trail that edges the marsh. In two spots, the trail turns to boardwalk and cuts directly across the wetlands. Be careful when the boardwalk is wet, as it becomes very slippery. After a short uphill stretch, you'll reach an intersection with the other end of 0.6-mile-long Beaver Dam Trail. Stay

Miocene-era fossils can sometimes be found on the beach.

straight, heading down a set of log steps. You'll soon reach an intersection, where you will turn right and proceed along a boardwalk that leads over the marshy meadow to an observation tower. From the wooden deck of the observation tower, you can observe a creek cutting across the meadow, and, looking left, you'll see the Potomac River and Fossil Beach. Marsh birds flitter from plant to plant.

Detour to the beach by descending from the tower and continuing straight along the boardwalk, where trumpet vine blooms in summer. When the boardwalk ends, turn right and hike about 0.1 mile to the beach. Search among the stones and shells for fossils, shark's teeth, and whale bones—the remains of marine animals from the Miocene period. Look to your left for views of Horsehead Cliffs.

When you're finished searching for fossils, return past the observation tower to Turkey Neck Trail, where you will turn right. You'll continue to edge along the marsh before climbing up above the ravine. Notice the mountain laurel as you make a prolonged ascent. A bench awaits you at the top of the climb, should you need a rest. From here, the trail is fairly level as it completes the loop. Turn right at the loop's end, and then turn right again at the intersection near the campground to retrace your steps and return to the parking area.

Options

Add 1.2 miles to your hike by taking a short out-and-back detour on Big Meadow Trail. After visiting Fossil Beach, turn right onto red-blazed Big Meadow Trail rather than turning left to go back past the observation tower. This trail climbs uphill through hardwood forest where deer like to graze. At the trail's end, cross the road to reach an overlook atop Horsehead Cliffs with broad views of the Potomac. Return via the same route to reconnect with Turkey Neck Trail and continue the hike previously described.

Directions

Take southbound I-95 to exit 130A to merge onto eastbound Route 3. Drive 40.8 miles on Route 3, and then turn left onto Route 347 to enter Westmoreland State Park. Continue through the entrance station to the Turkey Neck trailhead parking lot, which will be on your right after about 1.5 miles.

Information and Contact

There is a fee of $3 per vehicle on weekdays, $4 on weekends and holidays. Virginia State Park passes are accepted. Dogs on leash are allowed. The park is open from dawn to dusk daily. Maps are available at the entrance station. For more information, contact Westmoreland State Park, 1650 State Park Road, Montross, VA 22520, 804/493-8821, www.dcr.virginia.gov/state_parks/wes.shtml.

RESOURCES

MARYLAND STATE PARKS

Calvert Cliffs State Park

www.dnr.maryland.gov/publiclands/
southern/calvertcliffs.asp
c/o Smallwood State Park
2750 Sweden Point Road
Marbury, MD 20658
301/743-7613

Cedarville State Forest

www.dnr.maryland.gov/publiclands/
southern/cedarville.asp
10201 Bee Oak Road
Brandywine, MD 20613
301/888-1410

Cunningham Falls State Park

www.dnr.maryland.gov/publiclands/
western/cunningham.asp
14039 Catoctin Hollow Road
Thurmont, MD 21788
301/271-7574

Elk Neck State Park

www.dnr.maryland.gov/publiclands/
central/elkneck.asp
4395 Turkey Point Road
North East, MD 21901
410/287-5333

Gambrill State Park

www.dnr.maryland.gov/publiclands/
western/gambrill.asp
8602 Gambrill Park Road
Frederick, MD 21702
301/271-7574

Greenbrier State Park

www.dnr.maryland.gov/publiclands/
western/greenbrier.asp
c/o South Mountain Recreation Area
21843 National Pike
Boonsboro, MD 21713
301/791-4767

Green Ridge State Forest

www.dnr.maryland.gov/publiclands/
western/greenridgeforest.asp
28700 Headquarters Drive NE
Flintstone, MD 21530
301/478-3124

Gunpowder Falls State Park

www.dnr.maryland.gov/publiclands/
central/gunpowder.asp
2813 Jerusalem Road
P.O. Box 480
Kingsville, MD 21087
410/592-2897

Merkle Wildlife Sanctuary

www.dnr.maryland.gov/publiclands/
southern/merkle.asp
11704 Fenno Road
Upper Marlboro, MD 20772
301/888-1410

Patapsco Valley State Park

www.dnr.maryland.gov/publiclands/
central/patapsco.asp
8020 Baltimore National Pike
Ellicott City, MD 21043
410/461-5005

Rocks State Park

www.dnr.maryland.gov/publiclands/
central/rocks.asp
3318 Rocks Chrome Hill Road
Jarrettsville, MD 21084
410/557-7994

Rocky Gap State Park

www.dnr.maryland.gov/publiclands/
western/rockygap.asp
12500 Pleasant Valley Road
Flintstone, MD 21530
301/722-1480

Soldiers Delight Natural Environment Area

www.dnr.maryland.gov/publiclands/
central/soldiersdelight.asp
5100 Deer Park Road
Owings Mill, MD 21117
410/461-5005

Susquehanna State Park

www.dnr.maryland.gov/publiclands/
central/susquehanna.asp
4122 Wilkinson Road
Havre de Grace, MD 21078
410/557-7994

Tuckahoe State Park

www.dnr.maryland.gov/publiclands/
eastern/tuckahoe.asp
13070 Crouse Mill Road
Queen Anne, MD 21657
410/820-1668

Wye Island Natural Resources Management Area

www.dnr.maryland.gov/publiclands/
eastern/wyeisland.asp
632 Wye Island Road
Queenstown, MD 21658
410/827-7577

VIRGINIA STATE PARKS
Caledon Natural Area

www.dcr.virginia.gov/state_parks/cal.
shtml
11617 Caledon Road
King George, VA 22485
540/663-3861

Lake Anna State Park

www.dcr.virginia.gov/state_parks/lak.
shtml
6800 Lawyers Road
Spotsylvania, VA 22551
540/854-5503

Leesylvania State Park

www.dcr.virginia.gov/state_parks/lee.
shtml
2001 Daniel K. Ludwig Drive
Woodbridge, VA 22191
703/730-8205

Mason Neck State Park

www.dcr.virginia.gov/state_parks/mas.
shtml
7301 High Point Road
Lorton, VA 22079
703/339-2380

Pocahontas State Park

www.dcr.virginia.gov/state_parks/poc.shtml
10301 State Park Road
Chesterfield, VA 23832
804/796-4255

Westmoreland State Park

www.dcr.virginia.gov/state_parks/wes.shtml
1650 State Park Road
Montross, VA 22520
804/493-8821

WEST VIRGINIA STATE PARKS
Cacapon Resort State Park

www.cacaponresort.com
818 Cacapon Lodge Drive
Berkeley Springs, WV 25411
304/258-1022

NATIONAL PARKS
Antietam National Battlefield

www.nps.gov/anti

Park Headquarters
P.O. Box 158
Sharpsburg, MD 21782
301/432-7648

Visitors Center
5831 Dunker Church Road
Sharpsburg, MD 21782
301/432-5124

Catoctin Mountain Park

www.nps.gov/cato
6602 Foxville Road
Thurmont, MD 21788
301/663-9388

C&O Canal National Historical Park

www.nps.gov/choh

Park Headquarters
1850 Dual Highway, Suite 100
Hagerstown, MD 21740
301/739-4200

Great Falls Tavern Visitor Center
11710 MacArthur Boulevard
Potomac, MD 20854
301/767-3714

Fredericksburg and Spotsylvania National Military Park

www.nps.gov/frsp
120 Chatham Lane
Fredericksburg, VA 22405
540/786-2880

Great Falls Park

www.nps.gov/grfa
9200 Old Dominion Drive
McLean, VA 22102
703/285-2965

Harpers Ferry National Historical Park

www.nps.gov/hafe
P.O. Box 65
Harpers Ferry, WV 25425
304/535-6029

Kenilworth Park

www.nps.gov/keaq
1900 Anacostia Drive SE
Washington, DC 20020
202/426-6905

Manassas National Battlefield Park

www.nps.gov/mana
12521 Lee Highway
Manassas, VA 20109
703/361-7106

Prince William Forest Park

www.nps.gov/prwi
18100 Park Headquarters Road
Triangle, VA 22172
703/221-7181

Rock Creek Park

www.nps.gov/rocr

Park Headquarters

3545 Williamsburg Lane NW
Washington, DC 20008
202/895-6000

Nature Center

5200 Glover Road NW
Washington, DC 20015
202/895-6070

Shenandoah National Park

www.nps.gov/shen
3655 Highway 211 East
Luray, VA 22835
540/999-3500

Theodore Roosevelt Island

www.nps.gov/this
c/o Turkey Run Park
George Washington Memorial Parkway
McLean, VA 22101
703/289-2500

NATIONAL FORESTS
George Washington National Forest

www.fs.fed.us/r8/gwj

Lee Ranger District

95 Railroad Avenue
Edinburg, VA 22824
540/984-4101

OTHER
Appalachian Trail Conservancy

www.appalachiantrail.org
P.O. Box 807
799 Washington Street
Harpers Ferry, WV 25425-0807
304/535-6331

Fairfax County Park Authority

www.fairfaxcounty.gov/parks
12055 Government Center Parkway,
Suite 927
Fairfax, VA 22035
703/324-8702

Friends of the James River Park

www.jamesriverpark.org
P.O. Box 4453
Richmond, VA 23220
804/646-8911

G. Richard Thompson Wildlife Management Area

www.dgif.state.va.us/wmas/detail.asp?pid=31
Virginia Department of Game and Inland Fisheries
4010 West Broad Street
P.O. Box 11104
Richmond, VA 23230
804/367-1000

Mason Neck Wildlife Refuge

www.fws.gov/masonneck
12638 Darby Brooke Court
Woodbridge, VA 22192
703/490-4979

Montgomery County Department of Parks

www.montgomeryparks.org
9500 Brunett Avenue
Silver Spring, MD 20901
301/495-2595

Northern Virginia Regional Park Authority

www.nvrpa.org
5400 Ox Road
Fairfax Station, VA 22039
703/352-5900

Sugarloaf Mountain

www.sugarloafmd.com
Stronghold Inc.
7901 Comus Road
Dickerson, MD 20842
301/869-7846

U.S. National Arboretum

www.usna.usda.gov
3501 New York Avenue NE
Washington, DC 20002
202/245-2726

Wildcat Mountain Natural Area

www.nature.org
The Nature Conservancy
490 Westfield Road
Charlottesville, VA 22901
434/295-6106

PASSES AND PERMITS
America the Beautiful

This annual National Parks and Federal Recreation Lands Pass, good for one year from the date of issue, provides admission to national parks and federal recreation areas across the United States. At sites that charge by the vehicle, the pass admits all occupants of a noncommercial vehicle. At sites that charge per person, the pass admits the cardholder plus three adults (children under 16 are free). The pass costs $80. U.S. citizens and permanent residents aged 62 or older can obtain a senior pass, which is good for the passholder's lifetime, for only $10. Permanently disabled U.S. citizens and permanent residents can receive a free lifetime access pass with the same benefits as the senior pass. Standard passes can be obtained at any park or federal recreation area, by phone (888/275-8747), or on the Internet (http://store.

usgs.gov/pass). Senior passes and access passes must be obtained at the park or through the mail using a form that can be found at www.nps.gov/findapark/passes. Proper documentation of age or disability is required. Between 80 and 100 percent of the cost of the pass goes directly to improving and maintaining our nation's parks.

Maryland State Park Passport

The Maryland Department of Natural Resources offers a park pass that admits the passholder and up to nine other people in one vehicle into Maryland's parks and forests. The pass costs $75 for Maryland residents and $100 for nonresidents and is good for one calendar year; it also allows for free boat launching and provides a 10 percent discount on concessions and boat rentals. Seniors aged 62 or older can obtain a Golden Age Pass, which costs $10 and is good for the passholder's lifetime. The Golden Age Pass covers park admission and offers half-price camping Sunday–Thursday. A Universal Disability Pass is available at no cost to those with permanent disabilities and provides the passholder and one additional person with free admission to all Maryland parks. Information on and applications for all passes can be found online at www.dnr.maryland.gov/publicland/parkpass.asp.

Virginia Naturally Yours Passport Plus

The Virginia Department of Conservation and Recreation offers a variety of passes. The Naturally Yours Passport Plus costs $66 and provides admission to all Virginia state parks for everyone in the passholder's vehicle as well as discounts on amenities for one year from the date of purchase. For an additional fee, the pass can be amended to include boat launch and equestrian trailer parking. Seniors aged 62 or older can obtain a lifetime pass for $36. A Disability Passport provides those with disabilities free access to all parks. Information on and applications for all passes can be found online at www.dcr.virginia.gov/state_parks/passes.shtml.

MAP SOURCES

The sources listed here provide detailed topographic maps that can act as stand-alone trail maps or as supplements to the basic maps provided by parks.

National Geographic Maps
212 Beaver Brook Canyon Road
Evergreen, CO 80439
800/962-1643
www.natgeomaps.com

Potomac Appalachian Trail Club
118 Park Street SE
Vienna, VA 22180
703/242-0315
www.patc.net

U.S. Geological Survey
USGS National Center
12201 Sunrise Valley Drive
Reston, VA 20192
703/648-5953
www.usgs.gov

DC HIKING CLUBS
For camaraderie on the trails, check out
these local hiking clubs:

Capital Hiking Club
www.capitalhikingclub.org

Center Hiking Club
www.centerhikingclub.org

Mid-Atlantic Hiking Group
www.midatlantichiking.com

**Sierra Club Potomac
Region Outings**
www.sierrapotomac.org

Wanderbirds Hiking Club
www.wanderbirds.org

Washington Women Outdoors
www.washingtonwomenoutdoors.org

SUGGESTED READING

Bull, John. *National Audubon Society Field Guide to Birds: Eastern Region.* New York: Knopf, 1994.

Cohen, Stan. *The Tree Army: A Pictorial History of the Civilian Conservation Corps, 1933–1942.* Missoula, MT: Pictorial Histories Pub. Co., 1980.

Engle, Reed L. *Everything Was Wonderful: A Pictorial History of the Civilian Conservation Corps in Shenandoah National Park.* Luray, VA: Shenandoah Natural History Association, 1999.

Gupton, Oscar W., and Fred C. Swope. *Wildflowers of the Shenandoah Valley and Blue Ridge Mountains.* Richmond: University of Virginia Press, 2002.

Opler, Paul A. *Peterson First Guide to Butterflies and Moths.* Boston: Houghton Mifflin, 1994.

Petrides, George. *A Field Guide to Eastern Trees.* Boston: Houghton Mifflin, 1998.

INTERNET RESOURCES
Hiking Upward
www.hikingupward.com
This online guide features trip reports, reviews, and maps of trails in Maryland, Virginia, and West Virginia. It also hosts a forum where you can connect with other hikers.

Mid-Atlantic Hikes
www.midatlantichikes.com
This website features trip reports, reviews, and maps of trails in Maryland, Pennsylvania, Virginia, and West Virginia. It also includes information on gear, flora and fauna, and restaurants near trailheads.

Potomac Appalachian Trail Club

www.patc.net

The homepage of this organization, which maintains more than 1,200 miles of hiking trails in the region, provides trail news, information on volunteering, and a schedule of activities. You can also purchase maps and guides and make cabin reservations on the site.

Index

Notes

Notes

Notes

Notes

Notes

Notes

www.moon.com

DESTINATIONS | ACTIVITIES | BLOGS | MAPS | BOOKS

MOON.COM is ready to help plan your next trip! Filled with fresh trip ideas and strategies, author interviews, informative travel blogs, a detailed map library, and descriptions of all the Moon guidebooks, Moon.com is all you need to get out and explore the world—or even places in your own backyard. While at Moon.com, sign up for our monthly e-newsletter for updates on new releases, travel tips, and expert advice from our on-the-go Moon authors. As always, when you travel with Moon, expect an experience that is uncommon and truly unique.

KEEP UP WITH MOON ON FACEBOOK AND TWITTER
JOIN THE MOON PHOTO GROUP ON FLICKR